*The Roman and the Teuton*

# The Roman and the Teuton

## A Series of Lectures

BY
Charles Kingsley

WITH A PREFACE BY
F. Max Müller

*The first edition of these lectures was published in 1864*
*The text following is based on the 1891 edition*
*This edition was published in 2024*
ISBN 979-8869170392

# CONTENTS

# PREFACE

Never shall I forget the moment when for the last time I gazed upon the manly features of Charles Kingsley, features which Death had rendered calm, grand, sublime. The constant struggle that in life seemed to allow no rest to his expression, the spirit, like a caged lion, shaking the bars of his prison, the mind striving for utterance, the soul wearying for loving response,—all that was over. There remained only the satisfied expression of triumph and peace, as of a soldier who had fought a good fight, and who, while sinking into the stillness of the slumber of death, listens to the distant sounds of music and to the shouts of victory. One saw the ideal man, as Nature had meant him to be, and one felt that there is no greater sculptor than Death.

As one looked on that marble statue which only some weeks ago had so warmly pressed one's hand, his whole life flashed through one's thoughts. One remembered the young curate and the Saint's Tragedy; the chartist parson and Alton Locke; the happy poet and the Sands of Dee; the brilliant novel-writer and Hypatia and Westward-Ho; the Rector of Eversley and his Village Sermons; the beloved professor at Cambridge, the busy canon at Chester, the powerful preacher in Westminster Abbey. One thought of him by the Berkshire chalk-streams and on the Devonshire coast, watching the beauty and wisdom of Nature, reading her solemn lessons, chuckling too over her inimitable fun. One saw him in town-alleys, preaching the Gospel of godliness and cleanliness, while smoking his pipe with soldiers and navvies. One heard him in drawing-rooms, listened to with patient silence, till one of his vigorous or quaint speeches bounded forth, never to be forgotten. How children delighted in him! How young, wild men believed in him, and obeyed him too! How women were captivated by his chivalry, older men by his genuine humility and sympathy!

All that was now passing away—was gone. But as one looked on him for the last time on earth, one felt that greater than the curate, the poet, the professor, the canon, had been the man himself, with his warm heart, his honest purposes, his trust in his friends, his readiness to spend himself, his chivalry and humility, worthy of a better age.

Of all this the world knew little;—yet few men excited wider and stronger sympathies.

Who can forget that funeral on the 28th Jan., 1875, and the large sad throng that gathered round his grave? There was the representative of the Prince of Wales, and close by the gipsies of the Eversley common, who used to call him their Patrico-rai, their Priest-King. There was the old Squire of his village, and the labourers, young and old, to whom he had been a friend and a father. There were Governors of distant Colonies, officers, and sailors, the Bishop of his diocese, and the Dean of his abbey; there were the leading Nonconformists of the neighbourhood, and his own devoted curates, Peers and Members of the House of Commons, authors and publishers; and outside the church-yard, the horses and the hounds and the huntsman in pink, for though as good a clergyman as any, Charles Kingsley had been a good sportsman too, and had taken in his life many a fence as bravely as he took the last fence of all, without fear or trembling.  All that he had loved, and all that had loved him was there, and few eyes were dry when he was laid in his own yellow gravel bed, the old trees which he had planted and cared for waving their branches to him for the last time, and the grey sunny sky looking down with calm pity on the deserted rectory, and on the short joys and the shorter sufferings of mortal men.

All went home feeling that life was poorer, and every one knew that he had lost a friend who had been, in some peculiar sense, his own.  Charles Kingsley will be missed in England, in the English colonies, in America, where he spent his last happy year; aye, wherever Saxon speech and Saxon thought is understood.  He will be mourned for, yearned for, in every place in which he passed some days of his busy life.  As to myself, I feel as if another cable had snapped that tied me to this hospitable shore.

When an author or a poet dies, the better part of him, it is often said, is left in his works.  So it is in many cases.  But with Kingsley his life and his works were one.  All he wrote was meant for the day when he wrote it.  That was enough for him.  He hardly gave himself time to think of fame and the future.  Compared with a good work done, with a good word spoken, with a silent grasp of the hand from a young man he had saved from mischief, or with a 'Thank you, Sir,' from a poor woman to whom he had been a comfort, he would have despised what people call glory, like incense curling away in smoke. He was, in one sense of the word, a careless writer. He did his best at the time and for the time. He did it with a concentrated energy of will which broke through all difficulties. In his flights of imagination, in the light and fire of his language he had few equals, if any; but the perfection and classical finish which can be obtained by a sustained effort only, and by a patience which shrinks from no drudgery, these are wanting in most of his works.

However, fame, for which he cared so little, has come to him. His bust will stand in Westminster Abbey, in the Chapel of St. John the Baptist, by the side of his friend, Frederick Maurice; and in the Temple of Fame which will be consecrated to the period of Victoria and Albert, there will be a niche for Charles Kingsley, the author of Alton Locke and Hypatia.

Sooner or later a complete edition of his works will be wanted, though we may doubt whether he himself would have wished all his literary works to be preserved. From what I knew of him and his marvellous modesty, I should say decidedly not. I doubt more especially, whether he would have wished the present book, *The Roman and the Teuton*, to be handed down to posterity. None of his books was so severely criticised as this volume of Lectures, delivered before the University of Cambridge, and published in 1864. He himself did not republish it, and it seems impossible to speak in more depreciatory terms of his own historical studies than he does himself again and again in the course of his lectures. Yet these lectures, it should be remembered, were more largely attended than almost any other lectures at Cambridge. They produced a permanent impression on many a young mind. They are asked for again and again, and when the publishers wished for my advice as to the expediency of bringing out a new and cheaper edition, I could not hesitate as to what answer to give.

I am not so blinded by my friendship for Kingsley as to say that these lectures are throughout what academical lectures ought to be. I only wish some one would tell me what academical lectures at Oxford and Cambridge can be, as long as the present system of teaching and examining is maintained. It is easy to say what these lectures are not. They do not profess to contain the results of long continued original research. They are not based on a critical appreciation of the authorities which had to be consulted. They are not well arranged, systematic or complete. All this the suddenly elected professor of history at Cambridge would have been the first to grant. 'I am not here,' he says, 'to teach you history. I am here to teach you how to teach yourselves history.' I must say even more. It seems to me that these lectures were not always written in a perfectly impartial and judicial spirit, and that occasionally they are unjust to the historians who, from no other motive but a sincere regard for truth, thought it their duty to withhold their assent from many of the commonly received statements of mediaeval chroniclers.

But for all that, let us see what these Lectures are, and whether there is not room for them by the side of other works. First of all, according to the unanimous testimony of those who heard them delivered at Cambridge, they stirred up the interest of young men, and made them ask for books which Undergraduates had never asked for before at the University libraries. They made many people who read them afterwards, take a new interest in old and half-forgotten kings and battles, and they extorted even from unfriendly critics the admission that certain chapters, such as, for instance, 'The Monk as a Civiliser,' displayed in an unexpected way his power of appreciating the good points in characters, otherwise most antipathic to the apostle of Manly Christianity. They contain, in fact, the thoughts of a poet, a moralist, a politician, a theologian, and, before all, of a friend and counsellor of young men, while reading for them and with them one of the most awful periods in the history of mankind, the agonies of a dying Empire and the birth of new nationalities. History was but his text, his chief aim was that of the teacher and preacher, and as an eloquent interpreter of the purposes of history before an audience of young men to whom history is but too often a mere succession of events to be learnt by heart, and to be ready against periodical examinations, he achieved what he wished to achieve. Historians by profession would naturally be incensed at some portions of this book, but even they would probably admit by this time, that there are in it whole chapters full of excellence, telling passages, happy delineations, shrewd remarks, powerful outbreaks of real eloquence, which could not possibly be consigned to oblivion.

Nor would it have been possible to attempt to introduce any alterations, or to correct what may seem to be mistakes. The book is not meant as a text-book or as an authority, any more than Schiller's History of the Thirty Years' War; it should be read in future, as what it was meant to be from the first, Kingsley's thoughts on some of the moral problems presented by the conflict between the Roman and the Teuton. One cannot help wishing that, instead of lectures, Kingsley had given us another novel, like Hypatia, or a real historical tragedy, a Dietrich von Bern, embodying in living characters one of the fiercest struggles of humanity, the death of the Roman, the birth of the German world. Let me quote here what Bunsen said of Kingsley's dramatic power many years ago:

'I do not hesitate (he writes) to call these two works, the *Saint's Tragedy* and *Hypatia*, by far the most important and perfect of this genial writer. In these more particularly I find the justification of a hope which I beg to be allowed to express—that Kingsley might continue Shakspeare's historical plays. I have for several years made no secret of it, that Kingsley seems to me the genius of our century, called to place by the side of that sublime dramatic series from *King John* to *Henry VIII*, another series of equal rank, from *Edward VI* to the *Landing of William of Orange*. This is the only historical development of Europe which unites in itself all vital elements, and which we might look upon without overpowering pain. The tragedy of *St. Elizabeth* shows that Kingsley can grapple, not only with the novel, but with the more severe rules of dramatic art. And *Hypatia* proves, on the largest scale, that he can discover in the picture of the historical past, the truly human, the deep, the permanent, and that he knows how to represent it. How, with all this, he can hit the fresh tone of popular life, and draw humourous characters and complications with Shakspearian energy, is proved by all his works. And why should he not undertake this great task? There is a time when the true poet, the prophet of the present, must bid farewell to the questions of the day, which seem so great because they are so near, but are, in truth, but small and unpoetical. He must say to himself, "Let the dead bury their dead"—and the time has come that Kingsley should do so.'

A great deal has been written on mistakes which Kingsley was supposed to have made in these Lectures, but I doubt whether these criticisms were always perfectly judicial and fair. For instance, Kingsley's using the name of Dietrich, instead of Theodoric, was represented as the very gem of a blunder, and some critics went so far as to hint that he had taken Theodoric for a Greek word, as an adjective of Theodorus. This, of course, was only meant as a joke, for on page 120 Kingsley had said, in a note, that the name of *Theodoric*, *Theuderic*, *Dietrich*, signifies 'king of nations.' He therefore knew perfectly well that *Theodoric* was simply a Greek adaptation of the Gothic name *Theode-reiks*, *theod* meaning people, *reiks*, according to Grimm, *princeps*. But even if he had called the king Theodorus, the mistake would not have been unpardonable, for he might have appealed to the authority of Gregory of Tours, who uses not only Theodoricus, but also Theodorus, as the same name.

A more serious charge, however, was brought against him for having used the High-German form *Dietrich*, instead of the original form *Theodereiks* or *Theoderic*, or even *Theodoric*. Should I have altered this? I believe not; for it is clear to me that Kingsley had his good reasons for preferring Dietrich to Theodoric.

He introduces him first to his hearers as 'Theodoric, known in German song as Dietrich of Bern.' He had spoken before of the Visi-Gothic Theodoric, and of him he never speaks as Dietrich. Then, why should he have adopted this High-German name for the great Theodoric, and why should he speak of Attila too as Etzel?

One of the greatest of German historians, Johannes von Müller, does the same. He always calls Theodoric, Dietrich of Bern; and though he gives no reasons for it, his reasons can easily be guessed. Soon after Theodoric's death, the influence of the German legends on history, and of history on the German legends, became so great that it was impossible for a time to disentangle two characters, originally totally distinct, viz. *Thjóðrekr* of the Edda, the *Dietrich* of the German poetry on one side, and the King of the Goths, *Theodoric*, on the other. What had long been said and sung about Thjóðrekr and Dietrich was believed to have happened to King Theodoric, while at the same time historical and local elements in the life of Theodoric, residing at Verona, were absorbed by the legends of Thjóðrekr and Dietrich. The names of the legendary hero and the historical king were probably identical, though even that is not quite certain; but at all events, after Theodoric's death, all the numerous dialectic varieties of the name, whether in High or in Low-German, were understood by the people at large, both of the hero and of the king.

Few names have had a larger number of alias.'

They have been carefully collected by Graff, Grimm, Förstemann, Pott, and others. I here give the principal varieties of this name, as actually occurring in MSS., and arranged according to the changes of the principal consonants:—

(1) With *Th-d*: Theudoricus, Theudericus, Θευδέριχος, Θεοδέριχος, Thiodiricus, Thiodericus, Thiodric, Thiodricus, Thiodrih, Theodoricus, Theodericus, Theoderic, Theodrich, Thiadric, Thiadrich, Thiedorik, Thiederic, Thiederik, Thiederich, Thiedorich, Thiedric, Thiedrich, Thideric, Thiederich, Thidrich, Thodericus, Thiaedric, Thieoderich, Thederich, Thedric.

(2) With *T-d*: Teudericus, Teudricus, Tiodericus, Teodoricus, Teodericus, Teodric, Teodrich, Tiadric, Tiedrik, Tiedrich, Tiedric, Tidericus, Tiderich, Tederich.

(3) With *D-d*: Δειδοριξ, Diodericus, Deoderich, Deodrich, Diederich, Diderich.

(4) With *Th-t*: Thiotiricus, Thiotirih, Thiotiricus, Thiotrih, Theotoricus, Theotericus, Theoterih, Theotrih, Theotrich, Thiatric, Thieterich, Thietrih, Thietrich, Theatrih.

(5) With *T-t*: Teutrich, Teoterih, Teotrich, Teotrih, Tieterich, Teatrih, Tiheiterich.

(6) With *D-t*: Dioterih, Diotericus, Diotricus, Deotrich, Deotrih, Dieterih, Dieterich, Dietrich, Diterih, Ditricus.

(7) With *Th-th*: Theotherich, Theothirich.

(8) With *T-th*: *deest*.

(9) With *D-th*: Dietherich.

It is quite true that, strictly speaking, the forms with Th-d, are Low-German, and those with D-t, High-German, but before we trust ourselves to this division for historical purposes, we must remember three facts: (1) that Proper Names frequently defy Grimm's Law; (2) that in High-German MSS. much depends on the locality in which they are written; (3) that High-German is not in the strict sense of the word a corruption of Low-German, and, at all events, not, as Grimm supposed, chronologically posterior to Low-German, but that the two are parallel dialects, like Doric and Aeolic, the Low-German being represented by the earliest literary documents, Gothic and Saxon, the High-German asserting its literary presence later, not much before the eighth century, but afterwards maintaining its literary and political supremacy from the time of Charlemagne to the present day.

When Theodoric married Odeflede, the daughter of Childebert, and a sister of Chlodwig, I have little doubt that, at the court of Chlodwig or Clovis, his royal brother-in-law was spoken of in conversation as Dioterih, although in official documents, and in the history of Gregory of Tours, he appears under his classical name of Theodoricus, in Jornandes Theodericus. Those who, with Grimm, admit a transition of Low into High-German, and deny that the change of Gothic *Th* into High-German *D* took place before the sixth or seventh century, will find it difficult to account, in the first century, for the name of Deudorix, a German captive, the nephew of Melo the Sigambrian, mentioned by Strabo[1].

1 Förstemann mentions a Latin inscription of the third century found near

In the oldest German poem in which the name of Dietrich occurs, the song of Hildebrand and Hadebrand, written down in the beginning of the ninth century, we find both forms, the Low-German *Theotrîh*, and the High-German *Deotrîh*, used side by side.

Very soon, however, when High-German became the more prevalent language in Germany, German historians knew both of the old legendary hero and of the Ost-gothic king, by one and the same name, the High-German *Dietrich*.

If therefore Johannes von Müller spoke of Theodoric of Verona as Dietrich von Bern, he simply intended to carry on the historical tradition.  He meant to remind his readers of the popular name which they all knew, and to tell them,—This Dietrich with whom you are all acquainted from your childhood, this Dietrich of whom so much is said and sung in your legendary stories and poems, the famous Dietrich of Bern, this is really the Theoderic, the first German who ruled Italy for thirty-three years, more gloriously than any Roman Emperor before or after.  I see no harm in this, as long as it is done on purpose, and as long as the purpose which Johannes von Müller had in his mind, was attained.

No doubt the best plan for an historian to follow is to call every man by the name by which he called himself.  Theodoric, we know, could not write, but he had a gold plate made in which the first four letters of his name were incised, and when it was fixed on the paper, the King drew his pen through the intervals. Those four letters were ΘΕΟΔ, and though we should expect that,

<hr>

Wiesbaden with the Dative Toutiorigi.

as a Goth, he would have spelt his name *Thiudereik*, yet we have no right to doubt, that the vowels were *eo*, and not *iu*. But again and again historians spell proper names, not as they were written by the people themselves, but as they appear in the historical documents through which they became chiefly known. We speak of Plato, because we have Roman literature between us and Greece. American names are accepted in history through a Spanish, Indian names through an English medium. The strictly Old High-German form of Carolus Magnus would be Charal, A. S. Carl; yet even in the Oaths of Strassburg (842) the name appears as Karlus and as Karl, and has remained so ever since[1]. In the same document we find Ludher for Lothar, Ludhuwig and Lodhuvig for Ludovicus, the oldest form being Chlodowich: and who would lay down the law, which of these forms shall be used for historical purposes?

I have little doubt that Kingsley's object in retaining the name Dietrich for the Ost-gothic king was much the same as Johannes von Müller's. You know, he meant to say, of Dietrich of Bern, of all the wonderful things told of him in the Nibelunge and other German poems. Well, that is the Dietrich of the German people, that is what the Germans themselves have made of him, by transferring to their great Gothic king some of the most incredible achievements of one of their oldest legendary heroes. They have changed even his name, and as the children in the schools of Germany[2] still speak of him as

---

1 Grimm thinks that Charle-maigne and Charlemagne were originally corruptions of Karlo-man, and were interpreted later as Carolus magnus.

2 Weber, Lehrbuch der Weltgeschichte, § 245: 'Bei Verona von Theoderich (daher Dietrich von Bern) besiegt, barg sich Odoaker hinter die Mauern

their Dietrich von Bern, let him be to us too Dietrich, not simply the Ost-gothic Theoderic, but the German Dietrich.

I confess I see no harm in that, though a few words on the strange mixture of legend and history might have been useful, because the case of Theodoric is one of the most luculent testimonies for that blending of fact and fancy in strictly historical times which people find it so difficult to believe, but which offers the key, and the only true key, for many of the most perplexing problems, both of history and of mythology.

Originally nothing could be more different than the Dietrich of the old legend and the Dietrich of history. The former is followed by misfortune through the whole of his life. He is oppressed in his youth by his uncle, the famous Ermanrich; he has to spend the greater part of his life (thirty years) in exile, and only returns to his kingdom after the death of his enemy. Yet whenever he is called Dietrich of Bern, it is because the real Theodoric, the most successful of Gothic conquerors, ruled at Verona. When his enemy was called Otacher, instead of Sibich, it is because the real Theodoric conquered the real Odoacer. When the king, at whose court he passes his years of exile, is called Etzel, it is because many German heroes had really taken refuge in the camp of Attila. That Attila died two years before Theodoric of Verona was born, is no difficulty to a popular poet, nor even the still more glaring contradiction between the daring and

---

von Ravenna.' It is much more objectionable when Simrock in his translation of the Edda renders Thjodrekr by Dietrich, though he retains Theodolf and similar names. But it shows at the same time the wide popularity of that name.

ferocious character of the real Attila and the cowardice of his namesake Etzel, as represented in the poem of the Nibelunge. Thus was legend quickened by history.

On the other hand, if historians, such as Gregory I (Dial. iv. 36)[1], tell us that an Italian hermit had been witness in a vision to the damnation of Theodoric, whose soul was plunged, by the ministers of divine vengeance, into the volcano of Lipari, one of the flaming mouths of the infernal world, we may recognise in the heated imagination of the orthodox monk some recollection of the mysterious end of the legendary Dietrich[2]. Later on, the legendary and the real hero were so firmly welded together that, as early as the twelfth century, chroniclers are at their wits' end how to reconcile facts and dates.

Ekkehard, in his Chronicon Universale[3], which ends

---

1 Gibbon, chap. xxxix. sub fin.

2 Otto von Freising, in the first half of the twelfth century (Chronicon 5, 3), takes the opposite view, and thinks the fable derived from history: 'Ob ea non multis post diebus, xxx imperii sui anno, subitanea morte rapitur ac juxta beati Gregorii dialogum (4, 36) a Joanne et Symmacho in Aetnam praecipitatus, a quodam homine Dei cernitur. Hinc puto fabulam illam traductam, qua vulgo dicitur: *Theodoricus vivus equo sedens ad inferos descendit.*

3 Grimm, Deutsche Heldensage, p. 36. Chronicon Urspergense, 85a: Haec Jordanis quidam grammaticus, ex eorundem stirpe Gothorum progenitus, de Getarum origine et Amalorum nobilitate non omnia, quae de eis scribuntur et referuntur, ut ipse dicit, complexus exaravit, sed brevius pro rerum notitia huic opusculo inseruimus. His perlectis diligenterque perspectis perpendat, qui discernere noverit, quomodo illud ratum teneatur, quod non solum *vulgari fabulatione et cantilenarum modulatione* usitatur, verum etiam in *quibusdam chronicis* annotatur; scilicet quod *Hermenricus* tempore Martiani principis super omnes Gothos regnaverit, et *Theodoricum Dietmari filium, patruelem* suum, ut dicunt, *instimulante Odoacre,* item, ut ajunt, *patruele suo de Verona pulsum,* apud *Attilam Hunorum regem exulare coegerit,* cum historiographus narret, Ermenricum regem Gothorum multis regibus dominantem tempore Valentiniani et Valentis fratrum regnasse et a *duobus fratribus Saro et Ammio,* quos conjicimus eos fuisse, qui *vulgariter Sarelo et Hamidiecus dicuntur,* vulneratum in primordio egressionis

1126 A.D., points out the chronological contradiction between Jornandes, who places the death of Ermanrich long before Attila, and the popular story which makes him and Dietrich, the son of Dietmar, his contemporaries.

Otto von Freising[1], in the first half of the twelfth century, expresses the same perplexity when he finds that Theodoric is made a contemporary of Hermanricus and Attila, though it is certain that Attila ruled long after Hermanric, and that, after the death of Attila, Theodoric, when eight years old, was given by his father as a hostage to the emperor Leo.

Gottfried von Viterbo[2], in the second half of the twelfth century, expresses his difficulties in similar words.

All these chroniclers who handed down the historical traditions of Germany were High-Germans, and

---

Hunorum per Maeotidem paludem, quibus rex fuit Valamber, tam vulneris quam Hunorum irruptionis dolore defunctum fuisse, Attilam vero postea ultra LXX annos sub Martiano et Valentiniano cum Romanis et Wisigothis Aetioque duce Romanorum pugnasse et sub eisdem principibus regno vitaque decessisse. . . . Hinc rerum diligens inspector perpendat, quomodo *Ermenricus Theodoricum Dietmari filium apud Attilam exulare coegerit*, cum juxta hunc historiographum contemporalis ejus non fuit. Igitur aut hic falsa conscripsit, aut *vulgaris opinio fallitur et fallit*, aut alius Ermenricus et alms Theodoricus dandi sunt Attilae contemporanei, in quibus hujus modi rerum convenientia rata possit haberi. Hic enim Ermenricus longe ante Attilam legitur defunctus.

1 Chronicon, 5, 3: Quod autem rursum narrant, eum Hermanarico Attilaeque contemporaneum fuisse, omnino stare non potest, dum Attilam longe post Hermanaricum constat exercuisse tyrannidem istumque post mortem Attilae octennem a patre obsidem Leoni Augusto traditum.

2 Chronicon, 16, 481: Quod autem quidam dicunt, ipsum Theodoricum fuisse Hermenrico Veronensi et Attilae contemporaneum, non est verum. Constat enim Attilam longe post Hermenricum fuisse Theodoricum etiam longe post mortem Attilae, quum esset puer octennis, Leoni imperatori in obsidem datum fuisse.

thus it has happened that in Germany Theodoric the Great became Dietrich, as Strataburgum became Strassburg, or Turicum, Zürich.  Whether because English belongs to the Low German branch, it is less permissible to an English historian than to a German to adopt these High-German names, I cannot say: all I wished to point out was that there was a very intelligible reason why Kingsley should have preferred the popular and poetical name of Dietrich, even though it was High-German, either to his real Gothic name, Theodereik, or to its classical metamorphosis, Theodoricus or Theodorus.

Some other mistakes, too, which have been pointed out, did not seem to me so serious as to justify their correction in a posthumous edition.  It was said, for instance, that Kingsley ought not to have called Odoacer and Theodoric, Kings of Italy, as they were only lieutenants of the Eastern Caesar.  Cassiodorus, however, tells us that Odoacer assumed the name of king (nomen regis Odoacer assumpsit), and though Gibbon points out that this may only mean that he assumed the abstract title of a king, without applying it to any particular nation or country, yet that great historian himself calls Odoacer, King of Italy, and shows how he was determined to abolish the useless and expensive office of vicegerent of the emperor.  Kingsley guesses very ingeniously, that Odoacer's assumed title, King of nations, may have been the Gothic *Theode-reiks*, the very name of Theodoric. As to Theodoric himself, Kingsley surely knew his real status, for he says: 'Why did he not set himself up as Caesar of Rome?  Why did he always consider himself as son-in-arms, and quasi-vassal of the Caesar of Constantinople?'

Lastly, in speaking of the extinction of the Western Empire with Romulus Augustulus, Kingsley again simply followed the lead of Gibbon and other historians; nor can it be said that the expression is not perfectly legitimate, however clearly modern research may have shown that the Roman Empire, though dead, lived.

So much in defence, or at all events, in explanation, of expressions and statements which have been pointed out as most glaring mistakes in Kingsley's lectures. I think it must be clear that in all these cases alterations would have been impossible. There were other passages, where I should gladly have altered or struck out whole lines, particularly in the ethnological passages, and in the attempted etymologies of German proper names. Neither the one nor the other, I believe, are Kingsley's own, though I have tried in vain to find out whence he could possibly have taken them.

These, however, are minor matters which are mentioned chiefly in order to guard against the impression that, because I left them unchanged, I approved of them. The permanent interest attaching to these lectures does not spring from the facts which they give. For these, students will refer to Gibbon. They will be valued chiefly for the thoughts which they contain, for the imagination and eloquence which they display, and last, not least, for the sake of the man, a man, it is true, of a warm heart rather than of a cold judgment, but a man whom, for that very reason, many admired, many loved, and many will miss, almost every day of their life.

M. M.

# THE FOREST CHILDREN

I wish in this first lecture to give you some general conception of the causes which urged our Teutonic race to attack and destroy Rome.  I shall take for this one lecture no special text-book: but suppose you all to be acquainted with the Germania of Tacitus, and with the 9th Chapter of Gibbon.  And I shall begin, if you will allow me, by a parable, a myth, a saga, such as the men of whom I am going to tell you loved; and if it seem to any of you childish, bear in mind that what is childish need not therefore be shallow.  I know that it is not history.  These lectures will not be, in the popular sense, history at all.  But I beg you to bear in mind that I am not here to teach you history.  No man can do that.  I am here to teach you how to teach yourselves history.  I will give you the scaffolding as well as I can; you must build the house.

Fancy to yourself a great Troll-garden, such as our forefathers dreamed of often fifteen hundred years ago;—a fairy palace, with a fairy garden; and all around the primæval wood.  Inside the Trolls dwell, cunning and wicked, watching their fairy treasures, working at their magic forges, making and making always things rare and strange; and outside, the forest is full of children; such children as the world had never seen before, but children still: children in frankness, and purity, and affectionateness, and tenderness of conscience, and devout awe of the unseen; and children too in fancy, and silliness, and ignorance, and caprice, and jealousy, and quarrelsomeness, and love of excitement and adventure, and the mere sport of overflowing animal health. They play unharmed among the forest beasts, and conquer them in their play; but the forest is too dull and too poor for them; and they wander to the walls of the Troll-garden, and wonder what is inside. One can conceive easily for oneself what from that moment would begin to happen. Some of the more adventurous clamber in. Some, too, the Trolls steal and carry off into their palace. Most never return: but here and there one escapes out again, and tells how the Trolls killed all his comrades: but tells too, of the wonders he has seen inside, of shoes of swiftness, and swords of sharpness, and caps of darkness; of charmed harps, charmed jewels, and above all of the charmed wine: and after all, the Trolls were very kind to him—see what fine clothes they have given him—and he struts about awhile among his companions; and then returns, and not alone. The Trolls have bewitched him, as they will bewitch more. So the fame of the Troll-garden spreads; and more and more steal in, boys and maidens, and tempt their comrades over the wall, and tell of the jewels, and the dresses, and the wine, the joyous maddening wine, which equals men with gods; and forget to tell how the Trolls have bought them, soul as well as body, and taught them to be vain, and lustful, and slavish; and tempted them, too, often, to sins which have no name.

But their better nature flashes out at times. They will not be the slaves and brutes in human form, which the evil Trolls would have them; and they rebel, and escape, and tell of the horrors of that fair foul place. And then arises a noble indignation, and war between the Trolls and the forest-children. But still the Trolls can tempt and bribe the greedier or the more vain; and still the wonders inside haunt their minds; till it becomes a fixed idea among them all, to conquer the garden for themselves and bedizen themselves in the fine clothes, and drink their fill of the wine. Again and again they break in: but the Trolls drive them out, rebuild their walls, keep off those outside by those whom they hold enslaved within; till the boys grow to be youths, and the youths men: and still the Troll-garden is not conquered, and still it shall be. And the Trolls have grown old and weak, and their walls are crumbling away. Perhaps they may succeed this time—perhaps next.

And at last they do succeed—the fairy walls are breached, the fairy palace stormed—and the Trolls are crouching at their feet, and now all will be theirs, gold, jewels, dresses, arms, all that the Troll possesses—except his cunning.

For as each struggles into the charmed ground, the spell of the place falls on him. He drinks the wine, and it maddens him. He fills his arms with precious trumpery, and another snatches it from his grasp. Each envies the youth before him, each cries—Why had I not the luck to enter first? And the Trolls set them against each other, and split them into parties, each mad with excitement, and jealousy, and wine, till, they scarce know how, each falls upon his fellow, and all upon those who are crowding in from the forest, and they fight and fight, up and down the palace halls, till their triumph has become a very feast of the Lapithæ, and the Trolls look on, and laugh a wicked laugh, as they tar them on to the unnatural fight, till the gardens are all trampled, the finery torn, the halls dismantled, and each pavement slippery with brothers' blood. And then, when the wine is gone out of them, the survivors come to their senses, and stare shamefully and sadly round. What an ugly, desolate, tottering ruin the fairy palace has become! Have they spoilt it themselves? or have the Trolls bewitched it? And all the fairy treasure—what has become of it? no man knows. Have they thrown it away in their quarrel? have the cunningest hidden it? have the Trolls flown away with it, to the fairy land beyond the Eastern mountains? who can tell? Nothing is left but recrimination and remorse. And they wander back again into the forest, away from the doleful ruin, carrion-strewn, to sulk each apart over some petty spoil which he has saved from the general wreck, hating and dreading each the sound of his neighbour's footstep.

What will become of the forest children, unless some kind saint or hermit comes among them, to bind them in the holy bonds of brotherhood and law?

This is my saga, gentlemen; and it is a true one withal. For it is neither more nor less than the story of the Teutonic tribes, and how they overthrew the Empire of Rome.

Menzel, who though he may not rank very high as a historian, has at least a true German heart, opens his history with a striking passage.

'The sages of the East were teaching wisdom beneath the palms; the merchants of Tyre and Carthage were weighing their heavy anchors, and spreading their purple sails for far seas; the Greek was making the earth fair by his art, and the Roman founding his colossal empire of force, while the Teuton sat, yet a child, unknown and naked among the forest beasts: and yet unharmed and in his sport he lorded it over them; for the child was of a royal race, and destined to win glory for all time to come.'

To the strange and complicated education which God appointed for this race; and by which he has fitted it to become, at least for many centuries henceforth, the ruling race of the world, I wish to call your attention in my future lectures. To-day, I wish to impress strongly on your minds this childishness of our forefathers. For good or for evil they were great boys; very noble boys; very often very naughty boys—as boys with the strength of men might well be. Try to conceive such to yourselves, and you have the old Markman, Allman, Goth, Lombard, Saxon, Frank. And the notion may be more than a mere metaphor. Races, like individuals, it has been often said, may have their childhood, their youth, their manhood, their old age, and natural death. It is but a theory—perhaps nothing more. But at least, our race had its childhood. Their virtues, and their sad failings, and failures, I can understand on no other theory. The nearest type which we can see now is I fancy, the English sailor, or the English navvy. A great, simple, honest, baby—full of power and fun, very coarse and plain spoken at times: but if treated like a human being, most affectionate, susceptible, even sentimental and superstitious; fond of gambling, brute excitement, childish amusements in the intervals of enormous exertion; quarrelsome among themselves, as boys are, and with a spirit of wild independence which seems to be strength; but which, till it be disciplined into loyal obedience and self-sacrifice, is mere weakness; and beneath all a deep practical shrewdness, an indomitable perseverance, when once roused by need. Such a spirit as we see to this day in the English sailor—that is the nearest analogue I can find now. One gets hints here and there of what manner of men they were, from the evil day, when, one hundred and two years before Christ, the Kempers and Teutons, ranging over the Alps toward Italy, 300,000 armed men and 15,000 mailed knights with broad sword and lances, and in their helmets the same bulls'-horns, wings, and feathers, which one sees now in the crests of German princes, stumbled upon Marius and his Romans, and were destroyed utterly, first the men, then the women, who like true women as they were, rather than give up their honour to the Romans, hung themselves on the horns of the waggon-oxen, and were trampled to death beneath their feet; and then the very dogs, who fought on when men and women were all slain—from that fatal day, down to the glorious one, when, five hundred years after, Alaric stood beneath the walls of Rome, and to their despairing boast of the Roman numbers, answered, 'Come out to us then, the thicker the hay, the easier mowed,'—for five hundred years, I say, the hints of their character are all those of a boy-nature.

They were cruel at times: but so are boys—much more cruel than grown men, I hardly know why—perhaps because they have not felt suffering so much themselves, and know not how hard it is to bear. There were varieties of character among them. The Franks were always false, vain, capricious, selfish, taking part with the Romans whenever their interest or vanity was at stake—the worst of all Teutons, though by no means the weakest—and a miserable business they made of it in France, for some five hundred years. The Goths, Salvian says, were the most ignavi of all of them; great lazy lourdans; apt to be cruel, too, the Visigoths at least, as their Spanish descendants proved to the horror of the world: but men of honour withal, as those old Spaniards were. The Saxons were famed for cruelty—I know not why, for our branch of the Saxons has been, from the beginning of history, the least cruel people in Europe; but they had the reputation—as the Vandals had also—of being the most pure; Castitate venerandi. And among the uncivilized people coldness and cruelty go often together. The less passionate and sensitive the nature, the less open to pity. The Caribs of the West Indies were famed for both, in contrast to the profligate and gentle inhabitants of Cuba and Hispaniola; and in double contrast to the Red Indian tribes of North America, who combined, from our first acquaintance with them, the two vices of cruelty and profligacy, to an extent which has done more to extirpate them than all the fire-water of the white man.

But we must be careful how we compare our forefathers with these, or any other savages. Those who, like Gibbon, have tried to draw a parallel between the Red Indian and the Primæval Teuton, have done so at the expense of facts. First, they have overlooked the broad fact, that while the Red Indians have been, ever since we have known them, a decreasing race, the Teutons have been a rapidly increasing one; in spite of war, and famine, and all the ills of a precarious forest life, proving their youthful strength and vitality by a reproduction unparalleled, as far as I know, in history, save perhaps by that noble and young race, the Russian. These writers have not known that the Teuton had his definite laws, more simple, doubtless, in the time of Tacitus than in that of Justinian, but still founded on abstract principles so deep and broad that they form the groundwork of our English laws and constitution; that the Teuton creed concerning the unseen world, and divine beings, was of a loftiness and purity as far above the silly legends of Hiawatha as the Teuton morals were above those of a Sioux or a Comanche. Let any one read honest accounts of the Red Indians; let him read Catlin, James, Lewis and Clarke, Shoolbred; and first and best of all, the old 'Travaile in Virginia,' published by the Hakluyt Society: and then let him read the Germania of Tacitus, and judge for himself. For my part, I believe that if Gibbon was right, and if our forefathers in the German forests had been like Powhattan's people as we found them in the Virginian forests, the Romans would not have been long in civilizing us off the face of the earth.

No. All the notes which Tacitus gives us are notes of a young and strong race; unconscious of its own capabilities, but possessing such capabilities that the observant Romans saw at once with dread and awe that they were face to face with such a people as they had never met before; that in their hands, sooner or later, might be the fate of Rome. Mad Caracalla, aping the Teuton dress and hair, listening in dread to the songs of the Allman Alrunas, telling the Teutons that they ought to come over the Rhine and destroy the empire, and then, murdering the interpreters, lest they should repeat his words, was but babbling out in an insane shape the thought which was brooding in the most far-seeing Roman minds. He felt that they could have done the deed; and he felt rightly, madman as he was. They could have done it then, if physical power and courage were all that was needed, in the days of the Allman war. They could have done it a few years before, when the Markmen fought Marcus Aurelius Antoninus; on the day when the Cæsar, at the advice of his augurs, sent two lions to swim across the Danube as a test of victory; and the simple Markmen took them for big dogs, and killed them with their clubs. From that day, indeed, the Teutons began to conquer slowly, but surely. Though Antoninus beat the Markmen on the Danube, and recovered 100,000 Roman prisoners, yet it was only by the help of the Vandals; from that day the empire was doomed, and the Teutons only kept at bay by bribing one tribe to fight another, or by enlisting their more adventurous spirits into the Roman legions, to fight against men of their own blood;—a short-sighted and suicidal policy; for by that very method they were teaching the Teuton all he needed, the discipline and the military science of the Roman.

But the Teutons might have done it a hundred years before that, when Rome was in a death agony, and Vitellius and Vespasian were struggling for the purple, and

Civilis and the fair Velleda, like Barak and Deborah of old, raised the Teuton tribes. They might have done it before that again, when Hermann slew Varus and his legions in the Teutoburger Wald; or before that again, when the Kempers and Teutons burst over the Alps, to madden themselves with the fatal wines of the rich south. And why did the Teutons *not* do it? Because they were boys fighting against cunning men. Boiorich, the young Kemper, riding down to Marius' camp, to bid him fix the place and time of battle—for the Teuton thought it mean to use surprises and stratagems, or to conquer save in fair and open fight—is the type of the Teuton hero; and one which had no chance in a struggle with the cool, false, politic Roman, grown grey in the experience of the forum and of the camp, and still as physically brave as his young enemy. Because, too, there was no unity among them; no feeling that they were brethren of one blood. Had the Teuton tribes, at any one of the great crises I have mentioned, and at many a crisis afterwards, united for but three years, under the feeling of a common blood, language, interest, destiny, Rome would have perished. But they could not learn that lesson. They could not put aside their boyish quarrels.

They never learnt the lesson till after their final victory, when the Gospel of Christ—of a Being to whom they all owed equal allegiance, in whose sight they were all morally equal—came to unite them into a Christendom.

And it was well that they did not learn it sooner. Well for them and for the world, that they did not unite on any false ground of interest or ambition, but had to wait for the true ground of unity, the knowledge of the God-man, King of all nations upon earth.

Had they destroyed Rome sooner, what would not they have lost? What would not the world have lost? Christianity would have been stifled in its very cradle; and with Christianity all chance—be sure of it—of their own progress. Roman law, order, and discipline, the very things which they needed to acquire by a contact of five hundred years, would have been swept away. All classic literature and classic art, which they learnt to admire with an almost superstitious awe, would have perished likewise. Greek philosophy, the germs of physical science, and all that we owe to the ancients, would have perished; and we should have truly had an invasion of the barbarians, followed by truly dark ages, in which Europe would have had to begin all anew, without the help of the generations which had gone before.

Therefore it was well as it was, and God was just and merciful to them and to the human race. They had a glorious destiny, and glorious powers wherewith to fulfil it: but they had, as every man and people has, before whom there is a noble future, to be educated by suffering. There was before them a terrible experience of sorrow and disappointment, sin and blood, by which they gained the first consciousness of what they could do and what they could not. Like Adam of old, like every man unto this day, they ate of the tree of the knowledge of good and evil, and were driven out of the paradise of unconsciousness; had to begin again sadder and wiser men, and eat their bread in the sweat of their brow; and

so to rise, after their fall, into a nobler, wiser, more artificial, and therefore more truly human and divine life,
than that from which they had at first fallen, when they
left their German wilds.

One does not, of course, mean the parallel to fit in
all details. The fall of the Teuton from the noble simplicity in which Tacitus beheld and honoured him, was
a work of four centuries; perhaps it was going on in
Tacitus' own time. But the culminating point was the
century which saw Italy conquered, and Rome sacked,
by Visigoth, by Ostrogoth, by Vandal, till nothing was
left save fever-haunted ruins. Then the ignorant and
greedy child, who had been grasping so long after the
fair apples of Sodom, clutched them once and for all,
and found them turn to ashes in his hands.

Yes—it is thus that I wish you to look at the Invasion
of the Barbarians, Immigration of the Teutons, or whatsoever name you may call it. Before looking at questions
of migration, of ethnology, of laws, and of classes, look
first at the thing itself; and see with sacred pity—and
awe, one of the saddest and grandest tragedies ever per-
formed on earth. Poor souls! And they were so simple
withal. One pities them, as one pities a child who steals
apples, and makes himself sick with them after all. It is
not the enormous loss of life which is to me the most
tragic part of the story; it is that very simplicity of the
Teutons. Bloodshed is a bad thing, certainly; but after
all nature is prodigal of human life—killing her twenty
thousand and her fifty thousand by a single earthquake;
and as for death in battle—I sometimes am tempted
to think, having sat by many death beds, that our old

forefathers may have been right, and that death in battle may be a not unenviable method of passing out of this troublesome world. Besides, we have no right to blame those old Teutons, while we are killing every year more of her Majesty's subjects by preventible disease, than ever they killed in their bloodiest battle. Let us think of that, and mend that, ere we blame the old German heroes. No, there are more pitiful tragedies than any battlefield can shew; and first among them, surely, is the disappointment of young hopes, the degradation of young souls.

One pities them, I say. And they pitied themselves. Remorse, shame, sadness, mark the few legends and songs of the days which followed the fall of Rome. They had done a great work. They had destroyed a mighty tyranny; they had parted between them the spoils wrung from all the nations; they had rid the earth of a mighty man-devouring ogre, whose hands had been stretched out for centuries over all the earth, dragging all virgins to his den, butchering and torturing thousands for his sport; foul, too, with crimes for which their language, like our own (thank God) has scarcely found a name. Babylon the Great, drunken with the blood of the saints, had fallen at last before the simple foresters of the north: but if it looks a triumph to us, it looked not such to them. They could only think how they had stained their hands in their brothers' blood. They had got the fatal Nibelungen hoard: but it had vanished between their hands, and left them to kill each other, till none was left.

You know the Nibelungen Lied? That expresses, I

believe, the key-note of the old Teuton's heart, after his work was done. Siegfried murdered by his brother-in-law; fair Chriemhild turned into an avenging fury; the heroes hewing each other down, they scarce know why, in Hunnish Etzel's hall, till Hagen and Gunther stand alone; Dietrich of Bern going in, to bind the last surviving heroes; Chriemhild shaking Hagen's gory head in Gunther's face, himself hewed down by the old Hildebrand, till nothing is left but stark corpses and vain tears:—while all the while the Nibelungen hoard, the cause of all the woe, lies drowned in the deep Rhine until the judgment day.—What is all this, but the true tale of the fall of Rome, of the mad quarrels of the conquering Teutons? The names are confused, mythic; the dates and places all awry: but the tale is true—too true. Mutato nomine fabula narratur. Even so they went on, killing, till none were left. Deeds as strange, horrible, fratricidal, were done, again and again, not only between Frank and Goth, Lombard and Gepid, but between Lombard and Lombard, Frank and Frank. Yes, they were drunk with each other's blood, those elder brethren of ours. Let us thank God that we did not share their booty, and perish, like them, from the touch of the fatal Nibelungen hoard. Happy for us Englishmen, that we were forced to seek our adventures here, in this lonely isle; to turn aside from the great stream of Teutonic immigration; and settle here, each man on his forest-clearing, to till the ground in comparative peace, keeping unbroken the old Teutonic laws, unstained the old Teutonic faith and virtue, cursed neither with poverty nor riches, but fed with food sufficient for us. To us, indeed, after long centuries, peace brought sloth, and sloth foreign invaders and bitter woes: but better so, than that we should have cast away alike our virtue and our lives, in that mad quarrel over the fairy gold of Rome.

# THE DYING EMPIRE

It is not for me to trace the rise, or even the fall of the Roman Empire. That would be the duty rather of a professor of ancient history, than of modern. All I need do is to sketch, as shortly as I can, the state in which the young world found the old, when it came in contact with it.

The Roman Empire, toward the latter part of the fourth century, was in much the same condition as the Chinese or the Turkish Empire in our own days. Private morality (as Juvenal and Persius will tell you), had vanished long before. Public morality had, of course, vanished likewise. The only powers really recognised were force and cunning. The only aim was personal enjoyment. The only God was the Divus Cæsar, the imperial demigod, whose illimitable brute force gave him illimitable powers of self-enjoyment, and made him thus the paragon and ideal of humanity, whom all envied, flattered, hated, and obeyed. The palace was a sink of corruption, where eunuchs, concubines, spies, informers, freedmen, adventurers, struggled in the basest plots, each for his share of the public plunder. The senate only existed to register the edicts of their tyrant, and if need be, destroy each other, or any one else, by judicial murders, the willing tools of imperial cruelty. The government was administered (at least since the time of Diocletian) by an official bureaucracy, of which Professor Goldwin Smith well says, 'the earth swarmed with

the consuming hierarchy of extortion, so that it was said
that they who received taxes were more than those who
paid them.' The free middle class had disappeared, or
lingered in the cities, too proud to labour, fed on government bounty, and amused by government spectacles.
With them, arts and science had died likewise. Such
things were left to slaves, and became therefore, literally,
servile imitations of the past. What, indeed, was not
left to slaves? Drawn without respect of rank, as well
as of sex and age, from every nation under heaven by
an organized slave-trade, to which our late African one
was but a tiny streamlet compared with a mighty river;
a slave-trade which once bought 10,000 human beings
in Delos in a single day; the 'servorum nationes' were
the only tillers of the soil, of those 'latifundia' or great
estates, 'quæ perdidere Romam.' Denied the rights of
marriage, the very name of humanity; protected by no
law, save the interest or caprice of their masters; sub-
jected, for slight offences, to cruel torments, they were
butchered by thousands in the amphitheatres to make
a Roman holiday, or wore out their lives in 'ergastula'
or barracks, which were dens of darkness and horror.
Their owners, as 'senatores,' 'clarissimi,' or at least 'curiales,' spent their lives in the cities, luxurious and effeminate, and left their slaves to the tender mercy of 'villici,'
stewards and gang-drivers, who were themselves slaves
likewise.

More pampered, yet more degraded, were the crowds
of wretched beings, cut off from all the hopes of humanity, who ministered to the wicked pleasures of their masters, even in the palaces of nominally Christian emper-

ors—but over that side of Roman slavery I must draw a veil, only saying, that the atrocities of the Romans toward their slaves—especially of this last and darkest kind—notably drew down on them the just wrath and revenge of those Teutonic nations, from which so many of their slaves were taken[1].

And yet they called themselves Christians—to whom it had been said, 'Be not deceived, God is not mocked. For these things cometh the wrath of God on the children of disobedience.' And the wrath did come.

If such were the morals of the Empire, what was its political state? One of complete disorganization. The only uniting bond left seems to have been that of the bureaucracy, the community of tax-gatherers, who found it on the whole safer and more profitable to pay into the imperial treasury a portion of their plunder, than to keep it all themselves. It stood by mere vi inertiæ, just because it happened to be there, and there was nothing else to put in its place. Like an old tree whose every root is decayed, it did not fall, simply because the storm had not yet come. Storms, indeed, had come; but they had been partial and local. One cannot look into the pages of Gibbon, without seeing that the normal condition of the empire was one of revolt, civil war, invasion—Pretenders, like Carausius and Allectus in Britain, setting

1 The early romancers, and especially Achilles Tatius, give pictures of Roman prædial slavery too painful to quote. Roman domestic slavery is not to be described by the pen of an Englishman. And I must express my sorrow, that in the face of such notorious facts, some have of late tried to prove American slavery to be as bad as, or even worse than, that of Rome. God forbid! Whatsoever may have been the sins of the Southern gentleman, he is at least a Teuton, and not a Roman; a whole moral heaven above the effeminate wretch, who in the 4th and 5th centuries called himself a senator and a clarissimus.

themselves up as emperors for awhile—Bands of brigands, like the Bagaudæ of Gaul, and the Circumcelliones
of Africa, wandering about, desperate with hunger and
revenge, to slay and pillage—Teutonic tribes making
forays on the frontier, enlisted into the Roman armies,
and bought off, or hired to keep back the tribes behind
them, and perish by their brethren's swords.

What kept the empire standing, paradoxical as it
may seem, was its own innate weakness. From within, at
least, it could not be overthrown. The masses were too
crushed to rise. Without unity, purpose, courage, they
submitted to inevitable misery as to rain and thunder.
At most they destroyed their own children from poverty, or, as in Egypt, fled by thousands into the caves and
quarries, and turned monks and hermits; while the upper classes, equally without unity or purpose, said each
to himself, 'Let us eat and drink, for to-morrow we die.'

The state of things at Rome, and after the rise of
Byzantium under Constantine at Byzantium likewise,
was one altogether fantastic, abnormal, utterly unlike
anything that we have seen, or can imagine to ourselves
without great effort. I know no better method of illus-
trating it, than quoting, from Mr. Sheppard's excellent
book, *The Fall of Rome and the Rise of New Nationalities*,
a passage in which he transfers the whole comi-tragedy
from Italy of old to England in 1861.

'I have not thought it necessary to give a separate
and distinct reply to the theory of Mr. Congreve, that
Roman Imperialism was the type of all good government, and a desirable precedent for ourselves. Those
who feel any penchant for the notion, I should strongly

recommend to read the answer of Professor G. Smith, in the *Oxford Essays* for 1856, which is as complete and crushing as that gentleman's performances usually are. But in order to convey to the uninitiated some idea of the state of society under Cæsarian rule, and which a Cæsarian rule, so far as mere government is concerned, if it does not produce, has never shewn any tendency to prevent, let us give reins to imagination for a moment, and picture to ourselves a few social and political analogies in our own England of the nineteenth century.

'An entire revolution has taken place in our principles, manners, and form of government. Parliaments, meetings, and all the ordinary expressions of the national will, are no longer in existence. A free press has shared their fate. There is no accredited organ of public opinion; indeed there is no public opinion to record. Lords and Commons have been swept away, though a number of the richest old gentlemen in London meet daily at Westminster to receive orders from Buckingham Palace. But at the palace itself has broken out one of those sanguinary conspiracies which have of late become unceasing. The last heir of the house of Brunswick is lying dead with a dagger in his heart, and everything is in frightful confusion. The armed force of the capital are of course "masters of the situation," and the Guards, after a tumultuous meeting at Windsor or Knightsbridge, have sold the throne to Baron Rothschild, for a handsome donation of £25 a-piece. Lord Clyde, however, we may be sure, is not likely to stand this, and in a few months will be marching upon London at the head of the Indian Army. In the mean time the Channel Fleet has declared for its own commander, has seized upon Plymouth and Portsmouth, and intends to starve the metropolis by stopping the imports of "bread-stuffs" at the mouth of the Thames. And this has become quite possible; for half the population of London, under the present state of things, subsist upon free distributions of corn dispensed by the occupant of the throne for the time being. But a more fatal change than even this has come over the population of the capital and of the whole country. The free citizens and 'prentices of London; the sturdy labourers of Dorsetshire and the eastern counties; and the skilful artizans of Manchester, Sheffield and Birmingham; the mariners and shipwrights of Liverpool, have been long ago drafted into marching regiments, and have left their bones to bleach beneath Indian suns and Polar snows. Their place has been supplied by countless herds of negro slaves, who till the fields and crowd the workshops of our towns, to the entire exclusion of free labour; for the free population, or rather the miserable relics of them, disdain all manual employment: they divide their time between starvation and a degrading debauchery, the means for which are sedulously provided by the government. The time-honoured institutions of the bull-bait, the cockpit, and the ring, are in daily operation, under the most distinguished patronage. Hyde Park has been converted into a gigantic arena, where criminals from Newgate "set-to" with the animals from the Zoological Gardens. Every fortnight there is a Derby Day, and the whole population pour into the Downs with frantic excitement, leaving the city to the slaves. And then the moral condition of this immense mass! Of the doings about the palace we should be sorry to speak. But the lady patronesses of Almack's still more assiduously patronize the prize-fights, and one of them has been seen within the ropes, in battle array, by the side of Sayers himself. No tongue may tell the orgies enacted, with the aid of French cooks, Italian singers, and foreign artists of all sorts, in the gilded saloons of Park Lane and Mayfair. Suffice to say, that in them the worst passions of human nature have full swing, unmodified by any thought of human or divine restraints, and only dashed a little now and then by the apprehension that the slaves may rise, and make a clean sweep of the metropolis with fire and steel. But *n'importe—Vive la bagatelle*! Mario has just been appointed prime minister, and has made a chorus singer from the Opera Duke of Middlesex and Governor-General of India. All wise men and all good men despair of the state, but they are not permitted to say anything, much less to act. Mr. Disraeli lost his head a few days ago; Lords Palmerston and Derby lie in the Tower under sentence of death; Lord Brougham, the Archbishop of Canterbury, and Mr. Gladstone, opened their veins and died in a warm bath last week. Foreign relations will make a still greater demand on the reader's imagination. We must conceive of England no longer as

> "A precious stone set in the silver sea,
> Which serves it in the office of a wall,
> Or as a moat defensive of a house."

but rather as open to the inroad of every foe whom her

aggressive and colonizing genius has provoked. The red man of the West, the Caffre, the Sikh, and the Sepoy, Chinese braves, and fierce orientals of all sorts, are hovering on her frontiers in "numbers numberless," as the flakes of snow in the northern winter. They are not the impotent enemy which we know, but vigorous races, supplied from inexhaustible founts of population, and animated by an insatiate appetite for the gold and silver, purple and fine linen, rich meats and intoxicating drinks of our effete civilization. And we can no longer oppose them with those victorious legions which have fought and conquered in all regions of the world. The men of Waterloo and Inkermann are no more. We are compelled to recruit our armies from those very tribes before whose swords we are receding!

'Doubtless the ordinary reader will believe this picture to be overcharged, drawn with manifest exaggeration, and somewhat questionable taste. *Every single statement which it contains* may be paralleled by the circumstances and events of the decadence of the Roman Empire. The analogous situation was with the subjects of this type of all good government, *always a possible*, often an actual, state of things. We think this disposes of the theory of Mr. Congreve. With it may advantageously be contrasted the opinion of a man of more statesman-like mind. "The benefits of despotism are short-lived; it poisons the very springs which it lays open; if it display a merit, it is an exceptional one; if a virtue, it is created of circumstances; and when once this better hour has passed away, all the vices of its nature break forth with redoubled violence, and weigh down society in every direction." So writes M. Guizot. Is it the language of prophecy as well as of personal experience?'

Mr. Sheppard should have added, to make the picture complete, that the Irish have just established popery across St. George's Channel, by the aid of re-immigrants from America; that Free Kirk and National Kirk are carrying on a sanguinary civil war in Scotland; that the Devonshire Wesleyans have just sacked Exeter cathedral, and murdered the Bishop at the altar, while the Bishop of London, supported by the Jews and the rich churchmen (who are all mixed up in financial operations with Baron Rothschild) has just commanded all Dissenters to leave the metropolis within three days, under pain of death.

I must add yet one more feature to this fearful, but accurate picture, and say how, a few generations forward, an even uglier thing would be seen. The English aristocracy would have been absorbed by foreign adventurers. The grandchildren of these slaves and mercenaries would be holding the highest offices in the state and the army, naming themselves after the masters who had freed them, or disguising their barbarian names by English endings. The De Fung-Chowvilles would be Dukes, the Little-grizzly-bear-Joe-Smiths Earls, and the Fitz-Stanleysons, descended from a king of the gipsies who enlisted to avoid transportation, and in due time became Commander-in-Chief, would rule at Knowsley in place of the Earl of Derby, having inherited the same by the summary process of assassination. Beggars on horseback, only too literally; married, most of them, to Englishwomen of the highest rank; but looking on England merely as a prey; without patriotism, without principle; they would destroy the old aristocracy by legal murders, grind the people, fight against their yet barbarian cousins outside, as long as they were in luck: but the moment the luck turned against them, would call in those barbarian cousins to help them, and invade England every ten years with heathen hordes, armed no more with tulwar and matchlock, but with Enfield rifle and Whitworth cannon. And that, it must be agreed, would be about the last phase of the British empire. If you will look through the names which figure in the high places of the Roman empire, during the fourth and fifth centuries, you will see how few of them are really Roman. If you will try to investigate, not their genealogies—for they have none—not a grandfather among them—but the few facts of their lives which have come down to us; you will see how that Nemesis had fallen on her which must at last fall on every nation which attempts to establish itself on slavery as a legal basis. Rome had become the slave of her own slaves.

It is at this last period, the point when Rome has become the slave of her own slaves, that I take up the story of our Teutonic race.

I do not think that anyone will call either Mr. Sheppard's statements, or mine, exaggerated, who knows the bitter complaints of the wickedness and folly of the time, which are to be found in the writings of the Emperor Julian. Pedant and apostate as he was, he devoted his short life to one great idea, the restoration of the Roman Empire to what it had been (as he fancied) in the days of the virtuous stoic Emperors of the second century.  He found his dream a dream, owing to the dead heap of frivolity, sensuality, brutality, utter unbelief, not merely in the dead Pagan gods whom he vainly tried to restore, but in any god at all, as a living, ruling, judging, rewarding, punishing power.

No one, again, will call these statements exaggerated who knows the Roman history of his faithful servant and soldier, Ammianus Marcellinus, and especially the later books of it, in which he sets forth the state of the Empire after Julian's death, under Jovian, Procopius, Valentinian, (who kept close to his bed-chamber two she-bears who used to eat men, one called Golden Camel, and the other Innocence—which latter, when she had devoured a sufficiency of his living victims, he set free in the forests as a reward for her services—a brutal tyrant, whose only virtue seems to have been his chastity); and Valens, the shameless extortioner who perished in that great battle of Adrianople, of which more hereafter.  The last five remaining books of the honest soldier's story are a tissue of horrors, from reading which one turns away as from a slaughter-house or a witches' sabbath.

No one, again, will think these statements exaggerated who knows Salvian's De Gubernatione Dei.  It has been always and most justly held in high esteem, as one great authority of the state of Gaul when conquered by the Franks and Goths and Vandals.

Salvian was a Christian gentleman, born somewhere near Treves.  He married a Pagan lady of Cologne, converted her, had by her a daughter, and then persuaded her to devote herself to celibacy, while he did the like.

His father-in-law, Hypatius, quarrelled with him on this
account; and the letter in which he tries to soothe the
old man is still extant, a curious specimen of the style of
cultivated men in that day. Salvian then went down to
the south of France and became a priest at Marseilles,
and tutor to the sons of Eucherius, the Bishop of Lyons. Eucherius, himself a good man, speaks in terms of
passionate admiration of Salvian, his goodness, sanctity,
learning, talents. Gennadius (who describes him as still
living when he wrote, about 490) calls him among other
encomiums, the Master of Bishops; and both mention
familiarly this very work, by which he became notorious
in his own day, and which he wrote about 450 or 455,
during the invasion of the Britons. So that we may trust
fully that we have hold of an authentic contemporaneous work, written by a good man and true.

Let me first say a few words on the fact of his having—as many good men did then—separated from his
wife in order to lead what was called a religious life. It
has a direct bearing on the History of those days. One
must not praise him because he (in common with all
Christians of his day) held, no doubt, the belief that
marriage was a degradation in itself; that though the
Church might mend it somewhat by exalting it into a
sacrament, still, the less of a bad thing the better:—a
doctrine against which one need not use (thank God)
in England, the same language which Michelet has most
justly used in France. We, being safe from the poison,
can afford to talk of it calmly. But I boldly assert, that
few more practically immoral doctrines than that of
the dignity of celibacy and the defilement of marriage

(which was the doctrine of all Christian devotees for 1000 years) have, as far as I know, ever been preached to man. That is a strong statement. It will be answered perhaps, by the patent fact, that during those very 1000 years the morality of Europe improved more, and more rapidly, than it had ever done before. I know it; and I thank God for it. But I adhere to my statement, and rejoin—And how much more rapidly have the morals of Europe improved, since that doctrine has been swept away; and woman, and the love of woman, have been restored to their rightful place in the education of man?

But if we do not praise Salvian, we must not blame him, or any one else who meant to be an honest and good man. Such did not see to what their celibate notions would lead. If they had, we must believe that they would have acted differently. And what is more, their preference for celibacy was not fancy, but common sense of a very lofty kind. Be sure that when two middle-aged Christian people consider it best to part, they have very good reasons for such a solemn step, at which only boys or cynics will laugh. And the reasons, in Salvian's case, and many more in his day, are patent to common human understanding. Do not fancy that he had any private reason, such as we should very fairly assign now: public reasons, and those, such as God grant no living man may see, caused wise men to thank God that they were not burdened with wife and child. Remember the years in which Salvian lived—from 416 perhaps to 490. It was a day of the Lord such as Joel saw; 'a day of clouds and of thick darkness, as the morning spread upon the mountains; a great people and strong; there had not been ever the like, neither should be any more after it: the land was a garden of Eden before them, and behind them a desolate wilderness: Yea, and nothing should escape them.' All things were going to wrack; the country was overrun by foreign invaders; bankruptcy, devastation, massacre, and captivity were for perhaps 100 years the normal state of Gaul, and of most other countries besides. I have little doubt that Salvian was a prudent man, when he thought fit to bring no more human beings into the world. That is an ugly thought—I trust that you feel how ugly, unnatural, desperate a thought it is. If you do not, think over it till you do, till it frightens you. You will gain a great step thereby in human sympathy, and therefore in the understanding of history. For many times, and in many places, men have said, rightly or wrongly, 'It is better to leave none behind me like myself. The miseries of life (and of what comes after this life) are greater than its joys. I commit an act of cruelty by bringing a fresh human being into the world.' I wish you to look at that thought steadily, and apply it for yourselves. It has many applications: and has therefore been a very common one.

But put to yourselves—it is too painful for me to put to you—the case of a married gentleman who sees his country gradually devastated and brought to utter ruin by foreign invaders; and who feels—as poor Salvian felt, that there is no hope or escape; that the misery is merited, deserved, fairly *earned* (for that is the true meaning of those words), and therefore must come. Conceive him seeing around him estates destroyed, farms burnt, ladies and gentlemen, his own friends and relations, reduced in an hour to beggary, plundered, stript, driven off in gangs—I do not choose to finish the picture: but ask yourselves, would an honourable man wish to bring sons—much more daughters—into the world to endure that?

Put yourselves in Salvian's place. Forget for a few minutes that you are Englishmen, the freest and bravest nation upon earth, strong in all that gives real strength, and with a volunteer army which is now formidable by numbers and courage—which, did the terrible call come, might be increased ten times in as many months. Forget all that awhile; and put yourselves in Salvian's place, the gentleman of Gaul, while Franks and Goths, Burgunds and Vandals were sweeping, wave after wave, over that lovely land; and judge him rationally, and talk as little as possible of his superstition, and as much as possible of his human feeling, prudence, self-control, and common sense. Believe me, neither celibacy, nor any other seemingly unnatural superstition would have held its ground for a generation if there had not been some practical considerations of common sense to back them. We wonder why men in old times went into monasteries. The simplest answer is, common sense sent them thither. They were tired of being the slaves of their own passions; they were tired of killing, and of running the chance of being killed. They saw society, the whole world, going to wrack, as they thought, around them: what could they do better, than see that their own characters, morals, immortal souls did not go to wrack with the rest. We wonder why women, especially women of rank, went into convents; why, as soon as a community of monks was founded, a community of nuns sprung up near them. The simplest answer is, common sense sent them thither. The men, especially of the upper fighting classes, were killed off rapidly; the women were not killed off, and a large number always remained, who, if they had wished to marry, could not. What better for them than to seek in convents that peace which this world could not give?

They may have mixed up with that simple wish for peace the notion of being handmaids of God, brides of Christ, and so forth. Be it so. Let us instead of complaining, thank heaven that there was some motive, whether quite right or not, to keep alive in them self-respect, and the feeling that they were not altogether useless and aimless on earth. Look at the question in this light, and you will understand two things; first, how horrible the times were, and secondly, why there grew up in the early middle age a passion for celibacy.

Salvian, in a word, had already grown up to manhood and reason, when he saw a time come to his native country, in which were fulfilled, with fearful exactness, the words of the prophet Isaiah:—

'Behold, the Lord maketh the land empty, and maketh it waste, and turneth it upside down, and scattereth abroad the inhabitants thereof. And it shall be, as with the people, so with the priest; as with the slave, so with his master; as with the maid, so with her mistress; as with the seller, so with the buyer; as with the lender, so with the borrower; as with the taker of usury, so with the giver of usury to him. The land shall be utterly emptied, and utterly spoiled; for the Lord hath spoken this word.'

And Salvian desired to know the reason why the Lord had spoken that word, and read his Bible till he found out, and wrote thereon his book De Gubernatione Dei, of the government of God; and a very noble book it is. He takes his stand on the ground of Scripture, with which he shews an admirable acquaintance. The few good were expecting the end of the world. Christ was coming to put an end to all these horrors: but why did he delay his coming? The many weak were crying that God had given up the world; that Christ had deserted his Church, and delivered over Christians to the cruelties of heathen and Arian barbarians. The many bad were openly blaspheming, throwing off in despair all faith, all bonds of religion, all common decency, and crying, Let us eat and drink, for to-morrow we die. Salvian answers them like an old Hebrew prophet: 'The Lord's arm is not shortened. The Lord's eyes are not closed. The Lord is still as near as ever. He is governing the world as He has always governed it: by the everlasting moral laws, by which the wages of sin are death. Your iniquities have withheld good things from you. You have earned exactly what God has paid you. Yourselves are your own punishment. You have been wicked men, and therefore weak men; your own vices, and not the Goths, have been your true conquerors.' As I said in my inaugural lecture—that is after all the true theory of history. Men may forget it in piping times of peace. God grant that in the dark hour of adversity,

God may always raise up to them a prophet, like good old Salvian, to preach to them once again the everlasting judgments of God; and teach them that not faulty constitutions, faulty laws, faulty circumstances of any kind, but the faults of their own hearts and lives, are the causes of their misery.

M. Guizot, in his elaborate work on the History of Civilization in France, has a few curious pages, on the causes of the decline of civil society in Roman Gaul, and its consequent weakness and ruin. He tells you how the Senators or Clarissimi did not constitute a true aristocracy, able to lead and protect the people, being at the mercy of the Emperor, and nominated and removed at his pleasure. How the Curiales, or wealthy middle class, who were bound by law to fulfil all the municipal offices, and were responsible for the collection of the revenue, found their responsibilities so great, that they by every trick in their power, avoided office. How, as M. Guizot well puts it, the central despotism of Rome stript the Curiales of all they earned, to pay its own functionaries and soldiers; and gave them the power of appointing magistrates, who were only after all the imperial agents of that despotism, for whose sake they robbed their fellow-citizens. How the plebs, comprising the small tradesmen and free artizans, were utterly unable to assert their own opinions or rights. How the slave population, though their condition was much improved, constituted a mere dead weight of helpless brutality.

And then he says, that the Roman Empire was dying. Very true: but often as he quotes Salvian, he omits always to tell us what Roman society was dying of. Salvian says, that it was dying of vice. Not of bad laws and class arrangements, but of bad men. M. Guizot belongs to a school which is apt to impute human happiness and prosperity too exclusively to the political constitution under which they may happen to live, irrespectively of the morality of the people themselves. From that, the constitutionalist school, there has been of late a strong reaction, the highest exponent, nay the very coryphæus of which is Mr. Carlyle. He undervalues, even despises, the influence of laws and constitutions: with him private virtue, from which springs public virtue, is the first and sole cause of national prosperity. My inaugural lecture has told you how deeply I sympathize with his view—taking my stand, as Mr. Carlyle does, on the Hebrew prophets.

There is, nevertheless, a side of truth in the constitutionalist view, which Mr. Carlyle, I think, overlooks. A bad political constitution does produce poverty and weakness: but only in as far as it tends to produce moral evil; to make men bad. That it can help to do. It can put a premium on vice, on falsehood, on peculation, on laziness, on ignorance; and thus tempt the mass to moral degradation, from the premier to the slave. Russia has been, for two centuries now but too patent a proof of the truth of this assertion. But even in this case, the moral element is the most important, and just the one which is overlooked. To have good laws, M. Guizot is apt to forget, you must first have good men to make them; and second, you must have good men to carry them out, after they are made. Bad men can abuse the best of laws, the best of constitutions. Look at the working of our parliaments during the reigns of William III and Anne, and see how powerless good constitutions are, when the men who work them are false and venal. Look, on the other hand, at the Roman Empire from the time of Vespasian to that of the Antonines, and see how well even a bad constitution will succeed, when good men are working it.

Bad laws, I say, will work tolerably under good men, if fitted to the existing circumstances by men of the world, as all Roman laws were. If they had not been such, how was the Roman Empire, at least in its first years, a blessing to the safety, prosperity, and wealth of every country it enslaved? But when defective Roman laws began to be worked by bad men, and that for 200 years, then indeed came times of evil. Let us take, then, Salvian's own account of the cause of Roman decay. He, an eye-witness, imputes it all to the morals of Roman citizens. They were, according to him, of the very worst. To the general dissoluteness he attributes, in plain words, the success of the Frank and Gothic invaders. And the facts which he gives, and which there is no reason to doubt, are quite enough to prove him in the right. Every great man's house, he says, was a sink of profligacy. The women slaves were at the mercy of their master; and the slaves copied his morals among themselves. It is an ugly picture: but common sense will tell us, if we but think a little, that such will, and must, be the case in slave-holding countries, wherever Christianity is not present in its purest and strongest form, to control the passions of arbitrary power.

But there was not merely profligacy among these

Gauls. That alone would not have wrought their immediate ruin. Morals were bad enough in old Greece and Rome; as they were afterwards among the Turks: nevertheless as long as a race is strong; as long as there is prudence, energy, deep national feeling, outraged virtue does not avenge itself at once by general ruin. But it avenges itself at last, as Salvian shews—as all experience shews. As in individuals so in nations, unbridled indulgence of the passions must produce, and does produce, frivolity, effeminacy, slavery to the appetite of the moment, a brutalized and reckless temper, before which, prudence, energy, national feeling, any and every feeling which is not centered in self, perishes utterly. The old French noblesse gave a proof of this law, which will last as a warning beacon to the end of time. The Spanish population of America, I am told, gives now a fearful proof of this same terrible penalty. Has not Italy proved it likewise, for centuries past? It must be so, gentlemen. For national life is grounded on, is the development of, the life of the family. And where the root is corrupt, the tree must be corrupt likewise. It must be so. For Asmodeus does not walk alone. In his train follow impatience and disappointment, suspicion and jealousy, rage and cruelty, and all the passions which set man's hand against his fellow-man. It must be so. For profligacy is selfishness; and the family, and the society, the nation, exists only by casting away selfishness and by obeying law:—not only the outward law, which says in the name of God, 'Thou shalt not,' but the inward law, the Law of Christ, which says, 'Thou must;' the law of self-sacrifice, which selfish lust tramples under foot, till there is no more cohesion left between man and man, no more trust, no more fellow-help, than between the stags who fight for the hinds; and God help the nation which has brought itself to that!

No wonder, therefore, if Salvian's accounts of Gaulish profligacy be true, that Gaulish recklessness reached at last a pitch all but incredible.  It is credible, however shocking, that as he says, he himself saw, both at Treves, and another great city (probably Cologne, Colonia Agrippina, or 'The Colony' par excellence) while the destruction of the state was imminent, 'old men of rank, decrepit Christians, slaves to gluttony and lust, rabid with clamour, furious with bacchanalian orgies.' It is credible, however shocking, that all through Gaul the captivity was 'foreseen, yet never dreaded.'  And 'so when the barbarians had encamped almost in sight, there was no terror among the people, no care of the cities.  All was possest by carelessness and sloth, gluttony, drunkenness, sleep, according to that which the prophet saith: A sleep from the Lord had come over them.'  It is credible, however shocking, that though Treves was four times taken by the barbarians, it remained just as reckless as ever; and that—I quote Salvian still—when the population was half destroyed by fire and sword, the poor dying of famine, corpses of men and women lying about the streets breeding pestilence, while the dogs devoured them, the few nobles who were left comforted themselves by sending to the Emperor to beg for Circensian games.

Those Circensian games, and indeed all the public spectacles, are fresh proofs of what I said just now; that if a bad people earn bad government, still a bad government makes a bad people.

They were the most extraordinary instance which the world ever saw, of a government setting to work at a vast expense to debauch its subjects. Whether the Roman rulers set that purpose consciously before them, one dare not affirm. Their notion probably was (for they were as worldly wise as they were unprincipled) that the more frivolous and sensual the people were, the more quietly they would submit to slavery; and the best way to keep them frivolous and sensual, the Romans knew full well; so well, that after the Empire became Christian, and many heathen matters were done away with, they did not find it safe to do away with the public spectacles. The temples of the Gods might go: but not the pantomimes.

In one respect, indeed, these government spectacles became worse, not better, under Christianity. They were less cruel, no doubt: but also they were less beautiful. The old custom of exhibiting representations of the old Greek myths, which had something of grace and poetry about them, and would carry back the spectators' thoughts to the nobler and purer heroic ages, disappeared before Christianity; but the old vice did not. That was left; and no longer ennobled by the old heroic myths round which it had clustered itself, was simply of the silliest and most vulgar kind. We know in detail the abominations, as shameless and ridiculous, which went on a century after Salvian, in the theatres of Constantinople, under the eyes of the most Christian Emperor Justinian, and which won for that most infamous woman, Theodora, a share in his imperial crown, and the right to dictate doctrine to the Christian Bishops of the East, and to condemn the soul of Origen to everlasting damnation, for having exprest hopes of the final pardon of sinners. We can well believe, therefore, Salvian's complaints of the wickedness of those pantomimes of which he says, that 'honeste non possunt vel accusari;' he cannot even accuse them without saying what he is ashamed to say; I believe also his assertion, that they would not let people be modest, even if they wished; that they inflamed the passions, and debauched the imaginations of young and old, man and woman, and— but I am not here to argue that sin is sin, or that the population of London would be the worse if the most shameless persons among them were put by the Government in possession of Drury Lane and Covent Garden; and that, and nothing less than that, did the Roman pantomimes mean, from the days of Juvenal till those of the most holy and orthodox Empress Theodora.

'Who, knowing the judgment of God, that they who do such things are worthy of death, not only do the same, but have pleasure in them that do them.'

Now in contrast to all these abominations, old Salvian sets, boldly and honestly, the superior morality of the barbarians. That, he says, is the cause of their strength and our weakness. We, professing orthodoxy, are profligate hypocrites. They, half heathens, half Arians, are honester men, purer men than we. There is no use, he says, in despising the Goths as heretics, while they are better men than we. They are better Christians than the Romans, because they are better men. They pray to God for success, and trust in him, and we presumptuously trust in ourselves. We swear by Christ: but what do we do but blaspheme him, when we swear 'Per Christum tollo eum,' 'I will make away with him,' 'Per Christum hunc jugulo,' 'I will cut his throat,' and then believe ourselves bound to commit the murder which we have vowed? . . . 'The Saxons,' he says, 'are fierce, the Franks faithless, the Gepidæ inhuman, the Huns shameless. But is the Frank's perfidy as blameable as ours? Is the Alman's drunkenness, or the Alan's rapacity, as damnable as a Christian's? If a Hun or a Gepid deceives you, what wonder? He is utterly ignorant that there is any sin in falsehood. But what of the Christian who does the same? The Barbarians,' he says, 'are better men than the Christians. The Goths,' he says, 'are perfidious, but chaste. The Alans unchaste, but less perfidious. The Franks are liars, but hospitable; the Saxons ferociously cruel, but venerable for their chastity. The Visigoths who conquered Spain,' he says, 'were the most "ignavi" (heavy, I presume he means, and loutish) of all the barbarians: but they were chaste, and therefore they conquered.'

In Africa, if we are to believe Salvian, things stood even worse, at the time of the invasion of the Vandals. In his violent invectives against the Africans, however, allowance must be made. Salvian was a great lover of monks; and the Africans used, he says, to detest them, and mob them wherever they appeared; for which offence, of course, he can find no words too strong. St. Augustine, however, himself a countryman of theirs, who died, happily, just before the storm burst on that hapless land, speaks bitterly of their exceeding profligacy—of which he himself in his wild youth, had had but too sad experience. Salvian's assertion is, that the Africans were the most profligate of all the Romans; and that while each barbarian tribe had (as we have just seen) some good in them, the Africans had none.

But there were noble souls left among them, lights which shone all the more brightly in the surrounding darkness. In the pages of Victor Vitensis, which tell the sad story of the persecution of the African Catholics by the Arian Vandals, you will find many a moving tale which shews that God had his own, even among those degraded Carthaginians.

The causes of the Arian hatred to the Catholics is very obscure. You will find all that is known in Dean Milman's History of Latin Christianity. A simple explanation may be found in the fact that the Catholics considered the Arians, and did not conceal their opinion, as all literally and actually doomed to the torments of everlasting fire; and that, as Gibbon puts it, 'The heroes of the north, who had submitted with some reluctance, to believe that all their ancestors were in hell, were astonished and exasperated to learn, that they themselves had only changed the mode of their eternal condemnation.' The Teutons were (Salvian himself confesses it) trying to serve God devoutly, in chastity, sobriety, and honesty, according to their light. And they were told by the profligates of Africa, that this and no less, was their doom. It is not to be wondered at, again, if they mistook the Catholic creed for the cause of Catholic immorality. That may account for the Vandal custom of

re-baptizing the Catholics. It certainly accounts for the
fact (if after all it be a fact) which Victor states, that they
tortured the nuns to extort from them shameful confes-
sions against the priests. But the history of the African
persecution is the history of all persecutions, as confest
again and again by the old fathers, as proved by the analogies of later times. The sins of the Church draw down
punishment, by making her enemies confound her doctrine and her practice. But in return, the punishment of
the Church purifies her, and brings out her nobleness
afresh, as the snake casts his skin in pain, and comes out
young and fair once more; and in every dark hour of
the Church, there flashes out some bright form of human heroism, to be a beacon and a comfort to all future
time. Victor, for instance, tells the story of Dionysia,
the beautiful widow whom the Vandals tried to torture
into denying the Divinity of our Lord.—How when
they saw that she was bolder and fairer than all the other
matrons, they seized her, and went to strip her: and she
cried to them, 'Qualiter libet occidite: verecunda tamen
membra nolite nudare,' but in vain. They hung her up
by the hands, and scourged her till streams of blood ran
down every limb. Her only son, a delicate boy, stood by
trembling, knowing that his turn would come next; and
she saw it, and called to him in the midst of her shame
and agony. 'He had been baptized into the name of the
Blessed Trinity; let him die in that name, and not lose
the wedding-garment. Let him fear the pain that never ends, and cling to the life that endures for ever.' The
boy took heart, and when his turn came, died under the
torture; and Dionysia took up the little corpse, and bur-

ied it in her own house; and worshipped upon her boy's grave to her dying day.

Yes. God had his own left, even among those fallen Africans of Carthage.

But neither there, nor in Spain, could the Vandals cure the evil. 'Now-a-days,' says Salvian, 'there are no profligates among the Goths, save Romans; none among the Vandals, save Romans. Blush, Roman people, everywhere, blush for your morals. There is hardly a city free from dens of sin, and none at all from impurity, save those which the barbarians have begun to occupy. And do we wonder if we are surpassed in power, by an enemy who surpasses us in decency? It is not the natural strength of their bodies which makes them conquer us. We have been conquered only by the vices of our own morals.'

Yes. Salvian was right. Those last words were no mere outburst of national vanity, content to confess every sin, save that of being cowards. He was right. It was not the mere muscle of the Teuton which enabled him to crush the decrepit and debauched slave-nations, Gaul and Briton, Iberian and African, as the ox crushes the frogs of the marsh. The 'sera juvenum Venus, ideoque inexhausta pubertas,' had given him more than his lofty stature, and his mighty limbs. Had he had nought but them, he might have remained to the end a blind Samson, grinding among the slaves in Cæsar's mill, butchered to make a Roman holiday. But it had given him more, that purity of his; it had given him, as it may give you, gentlemen, a calm and steady brain, and a free and loyal heart; the energy which springs from health; the

self-respect which comes from self-restraint; and the
spirit which shrinks from neither God nor man, and
feels it light to die for wife and child, for people, and
for Queen.

# ON DR. LATHAM'S 'GERMANIA'

If I have followed in these lectures the better known and more widely received etymology of the name Goth, I have done so out of no disrespect to Dr. Latham; but simply because his theory seems to me adhuc sub judice. It is this, as far as I understand it. That 'Goth' was not the aboriginal name of the race. That they were probably not so called till they came into the land of the Getæ, about the mouths of the Danube. That the Teutonic name for the Ostrogoths was Grutungs, and that of the Visigoths (which he does not consider to mean West-Goths) Thervings, Thüringer. That on reaching the land of the Getæ they took their name; 'just as the Kentings of Anglo-Saxon England took name from the Keltic country of Kent;' and that the names Goth, Gothones, Gothini were originally given to Lithuanians by their Sclavonic neighbours. I merely state the theory, and leave it for the judgment of others.

The principal points which Dr. Latham considers himself to have established, are—

That the area and population of the Teutonic tribes have been, on the authority of Tacitus, much overrated; many tribes hitherto supposed to be Teutonic being really Sclavonic, &c.

This need not shock our pride, if proved—as it seems to me to be. The nations who have influenced the world's destiny have not been great, in the modern American sense of 'big;' but great in heart, as our forefathers were. The Greeks were but a handful at Salamis; so were the Romans of the Republic; so were the Spaniards of America; so, probably, were the Aztecs and Incas whom they overthrew; and surely our own conquerors and re-conquerers of Hindostan have shewn enough that it is not numbers, but soul, which gives a race the power to rule.

Neither need we object to Dr. Latham's opinion, that more than one of the tribes which took part in the destruction of the Empire were not aboriginal Germans, but Sclavonians Germanized, and under German leaders. It may be so. The custom of enslaving captives would render pure Teutonic blood among the lower classes of a tribe the exception and not the rule; while the custom of chiefs choosing the 'thegns,' 'gesitha,' or 'comites,' who lived and died as their companions-in-arms, from among the most valiant of the unfree, would tend to produce a mixed blood in the upper classes also, and gradually assimilate the whole mass to the manners and laws of their Teutonic lords. Only by some such actual superiority of the upper classes to the lower can I explain the deep respect for rank and blood, which distinguishes, and will perhaps always distinguish, the Teutonic peoples. Had there even been anything like a primæval equality among our race, a hereditary aristocracy could never have arisen, or if arising for a while, never could have remained as a fact which all believed in, from the lowest to the highest. Just, or unjust, the institution represented, I verily believe, an ethnological fact. The golden-haired hero said to his brown-haired bondsman, 'I am a gentleman, who have a "gens," a stamm, a pedigree, and know from whom I am sprung. I am a Garding, an Amalung, a Scylding, an Osing, or what not. I am a son of the gods. The blood of the Asas is in my veins. Do you not see it? Am I not wiser, stronger, more virtuous, more beautiful than you? You must obey me, and be my man, and follow me to the death. Then, if you prove a worthy thane, I will give you horse, weapons, bracelets, lands; and marry you, it may be, to my daughter or my niece. And if not, you must remain a son of the earth, grubbing in the dust of which you were made.' And the bondsman believed him; and became his lord's man, and followed him to the death; and was thereby not degraded, but raised out of selfish savagery and brute independence into loyalty, usefulness, and self-respect. As a fact, that is the method by which the thing was done: done;—very ill indeed, as most human things are done; but a method inevitable—and possibly right; till (as in England now) the lower classes became ethnologically identical with the upper, and equality became possible in law, simply because it existed in fact.

But the part of Dr. Latham's 'Germania' to which I am bound to call most attention, because I have not followed it, is that interesting part of the Prolegomena, in which he combats the generally received theory, that, between the time of Tacitus and that of Charlemagne, vast masses of Germans had migrated southward from between the Elbe and the Vistula; and that they had been replaced by the Sclavonians who certainly were there in Charlemagne's days.

Dr. Latham argues against this theory with a great variety of facts and reasons. But has he not overstated his case on some points?

Need the migrations necessary for this theory have been of 'unparalleled magnitude and rapidity'?

As for the 'unparalleled completeness' on which he lays much stress, from the fact that no remnants of Teutonic population are found in the countries evacuated:

Is it the fact that 'history only tells us of German armies having advanced south'? Do we not find four famous cases—the irruption of the Cimbri and Teutons into Italy; the passage of the Danube by the Visigoths; and the invasions of Italy first by the Ostrogoths, then by the Lombards—in which the nations came with men, women, and children, horses, cattle, and dogs, bag and baggage? May not this have been the custom of the race, with its strong feeling for the family tie; and may not this account for no traces of them being left behind?

Does not Dr. Latham's theory proceed too much on an assumption that the Sclavonians dispossest the Teutons by force? And is not this assumption his ground for objecting that the movement was effected improbably 'by that division of the European population (the Sclavonic and Lithuanian) which has, within the historic period, receded before the Germanic'?

Are these migrations, though 'unrepresented in any history' (i.e. contemporaneous), really 'unrepresented in any tradition'? Do not the traditions of Jornandes and Paulus Diaconus, that the Goths and the Lombards came from Scandinavia, represent this very fact?—and are they to be set aside as naught? Surely not. Myths of this kind generally embody a nucleus of truth, and must be regarded with respect; for they often, after all arguments about them are spent, are found to contain the very pith of the matter.

Are the 'phenomena of replacement and substitution' so very strange—I will not say upon the popular theory, but at least on one half-way between it and Dr. Latham's? Namely—

That the Teutonic races came originally, as some of them say they did, from Scandinavia, Denmark, the South Baltic, &c.

That they forced their way down, wave after wave, on what would have been the line of least resistance—the Marches between the Gauls, Romanized or otherwise, and the Sclavonians.  And that the Alps and the solid front of the Roman Empire turned them to the East, till their vanguard found itself on the Danube.

This would agree with Dr. Latham's most valuable hint, that Markmen, 'Men of the Marches,' was perhaps the name of many German tribes successively.

That they fought, as they went, with the Sclavonian and other tribes (as their traditions seem to report), and rolled them back to the eastward; and that as each Teutonic tribe past down the line, the Sclavonians rolled back again, till the last column was past.

That the Teutons also carried down with them, as slaves or allies, a portion of this old Sclavonic population (to which Dr. Latham will perhaps agree); and that this fact caused a hiatus, which was gradually filled by tribes who after all were little better than nomad hunters, and would occupy (quite nominally) a very large tract with a small population.

Would not this theory agree at once tolerably with

the old traditions and with Dr. Latham's new facts?

The question still remains—which is the question of all. What put these Germanic peoples on going South? Were there no causes sufficient to excite so desperate a resolve?

(1) Did they all go? Is not Paulus Diaconus' story that one-third of the Lombards was to emigrate by lot, and two-thirds remain at home, a rough type of what generally happened—what happens now in our modern emigrations? Was not the surplus population driven off by famine toward warmer and more hopeful climes?

(2) Are not the Teutonic populations of England, North Germany, and the Baltic, the descendants, much intermixed, and with dialects much changed, of the portions which were left behind? This is the opinion, I believe, of several great ethnologists. Is it not true? If philological objections are raised to this, I ask (but in all humility), Did not these southward migrations commence long before the time of Tacitus? If so, may they not have commenced before the different Teutonic dialects were as distinct as they were in the historic period? And are we to suppose that the dialects did not alter during the long journeyings through many nations? Is it possible that the Thervings and Grutungs could have retained the same tongue on the Danube, as their forefathers spoke in their native land? Would not the Moeso-Gothic of Ulfilas have been all but unintelligible to the Goth who, upon the old theory, remained in Gothland of Sweden?

(3) But were there not more causes than mere want, which sent them south? Had the peculiar restlessness

of the race nothing to do with it? A restlessness not no-
madic, but migratory: arising not from carelessness of
land and home, but from the longing to found a home in
a new land, like the restlessness of us, their children? As
soon as we meet them in historic times, they are always
moving, migrating, invading. Were they not doing the
same in pre-historic times, by fits and starts, no doubt
with periods of excitement, periods of collapse and rest?
When we recollect the invasion of the Normans; the
wholesale eastward migration of the Crusaders, men,
women, and children; and the later colonization by
Teutonic peoples, of every quarter of the globe, is there
anything wonderful in the belief that similar migratory
manias may have seized the old tribes; that the spirit of
Woden, 'the mover,' may have moved them, and forced
them to go ahead, as now? Doubtless the theory is
strange. But the Teutons were and are a strange people;
so strange, that they have conquered—one may almost
say that they are—all nations which are alive upon the
globe; and we may therefore expect them to have done
strange things even in their infancy.

The Romans saw them conquer the empire; and said,
the good men among them, that it was on account of
their superior virtue. But beside the virtue which made
them succeed, there must have been the adventurous-
ness which made them attempt. They were a people
fond of 'avanturen,' like their descendants; and they
went out to seek them; and found enough and to spare.

(4) But more, had they never heard of Rome? Surely they had, and at a very early period of the empire. We
are apt to forget, that for every discovery of the Ger-

mans by the Romans, there was a similar discovery of the Romans by the Germans, and one which would tell powerfully on their childish imagination. Did not one single Kemper or Teuton return from Marius' slaughter, to spread among the tribes (niddering though he may have been called for coming back alive) the fair land which they had found, fit for the gods of Valhalla; the land of sunshine, fruits and wine, wherein his brothers' and sisters' bones were bleaching unavenged? Did no gay Gaul of the Legion of the Lark, boast in a frontier wine-house to a German trapper, who came in to sell his peltry, how he himself was a gentleman now, and a civilized man, and a Roman; and how he had followed Julius Cæsar, the king of men, over the Rubicon, and on to a city of the like of which man never dreamed, where-in was room for all the gods of heaven? Did no captive tribune of Varus' legions, led with horrid shouts round Thor's altar in the Teutoburger Wald, ere his corpse was hung among the horses and goats on the primæval oaks, turn to bay like a Roman, and tell his wild captors of the Eternal City, and of the might of that Cæsar who would avenge every hair upon his head with a German life; and receive for answer a shout of laughter, and the cry—'You have come to us: and some day we will go to you?' Did no commissary, bargaining with a German for cattle to be sent over the frontier by such a day of the week, and teaching him to mistranslate into those names of Thor, Woden, Freya, and so forth, which they now carry, the Jewish-Assyrian-Roman days of the se'nnight, amuse the simple forester by telling him how the streets of Rome were paved with gold, and no one had anything to do there but to eat and bathe at the public expense, and to go to the theatre, and see 20,000 gladiators fight at once? Did no German 'Regulus,' alderman, or king, enter Rome on an embassy, and come back with uplifted eyes and hands, declaring that he had seen things unspeakable—a 'very fine plunder,' as Blucher said of London; and that if it were not for the walls, they might get it all; for not only the ladies, but the noblemen, went about in litters of silver and gold, and wore gauze dresses, the shameless wretches, through which you might see every limb, so that as for killing them, there was no more fear of them than of a flock of sheep: but that he did not see as well as he could have wished how to enter the great city, for he was more or less the worse for liquor the whole time, with wondrous stuff which they called wine? Or did no captive, escaped by miracle from the butcheries of the amphitheatre, return to tell his countrymen how all the rest had died like German men; and call on them to rise and avenge their brothers' blood? Yes, surely the Teutons knew well, even in the time of Tacitus, of the 'micklegard,' the great city and all its glory. Every fresh tribe who passed along the frontier of Gaul or of Noricum would hear more and more of it, see more and more men who had actually been there. If the glory of the city exercised on its own inhabitants an intoxicating influence, as of a place omnipotent, superhuman, divine—it would exercise (exaggerated as it would be) a still stronger influence on the barbarians outside: and what wonder if they pressed southwards at first in the hope of taking the mighty city; and afterwards, as her real strength became more known, of at least seizing some of those colonial cities, which were as superhuman in their eyes as Rome itself would have been?  In the crusades, the children, whenever they came to a great town, asked their parents if that was not Jerusalem.  And so, it may be, many a gallant young Teuton, on entering for the first time such a city as Cologne, Lyons, or Vienna, whispered half trembling to his lord—'Surely this must be Rome.'

Some such arguments as these might surely be brought in favour of a greater migration than Dr. Latham is inclined to allow: but I must leave the question for men of deeper research and wider learning, than I possess.

# THE HUMAN DELUGE

'I have taken in hand,' said Sir Francis Drake once to the crew of the immortal Pelican, 'that which I know not how to accomplish. Yea, it hath even bereaved me of my wits to think of it.'

And so I must say on the subject of this lecture. I wish to give you some notion of the history of Italy for nearly one hundred years; say from 400 to 500. But it is very difficult. How can a man draw a picture of that which has no shape; or tell the order of absolute disorder? It is all a horrible 'fourmillement des nations,' like the working of an ant-heap; like the insects devouring each other in a drop of water. Teuton tribes, Sclavonic tribes, Tartar tribes, Roman generals, empresses, bishops, courtiers, adventurers, appear for a moment out of the crowd, dim phantoms—nothing more, most of them—with a name appended, and then vanish, proving their humanity only by leaving behind them one more stain of blood.

And what became of the masses all the while? of the men, slaves the greater part of them, if not all, who tilled the soil, and ground the corn—for man must have eaten, then as now? We have no hint. One trusts that God had mercy on them, if not in this world, still in the world to come. Man, at least, had none.

Taking one's stand at Rome, and looking toward the north, what does one see for nearly one hundred years? Wave after wave rising out of the north, the land of night, and wonder, and the terrible unknown; visible only as the light of Roman civilization strikes their crests, and they dash against the Alps, and roll over through the mountain passes, into the fertile plains below. Then at last they are seen but too well; and you discover that the waves are living men, women, and children, horses, dogs, and cattle, all rushing headlong into that great whirlpool of Italy: and yet the gulf is never full. The earth drinks up the blood; the bones decay into the fruitful soil; the very names and memories of whole tribes are washed away. And the result of an immigration which may be counted by hundreds of thousands is this—that all the land is waste.

The best authorities which I can give you (though you will find many more in Gibbon) are—for the main story, Jornandes, De Rebus Geticis. Himself a Goth, he wrote the history of his race, and that of Attila and his Huns, in good rugged Latin, not without force and sense.

Then Claudian, the poet, a bombastic panegyrist of contemporary Roman scoundrels; but full of curious facts, if one could only depend on them.

Then the earlier books of Procopius De Bello Gothico, and the Chronicle of Zosimus.

Salvian, Ennodius and Sidonius Apollinaris, as Christians, will give you curious details, especially as to South France and North Italy; while many particulars of the first sack of Rome, with comments thereon which express the highest intellects of that day, you will find in St. Jerome's Letters, and St. Augustine's City of God.

But if you want these dreadful times *explained* to

you, I do not think you can do better than to take your Bibles, and to read the Revelations of St. John the Apostle. I shall quote them, more than once, in this lecture. I cannot help quoting them. The words come naturally to my lips, as fitter to the facts than any words of my own.

I do not come here to interpret the Book of Revelations. I do not understand that book. But I do say plainly, though I cannot interpret the book, that the book has interpreted those times to me. Its awful metaphors give me more living and accurate pictures of what went on than any that Gibbon's faithful details can give.

You may see, if you have spiritual eyes wherewith to see, the Dragon, the serpent, symbol of political craft and the devilish wisdom of the Roman, giving authority to the Beast, the symbol of brute power; to mongrel Ætiuses and Bonifaces, barbarian Stilichos, Ricimers and Aspars, and a host of similar adventurers, whose only strength was force.

You may see the world wondering after the beast, and worshipping brute force, as the only thing left to believe in.

You may see the nations of the world gnawing their tongues for pain, and blaspheming God, but not repenting of their deeds.

You may see the faith and patience of the saints— men like Augustine, Salvian, Epiphanius, Severinus, Deogratias of Carthage, and a host more, no doubt, whose names the world will never hear—the salt of the earth, which kept it all from rotting.

You may see Babylon the great fallen, and all the

kings and merchants of the earth bewailing her afar off, and watching the smoke of her torment.

You may see, as St. John warns you, that—after her fall, mind—if men would go on worshipping the beast, and much more his image—the phantom and shadow of brute force, after the reality had passed away—they should drink of the wine of the wrath of God, and be tormented for ever. For you may see how those degenerate Romans did go on worshipping the shadow of brute force, and how they were tormented for ever; and had no rest day or night, because they worshipped the Beast and his image.

You may see all the fowl of the heavens flocking together to the feast of the great God, to eat the flesh of kings and captains, horse and rider, bond and free.—All carrion-birds, human as well as brute—All greedy villains and adventurers, the scoundreldom of the whole world, flocking in to get their share of the carcass of the dying empire; as the vulture and the raven flock in to the carrion when the royal eagles have gorged their fill.

And lastly, you may see, if God give you grace, One who is faithful and true, with a name which no man knew, save Himself, making war in righteousness against all evil; bringing order out of disorder, hope out of despair, fresh health and life out of old disease and death; executing just judgment among all the nations of the earth; and sending down from heaven the city of God, in the light of which the nations of those who are saved should walk, and the kings of the earth should bring their power and their glory into it; with the tree of life in the midst of it, whose leaves should be for the healing of the nations.

Again, I say, I am not here to interpret the Book of Revelations; but this I say, that that book interprets those times to me.

Leaving, for the present at least, to better historians than myself the general subject of the Teutonic immigrations; the conquest of North Gaul by the Franks, of Britain by the Saxons and Angles, of Burgundy by the Burgundians, of Africa by the Vandals, I shall speak rather of those Teutonic tribes which actually entered and conquered Italy; and first, of course, of the Goths. Especially interesting to us English should their fortunes be, for they are said to be very near of kin to us; at least to those Jutes who conquered Kent. As Goths, Geats, Getæ, Juts, antiquarians find them in early and altogether mythic times, in the Scandinavian peninsula, and the isles and mainland of Denmark.

Their name, it is said, is the same as one name for the Supreme Being. Goth, Guth, Yuth, signifies war. 'God' is the highest warrior, the Lord of hosts, and the progenitor of the race, whether as an 'Eponym hero' or as the supreme Deity. Physical force was their rude notion of Divine power, and Tiu, Tiv, or Tyr, in like manner, who was originally the god of the clear sky, the Zeus or Jove of the Greeks and Romans, became by virtue of his warlike character, identical with the Roman Mars, till the dies Martis of the Roman week became the German Tuesday.

Working their way down from Gothland and Jutland, we know not why nor when, thrusting aside the cognate Burgunds, and the Sclavonic tribes whom they met on the road, they had spread themselves, in the third century, over the whole South of Russia, and westward over the Danubian Provinces, and Hungary. The Ostrogoths (East-goths) lay from the Volga to the Borysthenes, the Visigoths (West-goths?) from the Borysthenes to the Theiss. Behind them lay the Gepidæ, a German tribe, who had come south-eastward with them, and whose name is said to signify the men who had 'bided' (remained) behind the rest.

What manner of men they were it is hard to say, so few details are left to us. But we may conceive them as a tall, fair-haired people, clothed in shirts and smocks of embroidered linen, and gaiters cross-strapped with hide; their arms and necks encircled with gold and silver rings; the warriors, at least of the upper class, well horsed, and armed with lance and heavy sword, with chain-mail, and helmets surmounted with plumes, horns, towers, dragons, boars, and the other strange devices which are still seen on the crests of German nobles. This much we can guess; for in this way their ancestors, or at least relations, the War-Geats, appear clothed in the grand old song of Beowulf. Their land must have been tilled principally by slaves, usually captives taken in war: but the noble mystery of the forge, where arms and ornaments were made, was an honourable craft for men of rank; and their ladies, as in the middle age, prided themselves on their skill with the needle and the loom. Their language has been happily preserved to us in Ulfilas' Translation of the Scriptures. For these Goths, the greater number of them at least, were by this time Christians, or very nearly such. Good Bishop Ulfilas, brought up a Christian and consecrated by order of Constantine the Great, had been labouring for years to convert his adopted countrymen from the worship of Thor and Woden. He had translated the Bible for them, and had constructed a Gothic alphabet for that purpose. He had omitted, however (prudently as he considered) the books of Kings, with their histories of the Jewish wars. The Goths, he held, were only too fond of fighting already, and 'needed in that matter the bit, rather than the spur.' He had now a large number of converts, some of whom had even endured persecution from their heathen brethren. Athanaric, 'judge,' or alderman of the Thervings, had sent through the camp—so runs the story—the waggon which bore the idol of Woden, and had burnt, with their tents and their families, those who refused to worship.

They, like all other German tribes, were ruled over by two royal races, sons of Woden and the Asas. The Ostrogoth race was the Amalungs—the 'heavenly,' or 'spotless' race; the Visigoth race was the Balthungs— the 'bold' or 'valiant' race; and from these two families, and from a few others, but all believed to be lineally descended from Woden, and now much intermixed, are derived all the old royal families of Europe, that of the House of Brunswick among the rest.

That they were no savages, is shewn sufficiently by their names, at least those of their chiefs. Such names as Alaric, 'all rich' or 'all powerful,' Ataulf, 'the helping father,' Fridigern, 'the willing peace-maker,' and so forth— all the names in fact, which can be put back into their native form out of their Romanized distortions, are tokens of a people far removed from that barbarous state in which men are named after personal peculiarities, natural objects, or the beasts of the field. On this subject you may consult, as full of interest and instruction, the list of Teutonic names given in Muratori.

They had broken over the Roman frontier more than once, and taken cities. They had compelled the Emperor Gratian to buy them off. They had built themselves flat-bottomed boats without iron in them and sailed from the Crimea round the shores of the Black Sea, once and again, plundering Trebizond, and at last the temple itself of Diana at Ephesus. They had even penetrated into Greece and Athens, plundered the Parthenon, and threatened the capitol. They had fought the Emperor Decius, till he, and many of his legionaries, were drowned in a bog in the moment of victory. They had been driven with difficulty back across the Danube by Aurelian, and walled out of the Empire with the Allemanni by Probus's 'Teufels-Mauer,' stretching from the Danube to the Rhine. Their time was not yet come by a hundred years. But they had seen and tasted the fine things of the sunny south, and did not forget them amid the steppes and snows.

At last a sore need came upon them. About 350 there was a great king among them, Ermanaric, 'the powerful warrior,' comparable, says Jornandes, to Alexander himself, who had conquered all the conquered tribes around. When he was past 100 years old, a chief of the Roxolani (Ugrians, according to Dr. Latham; men of Ros, or Russia), one of these tribes, plotted against him, and sent for help to the new people, the

Huns, who had just appeared on the confines of Europe and Asia. Old Ermanaric tore the traitor's wife to pieces with wild horses: but the Huns came nevertheless. A magic hind, the Goths said, guided the new people over the steppes to the land of the Goths, and then vanished. They fought with the Goths, and defeated them. Old Ermanaric stabbed himself for shame, and the hearts of the Goths became as water before the tempest of nations. They were supernatural creatures, the Goths believed, engendered of witches and demons on the steppes; pig-eyed hideous beings, with cakes instead of faces, 'offam magis quam faciem,' under ratskin caps, armed with arrows tipped with bone, and lassos of cord, eating, marketing, sleeping on horseback, so grown into the saddle that they could hardly walk in their huge boots. With them were Acatzirs, painted blue, hair as well as skin; Alans, wandering with their waggons like the Huns, armed with heavy cuirasses of plaited horn, their horses decked with human scalps; Geloni armed with a scythe, wrapt in a cloak of human skin; Bulgars who impaled their prisoners—savages innumerable as the locust swarms. Who could stand against them?

In the year 375, the West Goths came down to the Danube-bank and entreated the Romans to let them cross. There was a Christian party among them, persecuted by the heathens, and hoping for protection from Rome. Athanaric had vowed never to set foot on Roman soil, and after defending himself against the Huns, retired into the forests of 'Caucaland.' Good Bishop Ulfilas and his converts looked longingly toward the Christian Empire. Surely the Christians would receive them as brothers, welcome them, help them. The simple German fancied a Roman even such a one as themselves.

Ulfilas went on embassy to Antioch, to Valens the Emperor. Valens, low-born, cruel, and covetous, was an Arian, and could not lose the opportunity of making converts. He sent theologians to meet Ulfilas, and torment him into Arianism. When he arrived, Valens tormented him himself. While the Goths starved he argued, apostasy was the absolute condition of his help, till Ulfilas, in a weak moment, gave his word that the Goths should become Arians, if Valens would give them lands on the South bank of the Danube. Then they would be the Emperor's men, and guard the marches against all foes. From that time Arianism became the creed, not only of the Goths, but of the Vandals, the Sueves, and almost all the Teutonic tribes.

It was (if the story be true) a sinful and foolish compact, forced from a good man by the sight of his countrymen's extreme danger and misery. It avenged itself, soon enough, upon both Goths and Romans.

To the Goths themselves the change must have seemed not only unimportant, but imperceptible. Unaccustomed to that accuracy of thought, which is too often sneered at by Gibbon as 'metaphysical subtlety,' all of which they would have been aware was the change of a few letters in a creed written in an unknown tongue. They could not know, (Ulfilas himself could not have known, only two years after the death of St. Athanasius at Alexandria; while the Nicæan Creed was as yet received by only half of the Empire; and while he meanwhile had been toiling for years in the Danubian wilds, ignorant perhaps of the controversy which had meanwhile convulsed the Church)—neither the Goths nor he, I say, could have known that the Arianism, which they embraced, was really the last, and as it were apologetic, refuge of dying Polytheism; that it, and not the Catholic Faith, denied the abysmal unity of the Godhead; that by making the Son inferior to the Father, as touching his Godhead, it invented two Gods, a greater and a lesser, thus denying the absoluteness, the infinity, the illimitability, by any category of quantity, of that One Eternal, of whom it is written, that God is a Spirit. Still less could they have guessed that when Arius, the handsome popular preacher (whose very name, perhaps, Ulfilas never heard) asked the fine ladies of Alexandria—'Had you a son before that son was born?'—'No.' 'Then God could have no son before that son was begotten, &c.'—that he was mingling up the idea of Time with the idea of that Eternal God who created Time, and debasing to the accidents of before and after that Timeless and Eternal Generation, of which it is written, 'Thou art my Son, this day have I begotten thee.' Still less could Ulfilas, or his Goths, have known, that the natural human tendency to condition God by Time, would be, in later ages, even long after Arianism was crushed utterly, the parent of many a cruel, gross, and stupid superstition. To them it would have been a mere question whether Woden, the All-father, was superior to one of his sons, the Asas: and the Catholic faith probably seemed to them an impious assumption of equality, on the part of one of those Asas, with Woden himself.

Of the battle between Arianism and Orthodoxy I

have said enough to shew you that I think it an internecine battle between truth and falsehood.  But it has
been long ago judged by wager of battle: by the success
of that duel of time, of which we must believe (as our
forefathers believed of all fair duels) that God defends
the right.

So the Goths were to come over the Danube stream:
but they must give up their arms, and deliver their children (those of rank, one supposes), as hostages, to be
educated by the Romans, as Romans.

They crossed the fatal river; they were whole days in
crossing; those set to count them gave it up in despair;
Ammianus says: 'He who wishes to know their number,'

> 'Libyci velit æquoris idem
> Discere quam multæ Zephyro volvuntur arenæ.'

And when they were across, they gave up the children.  They had not the heart to give up the beloved
weapons.  The Roman commissioners let them keep the
arms, at the price of many a Gothic woman's honour.
Ugly and foul things happened, of which we have only
hints.  Then they had to be fed for the time being, till
they could cultivate their land.  Lupicinus and Maximus, the two governors of Thrace pocketed the funds
which Valens sent, and starved the Goths.  The markets
were full of carrion and dogs' flesh.  Anything was good
enough for a barbarian.  Their fringed carpets, their
beautiful linens, all went.  A little wholesome meat cost
10 pounds of silver.  When all was gone, they had to sell
their children.  To establish a slave-trade in the beautiful

boys and girls was just what the wicked Romans wanted.

At last the end came. They began to rise. Fridigern, their king, kept them quiet till the time was ripe for revenge. The Romans, trying to keep the West Goths down, got so confused, it seems, that they let the whole nation of the East Goths (of whom we shall hear more hereafter) dash across the Danube, and establish themselves in the north of the present Turkey, to the east of the West Goths.

Then at Marcianopolis, the capital of Lower Moesia, Lupicinus asked Fridigern and his chiefs to a feast. The starving Goths outside were refused supplies from the market, and came to blows with the guards. Lupicinus, half drunk, heard of it, and gave orders for a massacre. Fridigern escaped from the palace, sword in hand. The smouldering embers burst into flame, the war-cry was raised, and the villain Lupicinus fled for his life.

Then began war south of the Danube. The Roman legions were defeated by the Goths, who armed themselves with the weapons of the dead. Moesia was overrun with fire and sword. Adrianople was attacked, but in vain. The slaves in the gold mines were freed from their misery, and shewed the Goths the mountain-passes and the stores of grain. As they went on, the Goths recovered their children. The poor things told horrid tales; and the Goths, maddened, avenged themselves on the Romans of every age and sex. 'They left,' says St. Jerome, 'nothing alive—not even the beasts of the field; till nothing was left but growing brambles and thick forests.'

Valens, the Emperor, was at Antioch. Now he hurried to Constantinople, but too late. The East Goths had joined the West Goths; and hordes of Huns, Alans, and Taifalæ (detestable savages, of whom we know nothing but evil) had joined Fridigern's confederacy.

Gratian, Valens' colleague and nephew, son of Valentinian the bear-ward, had just won a great victory over the Allemanni at Colmar in Alsace; and Valens was jealous of his glory. He is said to have been a virtuous youth, whose monomania was shooting. He fell in love with the wild Alans, in spite of their horse-trappings of scalps, simply because of their skill in archery; formed a body-guard of them, and passed his time hunting with them round Paris. Nevertheless, he won this great victory by the help, it seems, of one Count Ricimer ('ever-powerful'), Count of the Domestics, whose name proclaims him a German.

Valens was jealous of Gratian's fame; he was stung by the reproaches of the mob of Constantinople; and he undervalued the Goths, on account of some successes of his lieutenants, who had recovered much of the plunder taken by them, and had utterly overpowered the foul Taifalæ, transporting them to lands about Modena and Parma in Italy. He rejected Count Ricimer's advice to wait till Gratian reinforced him with the victorious western legions, and determined to give battle a few miles from Adrianople. Had he waited for Gratian, the history of the whole world might have been different.

For on the ninth of August, A.D. 378, the fatal day, the second Cannæ, from which Rome never recovered as from that first, the young world and the old world met, and fought it out; and the young world won. The light Roman cavalry fled before the long lances and heavy swords of the German knights. The knights turned on the infantry, broke them, hunted them down by charge after charge, and left the footmen to finish the work.

Two-thirds of the Roman army were destroyed; four Counts of the Empire; generals and officers without number. Valens fled wounded to a cottage. The Goths set it on fire, and burned him and his staff therein, ignorant that they had in their hands the Emperor of Rome. Verily there is a God who judgeth the earth.

So thought the Catholics of that day, who saw in the fearful death of Valens a punishment for his having forced the Goths to become Arians. 'It was just,' says one, 'that he should burn on earth, by whose counsels so many barbarians will burn in hell for ever.' There are (as I have shewn) still darker counts in the conduct of the Romans toward the Goths; enough (if we believe our Bibles) to draw down on the guilty the swift and terrible judgments of God.

At least, this was the second Cannæ, the death-wound of Rome. From that day the end was certain, however slow. The Teuton had at last tried his strength against the Roman. The wild forest-child had found himself suddenly at death-grips with the Enchanter whom he had feared, and almost worshipped, for so long; and behold, to his own wonder, he was no more a child, but grown into a man, and the stronger, if not the cunninger of the two. There had been a spell upon him; the 'Romani nominis umbra.' But from that day the spell was broken. He had faced a Roman Emperor, a Divus Cæsar, the man-god by whose head all nations swore, rich with the magic wealth, wise with the magic cunning, of centuries of superhuman glory; and he had killed him, and behold he died, like other men. That he had done. What was there left for him now that he could not do?

The stronger he was, but not yet the cunninger of the two. The Goths could do no more. They had to leave Adrianople behind them, with the Emperor's treasures safe within its walls; to gaze with childish wonder at the Bosphorus and its palaces; to recoil in awe from the 'long walls' of Constantinople, and the great stones which the engines thereon hurled at them by 'arsmet-ricke and nigromancy,' as their descendants believed of the Roman mechanicians, even five hundred years after; to hear (without being able to avenge) the horrible news, that the Gothic lads distributed throughout Asia, to be educated as Romans, had been decoyed into the cities by promises of lands and honours, and then massacred in cold blood; and then to settle down, leaving their children unavenged, for twenty years on the rich land which we now call Turkey in Europe, waiting till the time was come.

Waiting, I say, till the time was come. The fixed idea that Rome, if not Constantinople, could be taken at last, probably never left the minds of the leading Goths after the battle of Adrianople. The altered policy of the Cæsars was enough of itself to keep that idea alive. So far from expelling them from the country which they had seized, the new Emperor began to flatter and to honour them.

They had been heretofore regarded as savages, either to be driven back by main force, or tempted to enlist in the Roman ranks. Theodosius regarded them as a nation, and one which it was his interest to hire, to trust, to indulge at the expense of his Roman subjects.

Theodosius has received the surname of Great—seemingly by comparison; 'Inter cæcos luscus rex;' and it was highly creditable to a Roman Emperor in those days to be neither ruffian nor villain, but a handsome, highbred, courteous gentleman, pure in his domestic life, an orthodox Christian, and sufficiently obedient to the Church to forgive the monks who had burnt a Jewish synagogue, and to do penance in the Cathedral of Milan for the massacre of Thessalonica. That the morals of the Empire (if Zosimus is to be at all believed) grew more and more effeminate, corrupt, reckless; that the soldiers (if Vegetius is to be believed) actually laid aside, by royal permission, their helmets and cuirasses, as too heavy for their degenerate bodies; that the Roman heavy infantry, which had conquered the world, ceased to exist, while its place was taken by that Teutonic heavy cavalry, which decided every battle in Europe till the English yeoman, at Crecy and Poictiers, turned again the balance of arms in favour of the men who fought on foot; that the Goths became the 'fœderati' or allies of the Empire, paid to fight its battles against Maximus the Spaniard, and Arbogast the Frank, the rebels who, after the murder of young Gratian, attempted to set up a separate empire in the west; that Stilicho the Vandal was the Emperor's trusted friend, and master of the horse; that Alaric the Balth, and other noble Goths, were learning to combine with their native courage those Roman tactics which they only needed to become masters of the world; that in all cities, even in the Royal Palace, the huge Goth swaggered in Roman costume, his neck and arms heavy with golden torcs and bracelets; or even (as in the case of Fravitta and Priulf) stabbed his enemy with impunity at the imperial table; that κινειν το Σκυθικον, to disturb the Goths, was a deadly offence throughout the Empire: all these things did not prevent a thousand new statues from rising in honour of the great Cæsar, and excited nothing more than grumblings of impotent jealousy from a people whose maxim had become, 'Let us eat and drink, for to-morrow we die.'

Three anecdotes will illustrate sufficiently the policy of Theodosius toward his inconvenient guests. Towards the beginning of his reign, when the Goths, after the death of the great Fridigern, were broken up, and quarreling among themselves, he tempted a royal Amal, Modar by name, by the title of Master-General, to attack and slaughter in their sleep a rival tribe of Goths, and carry off an immense spoil to the imperial camp. To destroy the German by the German was so old a method of the Roman policy, that it was not considered derogatory to the 'greatness' of Theodosius.

The old Athanaric, the Therving—he who had sworn never to set foot on Roman soil, and had burnt them who would not fall down and worship before Woden's waggon, came over the Danube, out of the forests of 'Caucaland,' and put himself at the head of the Goths. The great Cæsar trembled before the heathen hero; and they made peace together; and old Athanaric went to him at Constantinople, and they became as friends. And the Romani nominis umbra, the glamour of the Roman name, fell on the old man, too feeble now to fight; and as he looked, says Jornandes, on the site of the city, and on the fleets of ships, and the world-famous walls, and the people from all the nations upon earth, he said, 'Now I behold what I have often heard tell, and never believed. The Kaiser is a God on earth, and he who shall lift his hand against him, is guilty of his own blood.' The old hero died in Constantinople, and the really good-natured Emperor gave him a grand funeral, and a statue, and so delighted the simple Goths, that the whole nation entered his service bodily, and became the Emperor's men.

The famous massacre of Thessalonica, and the penance of Theodosius, immortalized by the pencil of Vandyke, is another significant example of the relation between Goth and Roman. One Botheric (a Vandal or other Teuton by his name) was military commandant of that important post. He put in prison a popular charioteer of the circus, for a crime for which the Teutonic language had to borrow a foreign name, and which the Teutons, like ourselves, punished with death, though it was committed with impunity in any Roman city. At the public games, the base mob clamoured, but in vain, for the release of their favourite; and not getting him, rose on Botheric, murdered him and his officers, and dragged their corpses through the streets.

This was indeed κινειν το Σκυθικον; and Theodosius, partly in honest indignation, partly perhaps in fear of the consequences, issued orders from Milan which seem to have amounted to a permission to the Goths to avenge themselves. The populace were invited as usual to the games of the circus, and crowded in, forgetful of their crime, heedless of danger, absorbed in the one greed of frivolous, if not sinful pleasure. The Gothic troops concealed around entered, and then began a 'murder grim and great.' For three hours it lasted. Every age and sex, innocent or guilty, native or foreigner, to the number of at least 7,000, perished, or are said to have perished; and the soul of Botheric had 'good company on its way to Valhalla.'

The Goths, doubtless, considered that they were performing an act of public justice upon villains: but the Bishops of the Church looked at the matter in another light. The circumstances of treachery, the confusion of the innocent with the guilty, the want of any judicial examination and sentence, aroused their sense of humanity and justice. The offence was aggravated by the thought that the victims were Roman and orthodox, the murderers barbarians and Arians; St. Ambrose, with a noble courage, stopped the Emperor at the door of the Basilica of Milan, and forbad him to enter, till he had atoned for the fatal order by public penance. The Cæsar submitted nobly to the noble demand; and the repentance of Theodosius is the last scene in the downward career of the Cæsars, which can call forth a feeling of admiration and respect.

In January 395 Theodosius died; and after him came the deluge.

The Empire was parted between his two worthless sons. Honorius had the west, Arcadius the east; while the real master of the Empire was Stilicho the Vandal, whose virtues and valour and mighty stature are sung (and not undeservedly) in the pompous verses of Claudian. Of the confusion which ensued; of the murder (well-deserved) of Rufinus, the infamous minister whose devout hypocrisy had so long cajoled Theodosius; of the revolt and atrocities of Gildo in Africa, you must read in the pages of Gibbon. These lectures confine themselves, at present, to the history of the Goths.

In January 395, I said, Theodosius died. Before the end of the winter the Goths were in arms, with Alaric the Balth at their head. They had been refused, at least for the time, the payment of their usual subsidy. He had been refused the command of the Roman armies. Any excuse was sufficient. The fruit was ripe for plucking. The wrongs of centuries were to be avenged. Other tribes crost the Danube on the ice, and joined the Goths; and the mighty host swept down through Greece, passing Thermopylæ unopposed, ransoming Athens (where Alaric enjoyed a Greek bath and a public banquet, and tried to behave for a day like a Roman gentleman); sacking Corinth, Argos, Sparta, and all the cities and villages far and wide, and carrying off plunder inestimable, and troops of captive women.

Stilicho threw himself into the Peloponnese at Corinth to cut off the Goths, and after heavy fighting, Alaric, who seems to have been a really great general, out-manoeuvred him, crost the Gulf of Corinth at Rhium, with all his plunder and captives, and got safe away into northern Greece.

There Arcadius, the terrified Emperor of the East,

punished him for having devastated Greece, by appointing him Master-General of the very country which he had ravaged. The end was coming very near. The Goths lifted him on the shield, and proclaimed him King of the West Goths; and there he staid, somewhere about the head of the Adriatic, poised like an eagle in mid-air, watching Rome on one side, and Byzant on the other, uncertain on which quarry he should swoop.

He made up his mind for Rome. He would be the man to do the deed at last. There was a saga in which he trusted. Claudian gives it in an hexameter,

'Alpibus Italiæ ruptis penetrabis ad urbem.'

Yes, he would take The City, and avenge the treachery of Valens, and all the wrongs which Teutons had endured from the Romans for now four centuries. And he did it.

But not the first time. He swept over the Alps. Honorius fled to Asta, and Alaric besieged him there. The faithful Stilicho came to the rescue; and Alaric was driven to extremities. His warriors counselled him to retreat. No, he would take Rome, or die. But at Pollentia, Stilicho surprised him, while he and his Goths were celebrating Easter Sunday, and a fearful battle followed. The Romans stormed his camp, recovered the spoils of Greece, and took his wife, decked in the jewels in which she meant to enter Rome. One longs to know what became of her.

At least, so say the Romans: the Goths tell a very different story; and one suspects that Pollentia may be one more of those splendid paper victories, in which the Teutons were utterly exterminated, only to rise out of the ground, seemingly stronger and more numerous than ever. At least, instead of turning his head to the Alps, he went on toward Rome. Stilicho dared not fight him again, and bought him off. He turned northward toward Gaul, and at Verona Stilicho got him at an advantage, and fought him once more, and if we are to believe Rosino and Claudian, beat him again. 'Taceo de Alarico, sæpe victo, sæpe concluso, semperque dimisso.' 'It is ill work trapping an eagle,' says some one. When you have caught him, the safest thing very often is to let him go again.

Meanwhile poured down into Italy, as far as Florence (a merely unimportant episode in those fearful days), another wave of German invaders under one Radogast, 200,000 strong. Under the walls of Florence they sat down, and perished of wine, and heat, and dysentery. Like water they flowed in, and like water they sank into the soil: and every one of them a human soul.

Stilicho and Honorius went to Rome, and celebrated their triumph over the Goths, with (for the last time in history) gladiatorial sports. Three years past, and then Stilicho was duly rewarded for having saved Rome, in the approved method for every great barbarian who was fool enough to help the treacherous Roman; namely, by being murdered.

Alaric rose instantly, and with him all the Gothic tribes. Down through Italy he past, almost without striking a blow. Ravenna, infamous, according to Sidonius, for its profligacy, where the Emperor's court was, he past disdainfully, and sat down before the walls of Rome. He did not try to storm it. Probably he could not. He had no such machines, as those with which the Romans battered walls. Quietly he sat, he and his Goths, 'as wolves wait round the dying buffalo;' waiting for the Romans within to starve and die. They did starve and die; men murdered each other for food; mothers ate their own babes; but they sent out embassies, boasting of their strength and numbers. Alaric laughed,—'The thicker the hay, the easier it is mowed.' What terms would he take? 'All your gold, all your silver, the best of your precious things. All your barbarian slaves.' That last is significant. He would deliver his own flesh and blood. The Teuton man should be free. The trolls should drag no more of the forest children into their accursed den. 'What then will you leave us?' 'Your lives.'

They bought him off with a quaint ransom: 5000 pounds weight of gold, 30,000 of silver, 4000 robes of silk, 3000 pieces of scarlet cloth, and 3000 lbs. of pepper, possibly spices of all kinds. Gold, and finery, and spices—gifts fit for children, such as those Goths were.

But he got, too, 40,000 Teuton slaves safe out of the evil place, and embodied them into his army. He had now 100,000 fighting men. Why did he not set up as king of Italy? Was it that the awe of the place, the prestige of the Roman name, cowed him? It cowed each of the Teutonic invaders successively. To make themselves emperors of Rome was a thing of which they dared not dream. Be that as it may, all he asked was, to be received as some sort of vassal of the Emperor. The Master-Generalship of Italy, subsidies for his army, an independent command in the Tyrolese country, whence he had come, were his demand.

Overblown with self-conceit, the Romans refused him. They would listen to no conditions. They were in a thoroughly Chinese temper. You will find the Byzantine empire in the same temper centuries after; blinded to present weakness by the traditions of their forefathers' strength. They had worshipped the beast. Now that only his image was left, they worshipped that.

Alaric seized Ostia, and cut off their supplies. They tried to appease him by dethroning Honorius, and setting up some puppet Attalus. Alaric found him plotting; or said that he had done so; and degraded him publicly at Rimini before his whole army. Again he offered peace. The insane Romans proclaimed that his guilt precluded him for ever from the clemency of the Empire.

Then came the end. He marched on Rome. The Salarian gate was thrown open at midnight, probably by German slaves within; and then, for five dreadful days and nights, the wicked city expiated in agony the sins of centuries.

And so at last the Nibelungen hoard was won.

'And the kings of the earth who had lived delicately with her, and the merchants of the earth who were made rich by her, bewailed her, standing afar off for the fear of her torment, and crying, Alas! alas, that great Babylon! for in one hour is thy judgment come.'

St. John passes in those words from the region of symbol to that of literal description. A great horror fell upon all nations, when the news came. Rome taken?

Surely the end of all things was at hand. The wretch-
ed fugitives poured into Egypt and Syria—especially to
Jerusalem; perhaps with some superstitious hope that
Christ's tomb, or even Christ himself, might save them.

St. Jerome, as he saw day by day patrician men and
women who had passed their lives in luxury, begging
their bread around his hermitage at Bethlehem, wrote
of the fall of Rome as a man astonied.

St. Augustine, at Hippo, could only look on it as the
end of all human power and glory, perhaps of the earth
itself. Babylon the great had fallen, and now Christ
was coming in the clouds of heaven to set up the city of
God for ever. In that thought he wrote his De Civitate
Dei. Read it, gentlemen—especially you who are to be
priests—not merely for its details of the fall of Rome,
but as the noblest theodicy which has yet proceeded
from a human pen.

Followed by long trains of captives, long trains of
waggons bearing the spoils of all the world, Alaric went
on South, 'with the native instinct of the barbarian,' as
Dr. Sheppard well says. Always toward the sun. Away
from Muspelheim and the dark cold north, toward the
sun, and Valhalla, where Odin and the Asas dwell in everlasting light.

He tried to cross into Sicily: but a storm wrecked his
boats, and the Goths were afraid of the sea. And after a
while he died. And the wild men made a great mourning over him. They had now no plan left; no heart to go
south, and look for Odin over the sea. But of one thing
they were resolved, that the base Romans should not dig
up Alaric out of his barrow and scatter his bones to the

winds.

So they put no barrow over the great king; but under
the walls of Cosenza they turned the river-bed, and in
that river-bed they set Alaric, armed and mailed, upright
upon his horse, with gold, and jewels, and arms, and it
may be captive youths and maids, that he might enter
into Valhalla in royal pomp, and make a worthy show
among the heroes in Odin's hall. And then they turned
back the river into its bed, and slew the slaves who had
done the work, that no man might know where Alaric
lies: and no man does know till this day.

As I said, they had no plan left now. Two years they
stayed in Campania, basking in the villas and gardens,
drinking their fill of the wine; and then flowed away
northward again, no one knows why. They had no wish
to settle, as they might have done. They followed some
God-given instinct, undiscoverable now by us. Ataulf,
Alaric's kinsman, married Placidia, the Emperor's beautiful young sister, and accepted from him some sort of
commission to fight against his enemies in Gaul. So
to the south of Gaul they went, and then into Spain,
crushing before them Alans, Sueves, and Vandals, and
quarrelling among themselves. Ataulf was murdered,
and all his children; Placidia put to shame. Then she
had her revenge. To me it is not so much horrible as
pitiful. They had got the Nibelungen hoard; and with it
the Nibelungen curse.

A hundred years afterwards, when the Franks pil-
laged the Gothic palace of Narbonne, they found the
remnants of it. Things inestimable, indescribable; tables
of solid emerald; the Missorium, a dish 2500 lbs. weight,

covered with all the gems of India. They had been in Solomon's Temple, fancied the simple Franks—as indeed some of them may well have been. The Arabs got the great emerald table at last, with its three rows of great pearls. Where are they all now? What is become, gentlemen, of the treasures of Rome? Jewels, recollect, are all but indestructible; recollect, too, that vast quantities were buried from time to time, and their places forgotten. Perhaps future generations will discover many such hoards. Meanwhile, many of those same jewels must be in actual use even now. Many a gem which hangs now on an English lady's wrist saw Alaric sack Rome—and saw before and since—What not? The palaces of the Pharaohs, or of Darius; then the pomp of the Ptolemies, or of the Seleucids—came into Europe on the neck of some vulgar drunken wife of a Roman proconsul, to glitter for a few centuries at every gladiator's butchery in the amphitheatre; then went away with Placidia on a Gothic ox-waggon, to pass into an Arab seraglio at Seville; and then, perhaps, back from Sultan to Sultan again to its native India, to figure in the peacock-throne of the Great Mogul, and be bought at last by some Armenian for a few rupees from an English soldier, and come hither—and whither next? When England shall be what Alexandria and Rome are now, that little stone will be as bright as ever.—An awful symbol, if you will take it so, of the permanence of God's works and God's laws, amid the wild chance and change of sinful man.

Then followed for Rome years of peace,—such peace as the wicked make for themselves—A troubled sea, casting up mire and dirt. Wicked women, wicked counts (mayors of the palace, one may call them) like Aetius and Boniface, the real rulers of a nominal Empire.

Puppet Valentinian succeeded his father, puppet Honorius. In his days appeared another great portent—another comet, sweeping down out of infinite space, and back into infinite space again.—Attila and his Huns. They lay in innumerable hordes upon the Danube, until Honoria, Valentinian's sister, confined in a convent at Constantinople for some profligacy, sent her ring to Attila. He must be her champion, and deliver her. He paused a while, like Alaric before him, doubting whether to dash on Constantinople or Rome, and at last decided for Rome. But he would try Gaul first; and into Gaul he poured, with all his Tartar hordes, and with them all the Teuton tribes, who had gathered in his progress, as an avalanche gathers the snow in its course. At the great battle of Châlons, in the year 451, he fought it out: Hun, Sclav, Tartar, and Finn, backed by Teutonic Gepid and Herule, Turkling, East Goth and Lombard, against Roman and West Goth, Frank and Burgund, and the Bretons of Armorica. Wicked Aetius shewed himself that day, as always, a general and a hero—the Marlborough of his time—and conquered. Attila and his hordes rolled away eastward, and into Italy for Rome.

That is the Hunnenschlacht; 'a battle,' as Jornandes calls it, 'atrox, multiplex, immane, pertinax.' Antiquity, he says, tells of nothing like it. No man who had lost that sight could say that he had seen aught worth seeing.—A fight gigantic, supernatural in vastness and horror, and the legends which still hang about the place.

You may see one of them in Von Kaulbach's immortal design—the ghosts of the Huns and the ghosts of the Germans rising from their graves on the battle-night in every year, to fight it over again in the clouds, while the country far and wide trembles at their ghostly hurrah. No wonder men remember that Hunnenschlacht. Many consider that it saved Europe; that it was one of the decisive battles of the world.

Not that Attila was ruined. Within the year he had swept through Germany, crossed the Alps, and devastated Italy almost to the walls of Rome. And there the great Pope Leo, 'the Cicero of preaching, the Homer of theology, the Aristotle of true philosophy,' met the wild heathen: and a sacred horror fell upon Attila, and he turned, and went his way, to die a year or two after no man knows how. Over and above his innumerable wives, he took a beautiful German girl. When his people came in the morning, the girl sat weeping, or seeming to weep; but Etzel, the scourge of God, lay dead in a pool of gore. She said that he had burst a blood-vessel. The Teutons whispered among themselves, that like a free-born Teuton, she had slain her tyrant. One longs to know what became of her.

And then the hordes broke up. Ardarich raised the Teuton Gepids and Ostrogoths. The Teutons who had obeyed Attila, turned on their Tartar conquerors, the only people who had ever subdued German men, and then only by brute force of overpowering numbers. At Netad, upon the great plain between the Drave and the Danube, they fought the second Hunnenschlacht, and the Germans conquered. Thirty thousand Huns fell on that dreadful day, and the rest streamed away into the heart of Asia, into the infinite unknown deserts from whence the foul miscreants had streamed forth, and left the Teutons masters of the world. The battle of Netad; that, and not Châlons, to my mind, was the saving battle of Europe.

So Rome was saved; but only for a few years. Puppet Valentinian rewarded Aetius for saving Rome, by stabbing with his own hand in his own palace, the hero of Châlons; and then went on to fill up the cup of his iniquity. It is all more like some horrible romance than sober history. Neglecting his own wife Eudoxia, he took it into his wicked head to ravish her intimate friend, the wife of a senator. Maximus stabbed him, retaliated on the beautiful empress, and made himself Emperor. She sent across the seas to Africa, to Genseric the Vandal, the cruel tyrant and persecutor. He must come and be her champion, as Attila had been Honoria's. And he came, with Vandals, Moors, naked Ausurians from the Atlas. The wretched Romans, in their terror, tore Maximus in pieces; but it was too late. Eudoxia met Genseric at the gates in royal robes and jewels. He stript her of her jewels on the spot, and sacked Rome; and that was her reward.

This is the second sack. More dreadful far than the first—455 is its date. Then it was that the statues, whose fragments are still found, were hurled in vain on the barbarian assailants. Not merely gold and jewels, but the art-treasures of Rome were carried off to the Vandal fleet, and with them the golden table and the seven-branched candlestick which Titus took from the

Temple of Jerusalem.

How had these things escaped the Goths forty years before? We cannot tell. Perhaps the Gothic sack, which only lasted five days, was less complete than this one, which went on for fourteen days of unutterable horrors. The plunderers were not this time sturdy honest Goths; not even German slaves, mad to revenge themselves on their masters: they were Moors, Ausurian black savages, and all the pirates and cut-throats of the Mediterranean.

Sixty thousand prisoners were carried off to Carthage. All the statues were wrecked on the voyage to Africa, and lost for ever.

And yet Rome did not die. She lingered on; her Emperor still calling himself an Emperor, her senate a senate; feeding her lazy plebs, as best she could, with the remnant of those revenues which former Emperors had set aside for their support—their public bread, public pork, public oil, public wine, public baths,—and leaving them to gamble and quarrel, and listen to the lawyers in rags and rascality, and to rise and murder ruler after ruler, benefactor after benefactor, out of base jealousy and fear of any one less base than themselves. And so 'the smoke of her torment went up continually.'

But if Rome would not die, still less would she repent; as it is written—'The remnant of the people repented not of their deeds, but gnawed their tongues for pain, and blasphemed the God of heaven.'

As the century runs on, the confusion becomes more and more dreadful. Anthemius, Olybrius, Orestes, and the other half-caste Romans with Greek names who become quasi-emperors and get murdered; Ricimer the

Sueve, the king-maker and king-murderer; even good Majorian, who as puppet Emperor set up by Ricimer, tries to pass a few respectable laws, and is only murdered all the sooner. None of these need detain us. They mean nothing, they represent no idea, they are simply kites and crows quarrelling over the carcase, and cannot possibly teach us anything, but the terrible lesson, that in all revolutions the worst men are certain to rise to the top.

But only for a while, gentlemen, only for a while. Villany is by its very essence self-destructive, and if rogues have their day, the time comes when rogues fall out, and honest men come by their own.

That day, however, was not come for wretched Rome. A third time she was sacked by Ricimer her own general; and then more villains ruled her; and more kites and crows plundered her. The last of them only need keep us a while. He is Odoacer, the giant Herule, Houdy-wacker, as some say his name really is, a soubriquet perhaps from his war-cry, 'Hold ye stoutly,' 'Stand you steady.' His father was Ædecon, Attila's secretary, chief of the little Turkling tribe, who, though Teutonic, had clung faithfully to Attila's sons, and after the battle of Netad, came to ruin. There are strange stories of Odoacer. One from the Lives of St. Severinus, how Odoacer and his brothers started over the Alps, knapsacks at back, to seek their fortunes in Italy, and take service with the Romans; and how they came to St. Severinus' cell near Vienna, and went in, heathens as they probably were, to get a blessing from the holy hermit; and how Odoacer had to stoop, and stand stooping, so huge he was. And

how the saint saw that he was no common lad, and said,
'Go into Italy, clothed in thy ragged sheep-skins: thou
shalt soon give greater gifts to thy friends.' So he went,
and his brother with him. One of them at least ought
to interest us. He was Onulf, Hunwulf, Wulf, Guelph,
the Wolf-cub, who went away to Constantinople, and
saw strange things, and did strange things likewise, and
at last got back to Germany, and settled in Bavaria, and
became the ancestor of all the Guelphs, and of Victoria,
queen of England. His son, Wulfgang, fought under
Belisarius against the Goths; his son again, Ulgang, under Belisarius against Persian and Lombard; his son or
grandson was Queen Brunhilda's confidant in France,
and became Duke of Burgundy; and after that the fortunes of his family were mixed up with the Merovingian
kings of France, and then again with the Lombards in
Italy, till one of them emerges as Guelf, count of Altorf,
the ancestor of our Guelphic line.

But to return to Odoacer. He came to Rome, seek-
ing his fortune. There he found in power Orestes, his
father's old colleague at Attila's court, the most unprincipled turn-coat of his day; who had been the Emper-
or's man, then Attila's man, and would be anybody's
man if needed: but who was now his own man, being
king-maker for the time being, and father of the puppet
Emperor, Romulus Augustulus, a pretty little lad, with
an ominous name.

Odoacer took service under Orestes in the body-
guards, became a great warrior and popular; watched
his time; and when Orestes refused the mercenaries,
Herules, Rugians, Scyrings, Turklings and Alans—all

the weak or half-caste frontier tribes who had as yet little or no share in the spoils of Italy—their demand of the third of the lands of Italy, he betrayed his benefactor; promised the mercenaries to do for them what Orestes would not, and raises his famous band of confederates. At last he called himself King of Nations, burnt Pavia, and murdered Orestes, as a due reward for his benefits. Stript of his purple, the last Emperor of Rome knelt crying at the feet of the German giant, and begged not to be murdered like his father. And the great wild beast's hard heart smote him, and he sent the poor little lad away, to live in wealth and peace in Lucullus' villa at Misenum, with plenty of money, and women, and gewgaws, to dream away his foolish life looking out over the fair bay of Naples—the last Emperor of Rome.

Then Odoacer set to work, and not altogether ill. He gave his confederates the third of Italy, in fief under himself as king, and for fourteen years (not without the help of a few more murders) he kept some sort of rude order and justice in the wretched land. Remember him, for, bad man as he is, he does represent a principle. He initiated, by that gift of the lands to his soldiers, the feudal system in Italy. I do not mean that he invented it. It seems rather to be a primæval German form, as old as the days of Tacitus, who describes, if you will recollect, the German war-kings as parting the conquered lands among their 'comites,' thanes, or companions in arms.

So we leave Odoacer king of Italy, for fourteen years, little dreaming, perhaps, of the day when as he had done unto others so should it be done to him. But for that tale of just and terrible retribution you must wait till the next lecture.

And now, to refresh us with a gleam of wholesome humanity after all these horrors, let us turn to our worthy West Goth cousins for a while. They have stopt cutting each other's throats, settled themselves in North Spain and South France, and good bishop Sidonius gets to like them. They are just and honest men on the whole, kindly, and respectable in morals, living according to their strange old Gothic Law. But above all Sidonius likes their king—Theodoric is his name. A man of blood he has been in his youth: but he has settled down, like his people; and here is a picture of him. A real photograph of a live old Goth, nearly 1400 years ago. Gibbon gives a good translation of it. I will give you one, but Sidonius is prolix and florid, and I have had to condense.

A middle-sized, stout man, of great breadth of chest, and thickness of limb, a large hand, and a small foot, curly haired, bushy eye-browed, with remarkably large eyes and eyelids, hook-nosed, thin-lipped; brilliant, cheerful, impassioned, full of health and strength in mind and body. He goes to chapel before day-light, sits till eight doing justice, while the crowd, let into a latticed enclosure, is admitted one by one behind a curtain into the presence. At eight he leaves the throne, and goes either to count his money, or look at his horses. If he hunts, he thinks it undignified to carry his bow, and womanish to keep it strung, a boy carries it behind him; and when game gets up, he asks you (or the Bishop, who seems to have gone hunting with him) what you would wish him to aim at; strings his bow, and then (says Sidonius) never misses his shot. He dines at noon, quietly in general, magnificently on Saturdays; drinks very little, and instead of sleeping after dinner, plays at tables and dice. He is passionately fond of his game, but never loses his temper, joking and talking to the dice, and to every one round him, throwing aside royal severity, and bidding all be merry (says the bishop); for, to speak my mind, what he is afraid of is, that people should be afraid of him. If he wins he is in immense good humour; then is the time to ask favours of him; and, says the crafty bishop, many a time have I lost the game, and won my cause thereby. At three begins again the toil of state. The knockers return, and those who shove them away return too; everywhere the litigious crowd murmurs round; and follows him at evening, when he goes to supper, or gets its matters settled by the officers of the court, who have to stay there till bed-time. At supper, though there are but rarely 'mimici sales,' which I cannot translate—some sort of jesting: but biting and cruel insults (common at the feasts of the Roman Emperors) are never allowed. His taste in music is severe. No water-organs, flute-player, lyrist, cymbal or harp-playing woman is allowed. All he delights in is the old Teutonic music, whose virtue (says the bishop) soothes the soul no less than does its sound the ear. When he rises from table the guards for the night are set, and armed men stand at all the doors, to watch him through the first hours of sleep.

# THE GOTHIC CIVILIZER

Let us follow the fortunes of Italy and of Rome. They are not only a type of the fortunes of the whole western world, but the fortunes of that world, as you will see, depend on Rome.

You must recollect, meanwhile, that by the middle of the fifth century, the Western Empire had ceased to exist. The Angles and Saxons were fighting their way into Britain. The Franks were settled in north France and the lower Rhineland. South of them, the centre of Gaul still remained Roman, governed by Counts of cities, who were all but independent sovereigns, while they confessed a nominal allegiance to the Emperor of Constantinople. Their power was destined soon to be annihilated by the conquests of Clovis and his Franks— as false and cruel ruffians as their sainted king, the first-born son of the Church. The history of Gaul for some centuries becomes henceforth a tissue of internecine horrors, which you must read for yourselves in the pages of M. Sismondi, or of Gregory of Tours. The Allemanni (whose name has become among the Franks the general name for Germans) held the lands from the Maine to the Rhætian Alps. The Burgunds, the lands to the south-west of them, comprising the greater part of south-east Gaul. The West Goths held the south-west of Gaul, and the greater part of Spain, having thrust the Sueves, and with them some Alans, into Gallicia, Asturias, and Portugal; and thrust, also, the Vandals across the straits of Gibraltar, to found a prosperous kingdom along the northern shore of Africa. The East Goths, meanwhile, after various wanderings to the north of the Alps, lay in the present Austria and in the Danube lands, resting after their great struggle with the Huns, and their crowning victory of Netad.

To follow the fortunes of Italy, we must follow those of these East Goths, and especially of one man among them, Theodoric, known in German song as Dietrich of Bern or Verona.

Interesting exceedingly to us should this great hero be. No man's history better shows the strange relations between the Teutons and the dying Empire: but more; his life is the first instance of a Teuton attempting to found a civilized and ordered state, upon experience drawn from Roman sources; of the young world trying to build itself up some sort of dwelling out of the ruins of the old. Dietrich failed, it is true. But if the thing had been then possible, he seems to have been the man to have done it. He lived and laboured like what he was—a royal Amal, a true son of Woden. Unable to write, he founded a great kingdom by native virtue and common sense. Called a barbarian, he restored prosperity to ruined Italy, and gave to it (and with it to the greater part of the western world), peace for three and thirty years. Brought up among hostile sects, he laid down that golden law of religious liberty which the nineteenth century has not yet courage and humanity enough to accept. But if his life was heroic, his death was tragic. He failed after all in his vast endeavours, from causes hidden from him, but visible, and most instructive, to us; and after

having toiled impartially for the good of conquerors
and of conquered alike, he died sadly, leaving behind
him a people who, most of them, believed gladly the
news that a holy hermit had seen his soul hurled down
the crater of Stromboli, as a just punishment for the inexpiable crime of being wiser than his generation.

Some have complained of Gibbon's 'hero-worship'
of Dietrich—I do not. The honest and accurate cyn-
ic so very seldom worshipped a hero, or believed in the
existence of any, that we may take his good opinion as
almost final and without appeal. One author, for whose
opinion I have already exprest a very high respect, says
that he was but a wild man of the woods to the last; pol-
ished over skin-deep with Roman civilization; 'Scratch
him, and you found the barbarian underneath.' It may
be true. If it be true, it is a very high compliment. It
was not from his Roman civilization, but from his 'barbarian' mother and father, that he drew the 'vive intel-
ligence des choses morales, et ces inspirations élevées et
heroïques,' which M. Thierry truly attributes to him.
If there was, as M. Thierry truly says, another nature
struggling within him—is there not such in every man?
And are not the struggles the more painful, the temptations more dangerous, the inconsistencies too often
the more shameful, the capacities for evil as well as for
good, more huge, just in proportion to the native force
and massiveness of the soul? The doctrine may seem
dangerous. It is dangerous, like many truths; and woe
to those who, being unlearned and unstable, wrest it to
their own destruction; and presume upon it to indulge
their own passions under Byronic excuses of 'genius,' or

'muscular Christianity.' But it is true nevertheless: so at least the Bible tells us, in its wonderful delineations of David, 'the man after God's own heart,' and of St. Peter, the chief of the apostles. And there are points of likeness between the character of Dietrich, and that of David, which will surely suggest themselves to any acute student of human nature. M. Thierry attributes to him, as his worse self, 'les instincts les plus violents; la cruauté, l'astuce, l'egoïsme impitoyable.' The two first counts are undeniable—at least during his youth: they were the common vices of the age. The two latter I must hold as not proven by facts: but were they proven, they would still be excusable, on the simple ground of his Greek education. 'Cunning and pitiless egotism' were the only moral qualities which Dietrich is likely to have seen exercised at the court of Constantinople: and what wonder, if he was somewhat demoralized by the abominable atmosphere which he breathed from childhood? Dietrich is an illustration of the saga with which these lectures began. He is the very type of the forest child, bewitched by the fine things of the wicked Troll garden. The key to the man's character, indeed the very glory of it, is the long struggle within him, between the Teutonic and the Greek elements. Dazzled and debauched, at times, by the sinful glories of the Bosphorus, its palaces, its gold, and its women, he will break the spell desperately. He will become a wild Goth and an honest man once more; he will revenge his own degradation on that court and empire which he knows well enough to despise, distrust and hate. Again and again the spell comes over him. His vanity and his passions make him once more a courtier among the Greeks; but the blood of Odin is strong within him still; again and again he rises, with a noble shame, to virtue and patriotism, trampling under foot selfish luxury and glory, till the victory is complete; and he turns away in the very moment of the greatest temptation, from the bewitching city, to wander, fight, starve, and at last conquer a new land for himself and for his nation; and shew, by thirty years of justice and wisdom, what that true Dietrich was, which had been so long overlaid by the false Dietrich of his sinful youth.

Look at the facts of his history, as they stand, and see whether they do not bear out this, and no other, theory of his character.

The year was 455, two years after Attila's death. Near Vienna a boy was born, of Theodemir one of the Gothic kings and his favourite Erleva. He was sent when eight years old to Constantinople as a hostage. The Emperor Leo had agreed to pay the Goths 300 pounds of gold every year, if they would but leave him in peace; and young Dietrich was the pledge of the compact. There he grew up amid all the wisdom of the Romans, watching it all, and yet never even learning to write. It seems to some that the German did not care to learn; it seems to me rather that they did not care to teach. He came back to his people at eighteen, delighted them by his strength and stature, and became, to all appearance, a Goth of the Goths; going adventures with six thousand volunteers against the Sarmatæ, who had just defeated the Greeks, and taken a city—which he retook, but instead of restoring it to the Emperor, kept himself. Food becoming scarce in Austria, the Ostrogoths moved some into Italy, some down on Illyria and Thessaly; and the Emperor gracefully presented them with the country of which they had already taken possession.

In every case, you see, this method went on. The failing Emperors bought off the Teutons where they could; submitted to them where they could not; and readily enough turned on them when they had a chance. The relations between the two parties can be hardly better explained, than by comparing them to those between the English adventurers in Hindostan and the falling Rajahs and Sultans of the last century.

After a while Theodoric, or Dietrich, found himself, at his father's death, sole king of the Ostrogoths. This period of his life is very obscure: but one hint at least we have, which may explain his whole future career. Side by side with him and with his father before him, there was another Dietrich—Dietrich the One-eyed, son of Triar, a low-born adventurer, who had got together the remnants of some low-caste tribes, who were called the Goths of Thrace, and was swaggering about the court of Constantinople, as, when the East Goths first met him, what we call Warden of the Marches, with some annual pay for his Goths. He was insolent to Theodemir and his family, and they retaliated by bitter hatred. It was intolerable for them, Amals, sons of Odin, to be insulted by this upstart. So they went on for years, till the miserable religious squabble fell out—you may read it in Gibbon—which ended in the Emperor Zeno, a low-born and cunning man, suspected of the murder of his own son by the princess Ariadne, being driven out of Constantinople by Basiliscus. We need not enter into such matters, except as far as they bear on the history of Dietrich the Amal. Dietrich the One-eyed helped Basiliscus—and then Zeno seems to have sent for Dietrich the Amal to help him. He came, but too late. Basiliscus' party had already broken up; Basiliscus and his family had taken refuge in a church, from whence Zeno enticed him, on the promise of shedding no blood, which he did not: but instead, put him, his wife and children, in a dry cistern, walled it up and left them.

Dietrich the Amal rose into power and great glory, and became 'son-in-arms' to the Emperor. But the young Amal longed for adventures. He offered to take his Ostrogoths into Italy, drive out Odoacer, and seat on the throne of the West, Nepos, one of the many puppets who had been hurled off it a few years before. Zeno had need of the young hero nearer home, and persuaded him to stay in Constantinople, eat, drink, and be merry.

Whereon Odoacer made Romulus Agustulus and the Roman Senate write to Zeno that they wanted no Emperor save him at Constantinople; that they were very happy under the excellent Odoacer, and that they therefore sent to Zeno, as the rightful owner, all the Imperial insignia and ornaments; things which may have been worn, some of them, by Augustus himself. And so ended, even in name, the Empire of Rome. All which the Amal saw, and, as will appear, did not forget.

Zeno gave the Amal all that the One-eyed had had before him, and paid the Ostrogoths yearly as he had paid the One-eye's men. The One-eyed was banished to his cantonments, and of course revolted. Zeno wanted to buy him off, but the Amal would not hear of it; he would not help the Romans against his rival, unless they swore perpetual enmity against him.

They did so, and he marched to the assistance of the wretched Empire. He was to be met by Roman reinforcements at the Hæmus. They never came; and the Amal, disgusted and disheartened, found himself entangled in the defiles of the Hæmus, starving and worn out; with the One-eyed entrenched on an inaccessible rock, where he dared not attack him.

Then followed an extraordinary scene. The One-eyed came down again and again from his rock, and rode round the Amal's camp, shouting to him words so true, that one must believe them to have been really spoken.

'Perjured boy, madman, betrayer of your race—do you not see that the Roman plan is as always to destroy Goths by Goths? Whichever of us falls, they, not we, will be the stronger. They never met you as they promised, at the cities, nor here. They have sent you out here to perish in the desert.'

Then the East Goths raised a cry. 'The One-eyed is right. The Amal cares not that these men are Goths like ourselves.'

Then the One-eyed appeals to the Goths themselves, as he curses the Amal.

'Why are you killing your kinsmen? Why have you made so many widows? Where is all their wealth gone, they who set out to fight for you? Each of them had two or three horses: but now they are walking on foot behind you like slaves,—free-men as well-born as yourself:—and you promised to measure them out gold by the bushel.'

Was it not true? If young Dietrich had in him (and he shewed that he had in after years) a Teuton's heart, may not that strange interview have opened his eyes to his own folly, and taught him that the Teuton must be his own master, and not the mercenary of the Romans?

The men cried out that it was true. He must make peace with the One-eyed, or they would do it themselves; and peace was made. They both sent ambassadors to Zeno; the Amal complaining of treachery; the One-eyed demanding indemnity for all his losses. The Emperor was furious. He tried to buy off the Amal by marrying him to a princess of the blood royal, and making him a Cæsar. Dietrich would not consent; he felt that it was a snare. Zeno proclaimed the One-eyed an enemy to the Empire; and ended by reinstating him in his old honours, and taking them from the Amal. The Amal became furious, burnt villages, slaughtered the peasants, even (the Greeks say) cut off the hands of his captives. He had broken with the Romans at last. The Roman was astride of him, and of all Teutons, like Sindbad's old man of the sea. The only question, as with Sindbad, was whether he should get drunk, and give them a chance of throwing the perfidious tyrant. And now the time was come. He was compelled to ask himself, not—what shall I be in relation to myself: but what shall I be in relation to the Kaiser of the Romans—a mercenary, a slave, or a conqueror—for one of the three I must be?

So it went on, year after year—sometimes with terrible reverses for Dietrich, till the year 480. Then the old One-eyed died, in a strange way. Mounting a wild horse at the tent-door, the beast reared before he could get his seat; afraid of pulling it over by the curb, he let it go. A lance, in Gothic fashion, was hanging at the tent-door, and the horse plunged the One-eyed against it. The point went deep into his side, and the old fighting man was at rest for ever.

And then came a strange peripeteia for the Amal. Zeno, we know not why, sent instantly for him. He had been ravaging, pursuing, defeating Roman troops, or being defeated by them. Now he must come to Rome. His Goths should have the Lower Danube. He should have glory and honour to spare. He came. His ideal, at this time, seems actually to have been to live like a Roman citizen in Constantinople, and help to govern the Empire. Recollect, he was still little more than five and twenty years old.

So he went to Constantinople, and I suppose with him the faithful mother, and faithful sister, who had been with him in all his wanderings. He had a triumph decreed him at the Emperor's expense, was made Consul Ordinarius ('which,' saith Jornandes, 'is accounted the highest good and chief glory in the world') and Master-general, and lodged in the palace.

What did it all mean? Dietrich was dazzled by it, at least for a while. What it meant, he found out too soon. He was to fight the Emperor's battles against all rebels, and he fought them, to return irritated, complaining (justly or unjustly) of plots against his life; to be pacified, like a child, with the honour of an equestrian statue; then to sink down into Byzantine luxury for seven inglorious years, with only one flashing out of the ancient spirit, when he demanded to go alone against the Bulgars, and killed their king with his own hand.

What woke him from his dream? The cry of his starving people.

The Goths, settled on the lower Danube, had been living, as wild men and mercenaries live, recklessly from hand to mouth, drinking and gambling till their families were in want. They send to the Amal. 'While thou art revelling at Roman banquets, we are starving—come back ere we are ruined.'

They were jealous, too, of the success of Odoacer and his mercenaries. He was growing now to be a great power; styling himself 'King of nations'[1], giving away to the Visigoths the Narbonnaise, the last remnant of the Western Empire; collecting round him learned Romans like Symmachus, Boethius, and Cassiodorus; respecting the Catholic clergy; and seemingly doing his best to govern well. His mercenaries, however, would not be governed. Under their violence and oppression agriculture and population were both failing; till Pope Gelasius speaks of 'Æmilia, Tuscia, ceteræque provinciæ in quibus nullus prope hominum existit.'

Meanwhile there seems to have been a deep hatred on the part of the Goths to Odoacer and his mercenaries. Dr. Sheppard thinks that they despised him himself as a man of low birth. But his father Ædecon had been chief of the Turklings, and was most probably of royal blood. It is very unlikely, indeed, that so large a number of Teutons would have followed any man who

---

1 Had he actually taken the name of Theodoric, Theuderic, Dietrich, which signifies much the same thing as 'King of nations'?

had not Odin's blood in his veins. Was there a stain on Odoacer from his early connexion with Attila? Or was the hatred against his men more than himself, contempt especially of the low-caste Herules,—a question of race, springing out of those miserable tribe-feuds, which kept the Teutons always divided and weak? Be that as it may, Odoacer had done a deed which raised this hatred to open fury. He had gone over the Alps into Rugiland (then Noricum, and the neighbourhood of Vienna) and utterly destroyed those of the Rugier who had not gone into Italy under his banner. They had plundered, it is said, the cell of his old friend St. Severinus, as soon as the saint died, of the garments laid up for the poor, and a silver cup, and the sacred vessels of the mass. Be that as it may, Odoacer utterly exterminated them, and carried their king Feletheus, or Fava, back to Italy, with Gisa his 'noxious wife;' and with them many Roman Christians, and (seemingly) the body of St. Severinus himself. But this had been a small thing, if he had not advised himself to have a regular Roman triumph, with Fava, the captive king, walking beside his chariot; and afterwards, in the approved fashion of the ancient Romans on such occasions, to put Fava to death in cold blood.

The records of this feat are to be found, as far as I know them, in one short chapter (I. xix.) of Paulus Diaconus, and in Muratori's notes thereto; but however small the records, the deed decided the fate of Italy. Frederic, son of Fava, took refuge with the Ostrogoths, and demanded revenge in the name of his royal race; and it is easy to conceive that the sympathies of the Goths would be with him. An attack (seemingly unprovoked) on an ancient Teutonic nation by a mere band of adventurers was—or could easily be made—a grievous wrong, and clear casus belli, over and above the innate Teutonic lust for fighting and adventures, simply for the sake of 'the sport.'

Dietrich went back, and from that day, the dream of eastern luxury was broken, and young Dietrich was a Goth again, for good and for evil.

He assembled the Goths, and marched straight on Constantinople, burning and pillaging as he went. So say, at least, the Greek historians, of whom, all through this strange story, no one need believe more than he likes. Had the Goths had the writing of the life of Dietrich, we should have heard another tale. As it is, we have, as it were, a life of Lord Clive composed by the court scribes of Delhi.

To no Roman would he tell what was in his mind. Five leagues from Constantinople he paused. Some say that he had compassion on the city where he had been brought up. Who can tell? He demanded to speak to Zeno alone, and the father in arms and his wild son met once more. There was still strong in him the old Teutonic feudal instinct. He was 'Zeno's man,' in spite of all. He asked (says Jornandes) Zeno's leave to march against Odoacer, and conquer Italy. Procopius and the Valesian Fragment say that Zeno sent him, and that in case of success, he was to reign there till Zeno came. Zeno was, no doubt, glad to get rid of him at any price. As Ennodius well says, 'Another's honour made him remember his own origin, and fear the very legions which obeyed him—for that obedience is suspected which serves the unworthy.' Rome was only nominally under Zeno's dominion; and it mattered little to him whether Herule or Gothic adventurer called himself his representative.

Then was held a grand function. Dietrich, solemnly appointed 'Patrician,' had Italy ceded to him by a 'Pragmatic' sanction, and Zeno placed on his head the sacrum velamen, a square of purple, signifying in Constantinople things wonderful, august, imperial—if they could only be made to come to pass. And he made them come to pass. He gathered all Teutonic heroes of every tribe, as well as his own; and through Roumelia, and through the Alps, a long and dangerous journey, went Dietrich and his Goths, with their wives and children, and all they had, packed on waggons; living on their flocks and herds, grinding their corn in hand-mills, and hunting as they went, for seven hundred miles of march; fighting as they went with Bulgars and Sarmatians, who had swarmed into the waste marches of Hungary and Carniola, once populous, cultivated, and full of noble cities; fighting a desperate battle with the Gepidæ, up to their knees in a morass; till over the passes of the Julian Alps, where icicles hung upon their beards, and their clothes cracked with frost, they poured into the Venetian plains. It was a daring deed; and needed a spirit like Dietrich's to carry it through.

Odoacer awaited him near the ruins of Aquileia. On the morning of the fight, as he was arming, Dietrich asked his noble mother to bring him some specially fine mantle, which she had embroidered for him, and put it over his armour, 'that all men may see how he goes gayer into the fight than ever he did into feast. For this day she shall see whether she have brought a man-child into the world, or no.'

And in front of Verona (where the plain was long white with human bones), he beat Odoacer, and after a short and sharp campaign, drove him to Ravenna. But there, Roman fortifications, and Roman artillery, stopped, as usual, the Goth; and Odoacer fulfilled his name so well, and stood so stout, that he could only be reduced by famine; and at last surrendered on terms, difficult now to discover.

Gibbon says, that there was a regular compact that they should enjoy equal authority, and refers to Procopius: but Procopius only says, that they should live together peaceably 'in that city.' Be that as it may, Odoacer and his party were detected, after awhile, conspiring against Dietrich, and put to death in some dark fashion. Gibbon, as advocatus diaboli, of course gives the doubt against Dietrich, by his usual enthymeme—All men are likely to be rogues, ergo, Dietrich was one. Rather hard measure, when one remembers that the very men who tell the story are Dietrich's own enemies. By far the most important of them, the author of the Valesian Fragment, who considers Dietrich damned as an Arian, and the murderer of Boethius and Symmachus, says plainly that Odoacer plotted against his life. But it was a dark business at best.

Be that as it may, Dietrich the Amal found himself in one day king of all Italy, without a peer. And now followed a three and thirty years' reign of wisdom, justice, and prosperity, unexampled in the history of those centuries. Between the days of the Antonines and those of Charlemagne, I know no such bright spot in the dark history of Europe.

As for his transferring the third of the lands of Italy, which had been held by Odoacer's men, to his own Goths,—that was just or unjust (even putting out of the question the rights of conquest), according to what manner of men Odoacer's mercenaries were, and what right they had to the lands. At least it was done so, says Cassiodorus, that it notoriously gave satisfaction to the Romans themselves. One can well conceive it. Odoacer's men had been lawless adventurers; and now law was installed as supreme. Dietrich, in his long sojourn at the Emperor's court, had discovered the true secret of Roman power, which made the Empire terrible even in her fallen fortunes; and that was Law. Law, which tells every man what to expect, and what is expected of him; and so gives, if not content, still confidence, energy, industry. The Goths were to live by the Gothic law, the Romans by the Roman. To amalgamate the two races would have been as impossible as to amalgamate English and Hindoos. The parallel is really tolerably exact. The Goth was very English; and the over-civilized, learned, false, profligate Roman was the very counterpart of the modern Brahmin. But there was to be equal justice between man and man. If the Goths were the masters of much of the Roman soil, still spoliation and oppression were forbidden; and the remarkable edict or code of Theodoric, shews how deeply into his great mind had sunk the idea of the divineness of Law. It is short, and of Draconic severity, especially against spoliation, cheating, false informers, abuse by the clergy of the rights of sanctuary, and all offences against the honour of women. I advise you all to study it, as an example of what an early Teutonic king thought men ought to do, and could be made to do.

The Romans were left to their luxury and laziness; and their country villas (long deserted) were filled again by the owners. The Goths were expected to perform military service, and were drilled from their youth in those military evolutions which had so often given the disciplined Roman the victory over the undisciplined Goth, till every pomoerium (boulevard), says Ennodius, might be seen full of boys and lads, learning to be soldiers. Everything meanwhile was done to soothe the wounded pride of the conquered. The senate of Rome was still kept up in name (as by Odoacer), her nobles flattered by sonorous titles, and the officers of the kingdom and the palace bore the same names as they would have done under Roman emperors. The whole was an attempt to develop Dietrich's own Goths by the only civilization which he knew, that of Constantinople: but to engraft on it an order, a justice, a freedom, a morality, which was the 'barbarian' element. The treasures of Roman art were placed under the care of government officers; baths, palaces, churches, aqueducts, were repaired or founded; to build seems to have been Dietrich's great delight; and we have left us, on a coin, some image of his own palace at Verona, a strange building with domes and minarets, something like a Turkish mosque; standing, seemingly, on the arcades of some older Roman building. Dietrich the Goth may, indeed, be called the founder of 'Byzantine' architecture throughout the Western world.

Meanwhile, agriculture prospered once more; the Pontine Marshes were drained; the imperial ports restored, and new cities sprang up. 'The new ones,' says Machiavelli, 'were Venice, Siena, Ferrara, Aquileia; and those which became extended were Florence, Genoa, Pisa, Milan, Naples, and Bologna.' Of these the great sea-ports, especially Venice, were founded not by Goths, but by Roman and Greek fugitives: but it was the security and liberality of Dietrich's reign which made their existence possible; and Venice really owes far more to the barbarian hero, than to the fabled patronage of St. Mark.

'From this devastation and new population,' continues Machiavelli, 'arose new languages, which, partaking of the native idiom of the new people, and of the old Roman, formed a new manner of discourse. Besides, not only were the names of provinces changed, but also of lakes, rivers, seas, and men; for France, Spain, and Italy are full of fresh names, wholly different from the ancient.'

This reign of Dietrich was, in fact, the birth-hour of modern Italy; and, as Machiavelli says, 'brought the country to such a state of greatness, that her previous sufferings were unrecognizable.' We shall see hereafter how the great Goth's work was all undone; and (to their everlasting shame) by whom it was undone.

The most interesting records of the time are, without doubt, the letters of Cassiodorus, the king's secretary and chancellor, which have come down to us in great

numbers. There are letters among them on all questions
of domestic and foreign policy: to the kings of the Var-
ni, kings of the Herules, kings of the Thuringer (who
were still heathens beyond the Black forest), calling on
them all to join him and the Burgundians, and defend
his son-in-law Alaric II., king of the Visigoths, against
Clovis and his Franks. There are letters, too, bearing on
the religious feuds of the Roman population, and on the
morals and social state of Rome itself, of which I shall
say nothing in this lecture, having cause to refer to them
hereafter. But if you wish to know the times, you must
read Cassiodorus thoroughly.

In his letters you will remark how most of the so-
called Roman names are Greek. You will remark, too,
as a sign of the decadence of taste and art, that though
full of wisdom and practical morality, the letters are
couched in the most wonderful bombast to be met with,
even in that age of infimæ Latinitatis. One can only explain their style by supposing that King Dietrich, having
supplied the sense, left it for Cassiodorus to shape it as
he thought best; and when the letter was read over to
him, took for granted (being no scholar) that that was
the way in which Roman Cæsars and other cultivated
personages ought to talk; admired his secretary's learning; and probably laughed in his sleeve at the whole
thing, thinking that ten words of honest German would
have said all that he meant. As for understanding these
flights of rhetoric, it is impossible that Dietrich could
have done so: perhaps not even Cassiodorus himself.
Take as one example, such a letter as this.—After a lofty
moral maxim, which I leave for you to construe—'In

partem pietatis recidit mitigata districtio; et sub benefi-
cio præstat, qui poenam debitam moderatione consid-
erata palpaverit,'—Jovinus the curial is informed, after
the most complex method, that having first quarrelled
with a fellow-curial, and then proceeded to kill him, he
is banished for life to the isle of Volcano, among the Li-
paris. As a curial is a gentleman and a government magistrate, the punishment is just enough; but why should
Cassiodorus (certainly not King Dietrich) finish a short
letter by a long dissertation on volcanoes in general, and
Stromboli in particular, insisting on the wonder that
the rocks, though continually burnt, are continually re-
newed by 'the inextricable potency of nature;' and only
returning to Jovinus to inform him that he will henceforth follow the example of a salamander, which always
lives in fire, 'being so contracted by natural cold, that
it is tempered by burning flame. It is a thin and small
animal, connected with worms, and clothed with a yellow colour;' . . . Cassiodorus then returns to the main
subject of volcanoes, and ends with a story of Stromboli
having broken out just as Hannibal poisoned himself
at the court of Prusias;—information which may have
been interesting, though not consoling, to poor Jovinus, in the prospect of living there; but of which one
would like to have had king Dietrich's opinion. Did he
felicitate himself like a simple Teuton, on the wonderful
learning and eloquence of his Greek-Roman secretary?
Or did he laugh a royal laugh at the whole letter, and
crack a royal joke at Cassiodorus and all quill-driving
schoolmasters and lawyers—the two classes of men
whom the Goths hated especially, and at the end to

which they by their pedantries had brought imperial
Rome? One would like to know. For not only was Dietrich no scholar himself, but he had a contempt for the
very scholarship which he employed, and forbade the
Goths to learn it—as the event proved, a foolish and
fatal prejudice. But it was connected in his mind with
chicanery, effeminacy, and with the cruel and degrading punishments of children. Perhaps the ferula had
been applied to him at Constantinople in old days. If
so, no wonder that he never learnt to write. 'The boy
who trembles at a cane,' he used to say, 'will never face a
lance.' His mother wit, meanwhile, was so shrewd that
'many of his sayings (says the unknown author of the
invaluable Valesian Fragment) remain among us to this
day.' Two only, as far as I know, have been preserved,
quaint enough:

'He that hath gold, or a devil, cannot hide it.'

And

'The Roman, when poor, apes the Goth: the Goth,
when rich, apes the Roman.'

There is a sort of Solomon's judgment, too, told of
him, in the case of a woman who refused to acknowledge her own son, which was effectual enough; but
somewhat too homely to repeat.

As for his personal appearance, it was given in a saga;
but I have not consulted it myself, and am no judge of
its authenticity. The traditional description of him is

that of a man almost beardless—a rare case among the Goths—with masses of golden ringlets, and black eyebrows over 'oculos cæsios,' the blue grey eyes common to so many conquerors. A complexion so peculiar, that one must believe it to be truly reported.

His tragic death, and the yet more tragic consequences thereof, will be detailed in the next lecture.

# DIETRICH'S END

I have now to speak to you on the latter end of Dietrich's reign—made so sadly famous by the death of Boethius—the last Roman philosopher, as he has been called for centuries, and not unjustly.  His De Consolatione Philosophiæ is a book good for any man, full of wholesome and godly doctrine.  For centuries it ranked as high as the highest classics; higher perhaps at times than any book save the Bible, among not merely scholars, but statesmen.  It is the last legacy of the dying old world to the young world which was trampling it out of life; and therefore it is full of sadness.  But beneath the sadness there is faith and hope; for God is just, and virtue must be triumphant and immortal, and the absolute and only good for man.  The whole story is very sad.  Dietrich was one of those great men, who like Henry VIII, Elizabeth, Napoleon, or the late Czar Nicholas, have lived too long for their own honour.  The old heathen would have attributed his misadventures to a φθονος θεων, an envy of the Gods, who will not abide to see men as prosperous as they themselves are.  We may attribute it more simply and more piously to the wear and tear of frail humanity.  For it may be that very few human souls can stand for many years the strain of a great rule.  I do not mean that they break down from overwork, but that they are pulled out of shape by it; and that, especially, the will becomes enormously developed at the expense of the other powers of the soul, till

the man becomes, as he grows older, imperious, careless
of, or irritated by counsel, determined to have his own
way because it is his own way. We see the same tendency in all accustomed for a long while to absolute rule,
even in petty matters;—in the old ship's captain, the old
head of a factory, the old master of hounds; and we do
not blame them for it. It is a disease incident to their
calling, as pedantry is to that of a scholar, or astuteness
to that of an attorney. But it is most dangerous in the
greatest minds, and in the highest places; and only to be
kept off by them, as by us, each in our place, by honest
self-examination, diligent prayer, and the grace of God
which comes thereby. Once or twice in the world's history a great ruler, like Charles the Fifth, cuts the Gord-
ian knot, and escapes into a convent: but how few can
or ought to do that? There are those who must go on
ruling, or see their country ruined; for all depends on
them. So had Queen Elizabeth to do; so had Dietrich of
Bern likewise. After them would come the deluge, and
did come; and they must endure to the last, whatever it
may cost to their own health of character, or peace of
mind.

But most painful, and most dangerous to the veter-
an sovereign, is it to have learnt to suspect, perhaps to
despise, those whom he rules; to have thrown away all
his labour upon knaves and fools; to have cast his pearls
before swine, and find them turning again and rending
him. That feeling, forced from Queen Elizabeth, in her
old age, that tragic cry, 'I am a miserable forlorn woman.
There is none about me whom I can trust.' She was a
woman, always longing for some one to love; and her

heart broke under it all. But do you not see that where the ruler is not an affectionate woman, but a strong proud man, the effect may be very different, and very terrible?—how, roused to indignation, scorn, suspicion, rage, he may turn to bay against his own subjects, with 'Scoundrels! you have seen the fair side of my character, and in vain. Now you shall see the foul, and beware for yourselves.'

Even so, I fancy, did old Dietrich turn to bay, and did deeds which have blackened his name for ever. Heaven forgive him! for surely he had provocation enough and to spare.

I have told you of the simple, half-superstitious respect which the Teuton had for the prestige of Rome. Dietrich seems to have partaken of it, like the rest. Else why did he not set himself up as Cæsar of Rome? Why did he always consider himself as son-in-arms, and quasi-vassal, of the Cæsar of Constantinople? He had been in youth overawed by the cunning civilization which he had seen in the great city. He felt, with a noble modesty, that he could not emulate it. He must copy it afar off. He must take to his counsels men like Cassiodorus, Symmachus, Boethius, born and bred in it; trained from childhood in the craft by which, as a patent fact, the Kaisers of Rome had been for centuries, even in their decay and degradation, the rulers of the nations. Yet beneath that there must have been a perpetual under-current of contempt for it and for Rome—the 'colluvies gentium'—the sink of the nations, with its conceit, its pomposity, its beggary, its profligacy, its superstition, its pretence of preserving the Roman law and rights, while

practically it cared for no law nor right at all.  Dietrich
had had to write letter upon letter, to prevent the green
and blue factions cutting each other's throats at the public spectacles; letters to the tribunus voluptatum, who
had to look after the pantomimes and loose women,
telling him to keep the poor wretches in some decent
order, and to set them and the city an example of a better life, by being a chaste and respectable man himself.
Letter upon letter of Cassiodorus', written in Dietrich's
name, disclose a state of things in Rome on which a
Goth could look only with disgust and contempt.

And what if he discovered (or thought that he discovered) that these prating coxcombs—who were actually living on government bounty, and had their daily
bread, daily bath, daily oil, daily pork, daily wine, found
for them at government expense, while they lounged
from the theatre to the church, and the church to the
theatre—were plotting with Justin the scoundrel and
upstart Emperor at Constantinople, to restore forsooth
the liberties of Rome?  And that that was their answer to
his three and thirty years of good government, respect,
indulgence, which had raised them up again out of all
the miseries of domestic anarchy and foreign invasion?

And what if he discovered (or thought that he discovered) that the Catholic Clergy, with Pope John at
their head, were in the very same plot for bringing in
the Emperor of Constantinople, on the grounds of religion; because he was persecuting the Arian Goths at
Constantinople, and therefore would help them to persecute them in Italy?  And that that was their answer to
his three and thirty years of unexampled religious lib-

erty?  Would not those two facts (even the belief that they were facts) have been enough to drive many a wise man mad?

How far they were facts, we never shall exactly know. Almost all our information comes from Catholic historians—and he would be a rash man who would pin his faith on any statement of theirs concerning the actions of a heretic.  But I think, even with no other help than theirs, we may see why Dietrich would have looked with horror on any intimacy between the Church of Rome and the Court of Constantinople.

We must remember first what the Greek Empire was then, and who was the new Emperor.  Anastasius the poor old Emperor, dying at eighty with his heart broken by monks and priests, had an ugly dream; and told it to Amantius the eunuch and lord chamberlain.  Whereon Amantius said he had had a dream too;—how a great hog flew at him as he was in waiting in the very presence, and threw him down and eat him fairly up.  Which came true—though not in the way Amantius expected.  On the death of Anastasius he determined to set up as Emperor a creature of his own.  For this purpose he must buy the guards; to which noble end he put a large sum of treasure into the hands of Justin, senator, and commander-in-chief of the said guards, who takes the money, and spends it on his own account; so that the miserable eunuch finds, not his man, but Justin himself, Emperor, and his hard-earned money spent against him. The mere rise of this unscrupulous swindler and his still more unscrupulous nephew, Justinian, would have been enough to rouse Dietrich's suspicion, if not fear.

Deep and unspeakable must have been the royal Amal's contempt for the man. For he must have known him well at Constantinople in his youth; known how he was a Goth or other Teuton after all, though he was called a Dardanian; how his real name was Uprauda (upright), the son of Stock—which Uprauda he had latinized into Justinus. The Amal knew well how he had entered the Emperor's guard; how he had intrigued and fought his way up (for the man did not lack courage and conduct) to his general's commission; and now, by a crowning act of roguery, to the Empire. He had known too, most probably, the man's vulgar peasant wife, who, in her efforts to ape royalty, was making herself the laughing-stock of the people, and who was urging on her already willing husband to persecute. And this man he saw ready to convulse his own Empire by beginning a violent persecution against the Arians. He was dangerous enough as a villain, doubly dangerous as a bigot also.

We must remember next what the Greek Church was then; a chaos of intrigue, villainy, slander, and wild fury, tearing to pieces itself and the whole Empire by religious feuds, in which the doctrine in question becomes invisible amid the passions and crimes of the disputants, while the Lords of the Church were hordes of wild monks, who swarm out of their dens to head the lowest mobs, or fight pitched battles with each other. The ecclesiastical history of the fifth century in the Eastern Empire is one, which not even the genius of a Gibbon or a Milman can make interesting, or even intelligible.

Recollect that Dietrich had seen much of this with his own eyes; had seen actually, as I told you, the rebellion of Basiliscus and the Eutychian Bishops headed by the mad Daniel the Stylite against his foster father the Emperor Zeno; had seen that Emperor (as Dean Milman forcibly puts it) 'flying before a naked hermit, who had lost the use of his legs by standing sixteen years upon a column.' Recollect that Dietrich and his Goths had helped to restore that Emperor to his throne; and then understand in what a school he had learnt his great ideas of religious toleration: how deep must have been the determination to have no such doings in his kingdom; how deep, too, the dread of any similar outbreak at Rome.

Recollect, also, that now in his old age he had just witnessed the same iniquities again rending the Eastern Empire; the old Emperor Anastasius hunted to death by armies of mad monks about the Monophysite Heresy; the cities, even the holiest places of the East, stained with Christian blood; everywhere mob-law, murder, treachery, assassination even in the house of God; and now the new Emperor Justin was throwing himself into the party of the Orthodox with all the blind rage of an ignorant peasant; persecuting, expelling, shutting up the Arian Churches of the Goths, refusing to hear Dietrich's noble appeals; and evidently organizing a great movement against those peaceable Arians, against whom, during the life-time of Dietrich, their bitterest enemies do not allege a single case of persecution.

Remember, too, that Dietrich had had experience of similar outbreaks of fanaticism at Rome; that the ordination of two rival Popes had once made the streets run with blood; that he had seen priests murdered,

monasteries fired, nuns insulted, and had had to interfere with the strong arm of the law, and himself decide
in favour of the Pope who had the most votes, and was
first chosen; and that in the quarrels, intrigues, and slanders, which followed that election, he had had too good
proof that the ecclesiastics and the mob of Rome, if he
but let them, could behave as ill as that of Constantinople; and, moreover, that this new Pope John, who seems
to have been a hot-headed fanatic, had begun his rule by
whipping and banishing Manichees—by whose permission, does not appear.

Recollect too, that for some reason or other, Dietrich,
when he had interfered in Eastern matters, had been always on the side of the Orthodox and the Council of
Chalcedon.  He had fought for the Orthodox against
Basiliscus.  He had backed the Orthodox and Vitalianus
their champion, against the late Emperor Anastasius;
and now as soon as the Orthodox got into power under
Justin, this was the reward of his impartiality.  If he did
not distrust and despise the Church and Emperor of the
East, he must have been not a hero, but a saint.

Recollect, too, that in those very days, Catholic bigotry had broken out in a general plunder of the Jews.
At Rome, at Milan, and Genoa their houses had been
sacked, and their synagogues burnt; and Dietrich, having compelled the Catholics to rebuild them at their
own expense, had earned the hatred of a large portion
of his subjects.  And now Pope John was doing all he
could to thwart him.  Dietrich bade him go to Constantinople, and plead with Justin for the persecuted Arians.
He refused.  Dietrich shipt him off, *nolentem volentem*.

But when he got to Constantinople he threw his whole weight into the Emperor's scale. He was received by Justin as if he was St. Peter himself, the Emperor coming out to meet him with processions and wax-lights, imploring his blessing; he did exactly the opposite to what Dietrich bade him do; and published on his return a furious epistle to the bishops of Italy, calling upon them to oppress and extirpate the Arian perfidy, so that no root of it is left: to consecrate the Arian churches wheresoever he found them, pleading the advice of the most pious and Christian Emperor Justin, talking of Dietrich as tainted inwardly and wrapt up outwardly with the pest of heresy. On which Cochlæus (who religiously believes that Dietrich was damned for his Arianism, and that all his virtues went for nothing because he had not charity, which exists, he says, alone within the pale of the Church), cannot help the naive comment, that if the Pontiff did really write that letter, he cannot wonder at Dietrich's being a little angry. Kings now, it is true, can afford to smile at such outbursts; they could not afford to do so in Dietrich's days. Such words meant murder, pillage, civil war, dethronement, general anarchy; and so Dietrich threw Pope John into prison. He had been in bad health before he sailed to Constantinople, and in a few months he died, and was worshipped as a saint.

As for the political conspiracy, we shall never know the truth of it. The 'Anonymus Valesii,' meanwhile says, that when Cyprian accused Albinus, Boethius answered, 'It is false: but if Albinus has done it, so have I, and the whole senate, with one consent. It is false, my Lord King!' Whatever such words may prove, they prove at least this, that Boethius, as he says himself, was the victim of his own chivalry. To save Albinus, and the senate, he thrust himself into the fore-front of the battle, and fell at least like a brave man. Whether Albinus, Boethius, and Symmachus did plot to bring in Justin; whether the senate did send a letter to him, I cannot tell. Boethius, in his De Consolatione, denies it all; and Boethius was a good man. He says that the letters in which he hoped for the liberty of Rome were forged; how could he hope for the impossible? but he adds, 'would that any liberty could have been hoped for! I would have answered the king as Cassius did, when falsely accused of conspiring by Caligula: "If I had known of it, you should not."' One knows not whether Dietrich ever saw those words: but they prove at least that all his confidence, justice, kindness to the patrician philosopher, had not won him from the pardonable conceit about the Romani nominis umbram.

Boethius' story is most probably true. One cannot think that that man would die with a lie in his mouth. One cannot pass by, as the utterances of a deliberate hypocrisy, those touching appeals to his guiding mistress, that heavenly wisdom who has led him so long upon the paths of truth and virtue, and who seems to him, in his miserable cell, to have betrayed him in his hour of need. Heaven forbid. Better to believe that Dietrich committed once in his life, a fearful crime, than that good Boethius' famous book is such another as the Eikon Basilike.

Boethius, again, says that the Gothic courtiers hated him, and suborned branded scoundrels to swear away his life and that of the senate, because he had opposed 'the hounds of the palace,' Amigast, Trigulla, and other greedy barbarians.  There was, of course, a Gothic party and a Roman party about the court; and each hated the other bitterly.  Dietrich had favoured the Romans. But the Goths could not have seen such men as Symmachus and Boethius the confidants and counsellors of the Amal, without longing for their downfall; and if, as Boethius and the Catholic historians say, the whole tragedy arose out of a Gothic plot to destroy the Roman party, such things have happened but too often in the world's history.  The only facts which make against the story are, that Cyprianus the accuser was a Roman, and that Cassiodorus, who must have belonged to the Roman party, not only is never mentioned during the whole tragedy, but was high in power under Theodatus and Athalaric afterwards.

Add to this, that there were vague but wide-spread reports that the Goths were in danger; that Dietrich at least could not be ignorant of the ambition and the talents of that terrible Justinian, Justin's nephew, who was soon to alter, for a generation, the fortunes of the whole Empire, and to sweep the Goths from Italy; that men's minds must have been perplexed with fear of change, when they recollected that Dietrich was seventy years old, without a son to succeed him, and that a woman and a child would soon rule that great people in a crisis, which they could not but foresee.  We know that the ruin came; is it unreasonable to suppose that the Goths foresaw it, and made a desperate, it may be a treacherous, effort to crush once and for all, the proud and not less treacherous senators of Rome?

So, maddened with the fancied discovery that the man whom he had honoured, trusted, loved, was conspiring against him, Dietrich sent Boethius to prison. He seems, however, not to have been eager for his death; for Boethius remained there long enough to write his noble book.

However, whether fresh proofs of his supposed guilt were discovered or not, the day came when he must die. A cord was twisted round his head (probably to extort confession), till his eyes burst from their sockets, and then he was put out of his misery by a club; and so ended the last Roman philosopher. Symmachus, his father-in-law, was beheaded; and Pope John, as we have heard, was thrown into prison on his return, and died after a few months. These are the tragedies which have stained for ever the name of 'Theodoric the Great.'

Pope John seems to have fairly earned his imprisonment. For the two others, we can only, I fear, join in the sacred pity in which their memories have been embalmed to all succeeding generations. But we must recollect, that after all, we know but one side of the question. The Romans could write; the Goths could not: they may have been able to make out a fair case for themselves; they may have believed truly in the guilt of Boethius; and if they did, nothing less could have happened, by such rules of public law and justice as were then in vogue, than did happen.

Be that as it may, the deed was done; and the punishment, if deserved, came soon enough. Sitting at dinner (so the story runs), the head of a fish took in Dietrich's fancy the shape of Symmachus' head, the upper teeth biting the lip, the great eyes staring at him. He sprang up in horror; took to his bed; and there, complaining of a mortal chill, wrapping himself up in heaps of blankets, and bewailing to his physician the death of his two victims, he died sadly in a few days. And a certain holy hermit, name not given, nor date of the vision, saw the ghosts of Boethius and Symmachus lead the Amal's soul up the cone of Stromboli, and hurl him in, as the English sailors saw old Boots, the Wapping usurer, hurled into the same place, for offences far more capable of proof.

So runs the story of Dietrich's death. It is perfectly natural, and very likely true. His contemporaries, who all believed it, saw in it proof of his enormous guilt, and the manifest judgment of God. We shall rather see in it a proof of the earnest, child-like, honest nature of the man, startled into boundless horror and self-abasement, by the sudden revelation of his crime. Truly bad men die easier deaths than that; and go down to the grave, for the most part, blind and self-contented, and, as they think, unpunished; and perhaps forgiven.

After Dietrich came the deluge. The royal head was gone. The royal heart remained in Amalasuentha 'the heavenly beauty,' a daughter worthy of her father.

One of her first acts was to restore to the widows and children of the two victims the estates which Dietrich had confiscated. That may, or may not, prove that she thought the men innocent. She may have only felt it royal not to visit the sins of the fathers on the children; and those fathers, too, her own friends and preceptors. Beautiful, learned, and wise, she too was, like her father, before her age. She, the pupil of Boethius, would needs bring up her son Athalaric in Roman learning, and favour the Romans in all ways; never putting to death or even fining any of them, and keeping down the rough Goths, who were ready enough, now Dietrich's hand was off them, to ill-use the conquered Italians. The Goths soon grew to dislike her, and her Roman tendencies, her Roman education of the lad. One day she boxed his ears for some fault. He ran crying out into the Heldensaal, and complained to the heroes. They sent a deputation to Amalasuentha, insolent enough. 'The boy should not be made a scholar of.' 'She meant to kill the boy and marry again. Had not old Dietrich forbidden free Goths to go to schoolmasters, and said, that the boy who was taught to tremble at a cane, would never face a lance?' So they took the lad away from the women, and made a ruffian of him. What with drink, women, idleness, and the company of wild young fellows like himself, he was early ruined, body and soul. Poor Amalasuentha, not knowing whither to turn, took the desperate resolution of offering Italy to the Emperor Justinian. She did not know that her cousin Theodatus had been beforehand with her—a bad old man, greedy and unjust, whose rapacity she had had to control again and again, and who hated her in return. Both send messages to Justinian. The wily Emperor gave no direct answer: but sent his ambassador to watch the course of events. The young prince died of debauchery, and the Goths whispered that his mother had poisoned him. Meanwhile Theodatus went on from bad to worse; accusations flowed in to Amalasuentha of his lawless rapacity: but he was too strong for her; and she, losing her head more and more, made the desperate resolve of marrying him, as the only way to keep him quiet.  He was the last male heir of the royal Amalungs.  The marriage would set him right in the eyes of the Goths, while it would free her from the suspicion of having murdered her son, in order to reign alone.  Theodatus meanwhile was to have the name of royalty; but she was to keep the power and the money—a foolish, confused plan, which could have but one ending.  Theodatus married her of course, and then cast her into prison, seized all her treasures, and threw himself into the arms of that party among the Goths, who hated Amalasuentha for having punished their oppressions.  The end was swift and sad.  By the time that Justinian's ambassador landed, Amalasuentha was strangled in her bath; and all that Peter the ambassador had to do was, to catch at the cause of quarrel, and declare 'inexpiable war' on the part of Justinian, as the avenger of the Queen.

And then began that dreadful East Goth war, which you may read for yourselves in the pages of an eye-witness, Procopius;—a war which destroyed utterly the civilization of Dietrich's long and prosperous reign, left Italy a desert, and exterminated the Roman people.

That was the last woe: but of it I must tell you in my next Lecture.

# THE NEMESIS OF THE GOTHS

Of this truly dreadful Gothic war I can give you but a hasty sketch; of some of the most important figures in it, not even a sketch. I cannot conceive to myself, and therefore cannot draw for you, the famous Belisarius. Was he really the strange compound of strength and weakness which Procopius, and after him Gibbon, represent him?—a caricature, for good and evil, of our own famous Marlborough? You must read and judge for yourselves. I cannot, at least as yet, offer you any solution of the enigma.

Still less can I conceive to myself Narses, living till his grey hairs in the effeminate intrigues of the harem, and then springing forth a general; the Warrior Eunuch; the misanthrope avenging his great wrong upon all mankind in bloody battle-fields; dark of counsel, and terrible of execution; him to whom in after years the Empress Sophia sent word that he was more fit to spin among maids than to command armies, and he answered, that he would spin her such a thread as she could not unravel; and kept his word (as legends say) by inviting the Lombards into Italy.

Least of all can I sketch Justinian the Great, the half-Teuton peasant, whom his uncle Justin sent for out of the Dardanian hills, to make him a demigod upon earth. Men whispered in after years that he was born of a demon, a demon himself, passing whole days without food, wandering up and down his palace corridors all night, resolving dark things, and labouring all day with Herculean force to carry them out. No wonder he was thought to be a demon, wedded to a demon-wife. The man is unfathomable, inexplicable;—marrying deliberately the wickedest of all women, plainly not for mere beauty's sake, but possibly because he saw in her a congenial intellect;—faithful and loving to her and she to him, amid all the crimes of their following years;—pious with exceeding devotion and orthodoxy, and yet with a piety utterly divorced from, unconscious of, the commonest morality;—discerning and using the greatest men, Belisarius and Narses for example, and throwing them away again, surely not in weak caprice, whenever they served him too well;—conquering Persians, Vandals, Goths; all but re-conquering, in fact, the carcase Roman Empire;—and then trying (with a deep discernment of the value of Roman law) to put a galvanic life into the carcase by codifying that law.

In whatever work I find this man, during his long life, he is to me inexplicable. Louis XI of France is the man most like Justinian whom I know, but he, too, is a man not to be fathomed by me. All the facts about Justinian you will find in Gibbon. I have no theory by which to arrange and explain them, and therefore can tell you no more than Gibbon does.

So to this Gothic war; which, you must remember, became possible for Justinian by Belisarius' having just destroyed the Vandals out of Africa. It began by Belisarius invading the south of Italy. Witigis was elected war-king of the Goths, 'the man of witty counsels,' who did not fulfil his name; while Theodatus (Theod-aht 'esteemed by the people' as his name meant) had fallen into utter disesteem, after some last villainy about money; had been struck down in the road by the man he had injured; and there had his throat cut, 'resupinus instar victimæ jugulatus.'

He had consulted a Jew diviner just before, who had given him a warning. Thirty pigs, signifying the unclean Gentiles, the Jew shut up in three sties; naming ten Goths, ten Romans, and ten Imperialists of Belisarius' army, and left them to starve. At the end they found dead all the Goths but two, hardly any of the Imperialists, and half the Romans: but the five Roman pigs who were left had lost their bristles—bare to the skin, as the event proved.

After that Theodatus had no heart to fight, and ended his dog's life by a dog's death, as we have seen.

Note also this, that there was a general feeling of coming ruin; that there were quaint signs and omens. We have heard of the pigs which warned the Goths. Here is another. There was a Mosaic picture of Theodoric at Naples; it had been crumbling to pieces at intervals, and every fresh downfall had marked the death of an Amal. Now the last remains went down, to the very feet, and the Romans believed that it foretold the end of the Amal dynasty. There was a Sibylline oracle too;

'Quintili mense Roma nihil Geticum metuet.'

Here, too, we find the last trace of heathenism, of that political mythology which had so inextricably interwoven itself with the life and history of the city. The shrine of Janus was still standing, all of bronze, only just large enough, Procopius says, to contain the bronze image of Janus Bifrons. The gates, during Christian centuries, had never been opened, even in war time. Now people went by night, and tried to force them open: but hardly succeeded.

Belisarius garrisoned Rome, and the Goths attacked it, but in vain. You must read the story of that famous siege in the really brilliant pages of old Procopius, the last good historian of the old world.

Moreover, and this is most important, Belisarius raised the native population against the Goths. As he had done in Africa, when in one short campaign he utterly destroyed the now effeminate aristocracy of the Vandals, so he did in Italy. By real justice and kindness; by proclaiming himself the deliverer of the conquered from the yoke of foreign tyrants, he isolated the slave-holding aristocracy of the Goths from the mass of the inhabitants of Italy.

Belisarius and the Goths met, and the Goths conquered. But to take Rome was beyond their power; and after that a long miserable war struggled and wrangled up and down over the wretched land; city after city was taken and destroyed, now by Roman, now by Goth. The lands lay waste, the people disappeared in tens of thousands. All great Dietrich's work of thirty years was trampled into mud.

There were horrible sieges and destructions by both parties;—sack of Milan by Goths, sack of Rimini and the country round by Romans; horrors of famine at Auximum; two women who kept an inn, killing and eating seventeen men, till the eighteenth discovered the trap and killed them. Everywhere, as I say, good Dietrich's work of thirty years trampled into gory mud.

Then Theudebert and his false Franks came down to see what they could get; all (save a few knights round the king) on foot, without bow or lance; but armed with sword, shield, and heavy short-handled double-edged francisc, or battle-axe. At the bridge over the Ticinus they (nominal Catholics) sacrificed Gothic women and children with horrid rites, fought alike Goths and Romans, lost a third of their army by dysentery, and went home again.

At last, after more horrors, Vitigis and his Goths were driven into Ravenna. Justinian treated for peace; and then followed a strange peripeteia, which we have, happily, from an eye-witness, Procopius himself. The Roman generals outside confessed their chance of success hopeless. The Goths inside, tired of the slow Vitigis, send out to the great Belisarius, Will he be their king? King over them there in Italy? He promised, meaning to break his promise; and to the astonishment and delight of the Romans, the simple and honest barbarians opened the gates of Ravenna, and let in him and his Romans, to find themselves betrayed and enslaved. 'When I saw our troops march in,' says Procopius, 'I felt it was God's doing, so to turn their minds. The Goths,' he says, 'were far superior in numbers and in strength; and their women, who had fancied these Romans to be mighty men of valour, spit in the faces of their huge husbands, and pointing to the little Romans, reproached them with having surrendered to such things as that.'

But the folly was committed. Belisarius carried them away captive to Constantinople, and so ended the first act of the Gothic war.

In the moment of victory the envy of the Byzantine court undid all that it had done. Belisarius returned with his captives to Rome, not for a triumph, but for a disgrace; and Italy was left open to the Goths, if they had men and heart to rise once more.

And they did rise. Among the remnant of the race was left a hero, Totila by name;—a Teuton of the ancient stamp. Totilas, 'free from death'—'the deathless one,' they say his name means. Under him the nation rose once more as out of the ground.

A Teuton of the ancient stamp he was, just and merciful exceedingly. Take but two instances of him, and know the man by them. He retook Naples. The Romans within were starving. He fed them; but lest they should die of the sudden repletion, he kept them in by guards at each gate, and fed them up more and more each day, till it was safe to let them out, to find food for themselves in the country. A Roman came to complain that a Goth had violated his daughter. He shall die, said Totila. He shall not die, said the Goths. He is a valiant hero. They came clamouring to the king. He answered them quietly and firmly. They may choose to-day, whether to let this man go unpunished, or to save the Gothic nation and win the victory. Do they not recollect how at the beginning of the war, they had brave soldiers, famous generals, countless treasures, horses, weapons, and all the forts of Italy? And yet under Theodatus, a man who loved gold better than justice, they had so angered God by their unrighteous lives, that—what had happened they knew but too well. Now God had seemed to have avenged himself on them enough. He had begun a new course with them. They must begin a new course with him; and justice was the only path. As for the man's being a valiant hero: let them know that the unjust and the ravisher were never brave in fight; but that according to a man's life, such was his luck in battle.

His noble words came all but true. The feeble generals who were filling Belisarius's place were beaten one by one, and almost all Italy was reconquered. Belisarius had to be sent back again to Italy: but the envy, whether of Justinian himself, or of the two wicked women who ruled his court, allowed him so small a force that he could do nothing.

Totila and the Goths came down once more to Rome. Belisarius in agony sent for reinforcements, and got them; but too late. He could not relieve Rome. The Goths had massed themselves round the city, and Belisarius, having got to Ostia (Portus) at the Tiber's mouth, could get no further. This was the last woe; the actual death-agony of ancient Rome. The famine grew and grew. The wretched Romans cried to Bessas and his garrison, either to feed them or to kill them out of their misery. They would do neither. They could hardly at last feed themselves. The Romans ate nettles off the ruins, and worse things still. There was not a dog or a rat left. They even killed themselves. One father of five children could bear no longer their cries for food. He wrapped his head in his mantle, and sprang into the Tiber, while the children looked on. The survivors wandered about like spectres, brown with hunger, and dropped dead with half-chewed nettles between their lips. To this, says Procopius, had fortune brought the Roman senate and people. Nay, not fortune, but wickedness. They had wished to play at being free, while they themselves were the slaves of sin.

And still Belisarius was coming,—and still he did not come. He was forcing his way up the Tiber; he had broken Totila's chain, burnt a tower full of Goths, and the city was on the point of being relieved, when one Isaac made a fool of himself, and was taken by the Goths. Belisarius fancied that Portus, his base of operations, with all his supplies, and Antonia, the worthless wife on whom he doted, were gone. He lost his head, was beaten terribly, fell back on Ostia, and then the end came. Isaurians from within helped in Goths by night. The Asinarian gate was opened, and Rome was in the hands of the Goths.

And what was left? What of all the pomp and glory, the spoils of the world, the millions of inhabitants?

Five or six senators, who had taken refuge in St. Peter's, and some five hundred of the plebs; Pope Pelagius crouching at Totila's feet, and crying for mercy; and Rusticiana, daughter of Symmachus, Boethius' widow, with other noble women, in slaves' rags, knocking without shame at door after door to beg a bit of bread. And that was what was left of Rome.

Gentlemen, I make no comment. I know no more awful page in the history of Europe. Through such facts as these God speaks. Let man be silent; and look on in fear and trembling, knowing that it was written of old time—The wages of sin are death.

The Goths wanted to kill Rusticiana.  She had sent money to the Roman generals; she had thrown down Dietrich's statues, in revenge for the death of her father and her husband.  Totila would not let them touch her. Neither maid, wife, nor widow, says Procopius, was the worse for any Goth.

Next day he called the heroes together.  He is going to tell them the old tale, he says—How in Vitigis' time at Ravenna, 7000 Greeks had conquered and robbed of kingdom and liberty 200,000 rich and well-armed Goths.  And now that they were raw levies, few, naked, wretched, they had conquered more than 20,000 of the enemy.  And why? Because of old they had looked to everything rather than to justice; they had sinned against each other and the Romans.  Therefore they must choose, and be just men henceforth, and have God with them, or unjust, and have God against them.

Then he sends for the wretched remnant of the senators and tells them the plain truth:—How the great Dietrich and his successors had heaped them with honour and wealth; and how they had returned his benefits by bringing in the Greeks.  And what had they gained by changing Dietrich for Justinian?  Logothetes, who forced them by blows to pay up the money which they had already paid to their Gothic rulers; and revenue exacted alike in war and in peace.  Slaves they deserve to be; and slaves they shall be henceforth.

Then he sends to Justinian.  He shall withdraw his army from Italy, and make peace with him.  He will be his ally and his son in arms, as Dietrich had been to the

Emperors before him, or if not, he will kill the senate, destroy Rome, and march into Illyricum.

Justinian leaves it to Belisarius.

Then Totila begins to destroy Rome. He batters down the walls, he is ready to burn the town. He will turn the evil place into a sheep-pasture. Belisarius flatters and cajoles him from his purpose, and he marches away with all his captives, leaving not a living soul in Rome.

But Totila shews himself a general unable to cope with that great tactician. He divides his forces, and allows Belisarius to start out of Ostia and fortify himself in Rome. The Goths are furious at his rashness: but it is too late, and the war begins again, up and down the wretched land, till Belisarius is recalled by some fresh court intrigue of his wicked wife, and another and even more terrible enemy appears on the field, Narses the eunuch, avenging his wrong upon his fellow-men by cunning and courage almost preternatural. He comes upon them with a mighty host: but not of Romans alone. He has gathered the Teuton tribes;—Herules, the descendants probably of Odoacer's confederates; Gepids, who have a long blood-feud against the Goths; and most terrible of all, Alboin with his five thousand more Burgundians, of whom you will hear enough hereafter. We read even of multitudes of Huns, and even of Persian deserters from the Chosroo. But Narses' policy is the old Roman one—Teuton must destroy Teuton. And it succeeds.

In spite of some trouble with the Franks, who are holding Venetia, he marches down victorious through

the wasted land, and Totila marches to meet him in the
Apennines. The hero makes his last speech. He says,
'There will be no need to talk henceforth. This day will
end the war. They are not to fear these hired Huns,
Herules, Lombards, fighting for money. Let them hold
together like desperate men.' So they fight it out. The
Goths depending entirely on the lance, the Romans on
a due use of every kind of weapon. The tremendous
charge of the Gothic knights is stopped by showers of
Hun and Herule arrows, and they roll back again and
again in disorder on the foot: but in spite of the far superior numbers of the Romans, it is not till nightfall that
Narses orders a general advance of his line. The Goths
try one last charge; but appalled by the numbers of the
enemy, break up, and, falling back on the foot, throw
them into confusion, and all is lost.

The foot are cut down flying. The knights ride for
their lives. Totila and five horsemen are caught up by
Asbad the Gepid chief. Asbad puts his lance in rest, not
knowing who was before him. 'Dog,' cries Totila's page,
'wilt thou strike thy lord?' But it is too late. Asbad's
lance goes through his back, and he drops on his horse's
neck. Scipwar (Shipward) the Goth wounds Asbad,
and falls wounded himself. The rest carry off Totila. He
dies that night, after reigning eleven stormy years.

The Goths flee across the Po. There is one more
struggle for life, and one more hero left. Teia by name,
'the slow one,' slow, but strong. He shall be king now.
They lift him on the shield, and gather round him desperate, but determined to die hard. He finds the treasure of Totila, hid in Pisa. He sends to Theudebald and

his Franks. Will they help him against the Roman, and they shall have the treasure; the last remnant of the Nibelungen hoard. No. The Luegenfelden will not come. They will stand by and see the butchery, on the chance of getting all Italy for themselves. Narses storms Rome— or rather a little part of it round Hadrian's Mole, which the Goths had fortified; and the Goths escape down into Campania, mad with rage.

That victory of Narses, says Procopius, brought only a more dreadful destruction on the Roman senate and people. The Goths, as they go down, murder every Roman they meet. The day of grace which Totila had given them is over. The Teutons in Narses' army do much the same. What matter to Burgunds and Herules who was who, provided they had any thing to be plundered of? Totila has allowed many Roman senators to live in Campania. They hear that Narses has taken Rome, they begin to flock to the ghastly ruin. Perhaps there will be once again a phantom senate, phantom consuls, under the Romani nominis umbram. The Goths catch them, and kill them to a man. And there is an end of the Senatus Populusque Romanus.

The end is near now. And yet these terrible Goths cannot be killed out of the way. On the slopes of Vesuvius, by Nuceria, they fortify a camp; and as long as they are masters of the neighbouring sea, for two months they keep Narses at bay. At last he brings up an innumerable fleet, cuts off their supplies; and then the end comes. The Goths will die like desperate men on foot. They burst out of camp, turn their horses loose, after the fashion of German knights—One hears of the fashion again and again in the middle age,—and rush upon the enemy in deep solid column.  The Romans have hardly time to form some sort of line; and then not the real Romans, I presume, but the Burgunds and Gepids, turn their horses loose like the Goths.  There is no need for tactics; the fight is hand to hand; every man, says Procopius, rushing at the man nearest him.

For a third of the day Teia fights in front, sheltered by his long pavisse, stabbing with a mighty lance at the mob which makes at him, as dogs at a boar at bay.  Procopius is awed by the man.  Most probably he saw him with his own eyes.  Second in valour, he says, to none of the Heroes.

Again and again his shield is full of darts.  Without moving a foot, without turning an inch right or left, says Procopius, he catches another from his shield-bearer, and fights on.  At last he has twelve lances in his shield, and cannot move it: coolly he calls for a fresh one, as if he were fixed to the soil, thrusts back the enemy with his left hand, and stabs at them with his right.  But his time is come.  As he shifts his shield for a moment his chest is exposed, and a javelin is through him.  And so ends the last hero of the East Goths.  They put his head upon a pole, and carry it round the lines to frighten the Goths.  The Goths are long past frightening.

All day long, and all the next day, did the Germans fight on, Burgund and Gepid against Goth, neither giving nor taking quarter, each man dying where he stood, till human strength could bear up no longer, while Narses sat by, like an ugly Troll as he was, smiling to see the Teuton slay the Teuton, for the sake of their common enemy. Then the Goths sent down to Narses. They were fighting against God. They would give in, and go their ways peaceably, and live with some other Teuton nations after their own laws. They had had enough of Italy, poor fellows, and of the Nibelungen hoard. Only Narses, that they might buy food on the journey back, must let them have their money, which he had taken in various towns of Italy.

Narses agreed. There was no use fighting more with desperate men. They should go in peace. And he kept his faith with them. Perhaps he dared not break it. He let them go, like a wounded lion crawling away from the hunter, up through Italy, and over the Po, to vanish. They and their name became absorbed in other nations, and history knows the East Goths no more.

So perished, by their own sins, a noble nation; and in perishing, destroyed utterly the Roman people. After war and famine followed as usual dreadful pestilence, and Italy lay waste for years. Henceforth the Italian population was not Roman, but a mixture of all races, with a most powerful, but an entirely new type of character. Rome was no more Senatorial, but Papal.

And why did these Goths perish, in spite of all their valour and patriotism, at the hands of mercenaries?

They were enervated, no doubt, as the Vandals had been in Africa, by the luxurious southern climate, with its gardens, palaces, and wines. But I have indicated a stronger reason already:—they perished because they were a slave-holding aristocracy.

We must not blame them. All men then held slaves: but the original sin was their ruin, though they knew it not. It helped, doubtless, to debauch them; to tempt them to the indulgence of those fierce and greedy passions, which must, in the long run, lower the morality of slaveholders; and which, as Totila told them, had drawn down on them the anger of heaven. But more; though they reformed their morals, and that nobly, under the stern teaching of affliction, that could not save them. They were ruined by the inherent weakness of all slave-holding states; the very weakness which had ruined, in past years, the Roman Empire. They had no middle class, who could keep up their supplies, by exercising for them during war the arts of peace. They had no lower class, whom they dare entrust with arms, and from whom they might recruit their hosts. They could not call a whole population into the field, and when beaten in that field, carry on, as Britain would when invaded, a guerilla warfare from wood to wood, and hedge to hedge, as long as a coign of vantage-ground was left. They found themselves a small army of gentlemen, chivalrous and valiant, as slaveholders of our race have always been; but lessening day by day from battle and disease, with no means of recruiting their numbers; while below them and apart from them lay the great mass of the population, helpless, unarmed, degraded, ready to side with any or every one who would give them bread, or let them earn it for themselves (for slaves must eat, even though their masters starve), and careless of, if not even hostile to, their masters' interests, the moment those masters were gone to the wars.

In such a case, nothing was before them, save certain defeat at last by an enemy who could pour in ever fresh troops of mercenaries, and who had the command of the seas.

I may seem to be describing the case of a modern and just as valiant and noble a people. I do not mention its name. The parallel, I fear, is too complete, not to have already suggested itself to you.

# PAULUS DIACONUS

And now I come to the final settlement of Italy and the Lombard race; and to do that well, I must introduce you to-day to an old chronicler—a very valuable, and as far as we know, faithful writer—Paul Warnefrid, alias Paul the Deacon.

I shall not trouble you with much commentary on him; but let him, as much as possible, tell his own story. He may not be always quite accurate, but you will get no one more accurate. In the long run, you will know nothing about the matter, save what he tells you; so be content with what you can get. Let him shew you what sort of an account of his nation, and the world in general, a Lombard gentleman and clergyman could give, at the end of the 8th century.

You recollect the Lombards, of whom Tacitus says, 'Longobardos paucitas nobilitat.' Paulus Warnefrid was one of their descendants, and his history carries out the exact truth of Tacitus' words. He too speaks of them as a very small tribe. He could not foresee how much the 'nobilitat' meant. He knew his folk as a brave semi-feudal race, who had conquered the greater part of Italy, and tilled and ruled it well; who were now conquered by Charlemagne, and annexed to the great Frank Empire, but without losing anything of their distinctive national character. He did not foresee that they would become the architects, the merchants, the goldsmiths, the bankers, the scientific agriculturists of all Europe. We know it. Whenever in London or any other great city, you see a 'Lombard Street,' an old street of goldsmiths and bankers—or the three golden balls of Lombardy over a pawnbroker's shop—or in the country a field of rye-grass, or a patch of lucerne—recollect this wise and noble people, and thank the Lombards for what they have done for mankind.

Paulus is a garrulous historian, but a valuable one, just because he is garrulous. Though he turned monk and deacon in middle life, he has not sunk the man in the monk, and become a cosmopolite, like most Roman ecclesiastics, who have no love or hate for human beings save as they are friends or enemies of the pope, or their own abbey. He has retained enough of the Lombard gentleman to be proud of his family, his country, and the old legends of his race, which he tells, half-ashamed, but with evident enjoyment.

He was born at beautiful Friuli, with the jagged snow-line of the Alps behind him, and before him the sun and the sea, and the plains of Po; he was a courtier as a boy in Desiderius' court at Pavia, and then, when Charlemagne destroyed the Lombard monarchy, seems to have been much with the great king at Aix. He certainly ended his life as a Benedictine monk, at Monte Casino, about 799; having written a Life of St. Gregory; Homilies long and many; the Appendix to Eutropius (the Historia Miscella, as it is usually called) up to Justinian's time; and above all, this history of the Lombards, his forefathers, which I shall take as my text.

To me, and I believe to the great German antiquaries, his history seems a model history of a nation. You watch the people and their story rise before you out of fable into fact; out of the dreary darkness of the unknown north, into the clear light of civilized Roman history.

The first chapter is 'Of Germany, how it nourishes much people, and therefore many nations go forth of it.' The reason which he gives for the immense population is significant. The further to the north, and the colder, the more healthy he considers the world to be, and more fit for breeding human beings; whereas the south, being nearer to the heat of the sun, always abounds with diseases. The fact really is, I presume, that Italy (all the south which he knew), and perhaps most of the once Roman empire, were during the 6th and 7th centuries pestilential. Ruined cities, stopt watercourses, cultivated land falling back into marsh and desert, a soil too often saturated with human corpses—offered all the elements for pestilence. If the once populous Campagna of Rome be now uninhabitable from malaria, what must it have been in Paul Warnefrid's time?

Be that as it may, this is his theory.

Then he tells us how his people were at first called Winils; and how they came out of Scania Insula. Sweden is often, naturally, an island with the early chroniclers; only the south was known to them. The north was magical, unknown, Quenland, the dwelling-place of Yotuns, Elves, Trolls, Scratlings, and all other uncanny inhumanities. The Winils find that they are growing too many for Scanland, and they divide into three parties. Two shall stay behind, and the third go out to seek their fortunes. Which shall go is to be decided by lot.

The third on whom the lot falls choose as war-kings, two brothers, Ayo and Ibor, and with them their mother, Gambara, the Alruna-wife, prudent and wise exceedingly—and they go forth.

But before Paul can go too, he has a thing or two to say, which he must not forget, about the wild mysterious north from which his forefathers came. First how, in those very extreme parts of Germany, in a cave on the ocean shore, lie the seven sleepers. How they got thither from Ephesus, I cannot tell, still less how they should be at once there on the Baltic shore, and at Ephesus—as Mohammed himself believed, and Edward the Confessor taught—and at Marmoutier by Tours, and probably elsewhere beside. Be that as it may, there they are, the seven martyrs, sleeping for ever in their Roman dresses, which some wild fellow tried to pull off once, and had his arms withered as a punishment. And Paul trusts that they will awake some day, and by their preaching save the souls of the heathen Wends and Finns who haunt those parts.

The Teutonic knights, however, and not the seven sleepers, did that good work.

Only their dog is not with them, it appears;—the sacred dog which watches them till the judgment day, when it is to go up to heaven, with Noah's dove, and Balaam's ass, and Alborah the camel, and all the holy beasts. The dog must have been left behind at Ephesus.

Then he must tell us about the Scritofinns of the Bothnia gulf; wild Lapps and Finns, who have now retreated before the Teutonic race. In Paul Warnefrid's eyes they are little wild hopping creatures—whence

they derive their name, he says—Scritofinns, the hopping, or scrambling Finns.

Scrattels, Skretles, often figure in the Norse tales as
hopping dwarfs, half magical[1]. The Norse discoverers of
America recognized the Skrællings in the Esquimaux,
and fled from them in panic terror; till that furious vira-
go Freydisa, Thorvard's wife, and Eirek the Red's daughter, caught up a dead man's sword, and put to flight, sin-
gle-handed, the legion of little imps.

Others, wiser, or too wise, say that Paul is wrong;
that Skrikfins is the right name, so called from their
'screeking', screaming, and jabbering, which doubtless
the little fellows did, loudly enough.

Be that as it may, they appear to Paul (or rather to his
informants, Wendish merchants probably, who came
down to Charlemagne's court at Aix, to sell their amber and their furs) as hopping about, he says, after the
rein-deer, shooting them with a little clumsy bow, and
arrows tipt with bone, and dressing themselves in their
skins. Procopius knew these Scritfins too (but he has
got (as usual) addled in his geography, and puts them in
ultima Thule or Shetland), and tells us, over and above
the reindeer-skin dresses, that the women never nursed
their children, but went out hunting with their husbands, hanging the papoose up to a tree, as the Lapps do
now, with a piece of deer's marrow in its mouth to keep
it employed; and moreover, that they sacrificed their
captives to a war-god (Mars he calls him) in cruel ugly
ways. All which we may fully believe.

---

1 With west-countrymen, to 'scrattle' still means to scramble, or shuffle
about.

Then Paul has to tell us how in the Scritfin country there is little or no night in midsummer, little or no day in winter; and how the shadows there are exceeding long, and shorten to nothing as they reach the equator,—where he puts not merely Egypt, but Jerusalem. And how on Christmas days a man's shadow is nine feet long in Italy, whereas at Totonis Villam (Thionville), as he himself has measured, it is nineteen feet and a half. Because, he says, shrewdly enough, the further you go from the sun, the nearer the sun seems to the horizon. Of all which if you answer—But this is not history: I shall reply—But it is better than history. It is the history of history. It helps you to see how the world got gradually known; how history got gradually to be written; how each man, in each age, added his little grain to the great heap of facts, and gave his rough explanation thereof; and how each man's outlook upon this wondrous world grew wider, clearer, juster, as the years rolled on.

And therefore I have no objection at all to listen to Paul in his next chapter, concerning the two navels of the ocean, one on each side Britain—abysses which swallow up the water twice a day, and twice a day spout it up again. Paul has seen, so he seems to say, the tide, the ’Ωκεανοιο ροας, that inexplicable wonder of the old Greeks and Romans, running up far inland at the mouths of the Seine and Loire; and he has to get it explained somehow, before he can go forward with a clear conscience. One of the navels seems to be the Mahlstrom in Norway. Of the place of the other there is no doubt. It is close to Evodia insula, seemingly Alderney. For a high noble of the French told him so; he was sucked into it, ships and all, and only escaped by clinging to a rock. And after awhile the margins of that abyss were all left bare, leaving the Frenchman high and dry, 'palpitating so with fear,' says Paul, 'that he could hardly keep his seat.' But when all the water had been sucked in, out and up it came pouring again, in huge mountains, and upon them the Frenchman's ships, to his intense astonishment, reappeared out of the bottomless pit; into one of which he jumped; being, like a true Frenchman, thoroughly master of the situation; and got safe home to tell Paul the deacon. It is not quite the explanation of the tides which one would have wished for: but if a French nobleman of high rank will swear that he saw it with his own eyes, what can Paul do, in common courtesy, but believe him?

Paul has observed, too, which is a fact, that there is a small tide in his own Adriatic; and suggests modestly that there may be a similar hole in the bottom of that sea, only a little one, the tide being very little. After which, 'his prælibatis,' he will return, he says, to his story. And so he goes back to the famous Langbard Saga, the old story, which he has turned out of living Teutonic verse into dead Latin prose, and calls De Woden et Frea quædam ridicula fabula; but can't help for the life of him telling it, apologizing all the time. How the Winils (his own folk) went out to fight the Wendels, many more than them in number; and how Gambara, the Alruna-wife, cried to Freia the goddess, and Freia told her that whichsoever of the two armies first greeted Woden at the sunrise should win. But the Winils are far away on the war-road, and there is no time to send

to them.  So Freia bids her take the Winil women, and
dress them as warriors, and plait their tresses over their
lips for beards, and cry to Woden; and Woden admires
their long beards, and thinks them such valiant 'war-
beasts,' that he grants them the victory.

Then Freia tells him how he has been taken in, and
the old god laughs till the clouds rattle again, and the
Winils are called Langbardr ever after.

But then comes in the antiquary, and says that the
etymology is worthless, and that Langbardr means long
axes—(bard = an axe)—a word which we keep in hal-
bert, a hall-axe, or guard's pole-axe; and perhaps the antiquary is right.

But again comes in a very learned man, Dr. Latham,
and more than hints that the name is derived from the
Lange Börde, the long meadows by the side of the Elbe:
and so a good story crumbles to pieces, and

> 'All charms do fly
> Beneath the touch of cold philosophy.'

Then follows another story, possibly from another saga.  How by reason of a great famine they had to
leave Scoringia, the shore-land, and go into Mauringia,
a word which Mr. Latham connects with the Merovin-
gi, or Meerwing conquerors of Gaul.  Others say that
it means the moorland, others something else.  All
that they will ever find out we may see for ourselves already.—A little tribe of valiant fair-haired men, whether all Teutons, or, as Mr. Latham thinks, Sclavonians
with Teuton leaders, still intimately connected with

our own English race both by their language and their laws, struggling for existence on the bleak brown bogs and moors, sowing a little barley and flax, feeding a few rough cattle, breeding a few great black horses; generation after generation fighting their way southward, as they exhausted the barren northern soils, or became too numerous for their marches, or found land left waste in front of them by the emigration of some Suevic, Vandal, or Burgund tribe.  We know nothing about them, and never shall know, save that they wore white linen gaiters, and carried long halberts, or pole-axes, and had each an immortal soul in him, as dear to God as yours or mine, with immense unconscious capabilities, which their children have proved right well.

Then comes another saga, how they met the Assipitti, of whom, whether they were Tacitus's Usipetes, of the Lower Rhine, or Asabiden, the remnant of the Asen, who went not to Scandinavia with Odin, we know not, and need not know; and how the Assipitti would not let them pass; and how they told the Lombards that they had dogheaded men in their tribe who drank men's blood, which Mr. Latham well explains by pointing out, in the Traveller's Song, a tribe of Hundings (Houndings) sons of the hound; and how the Lombards sent out a champion, who fought the champion of the Assipitti, and so gained leave to go on their way.

Forward they go, toward the south-east, seemingly along the German marches, the debateable land between Teuton and Sclav, which would, mechanically speaking, be the line of least resistance.  We hear of Gothland—wherever that happened to be just then; of

Anthaib, the land held by the Sclavonian Anten, and Bathaib, possibly the land held by the Gepidæ, or remnant of the Goths who bided behind (as Wessex men still say), while the Goths moved forward; and then of Burgundhaib, wherever the Burgunds might be then. I know not; and I will dare to say, no man can exactly know. For no dates are given, and how can they be? The Lombards have not yet emerged out of the dismal darkness of the north into the light of Roman civilization; and all the history they have are a few scraps of saga.

At last they take a king of the family of the Gungings, Agilmund, son of Ayo, like the rest of the nations, says Jornandes; for they will be no more under duces, elective war-kings. And then follows a fresh saga (which repeats itself in the myths of several nations), how a woman has seven children at a birth, and throws them for shame into a pond; and Agilmund the king, riding by, stops to see, and turns them over with his lance; and one of the babes lays hold thereof; and the king says, 'This will be a great man;' and takes him out of the pond, and calls him Lamissohn, 'the son of the fishpond,' (so it is interpreted;) who grows to be a mighty Kemper-man, and slays an Amazon. For when they come to a certain river, the Amazons forbid them to pass, unless they will fight their she-champion; and Lamissohn swims over and fights the war-maiden, and slays her; and they go on and come into a large land and quiet, somewhere about Silesia, it would seem, and abode there a long while.

Then down on them come the savage Bulgars by night, and slay king Agilmund, and carry off his daughter; and Lamissohn follows them, and defeats them with a great slaughter, and is made king; and so forth: till at last they have got—how we shall never know—near history and historic lands. For when Odoacer and his Turklings and other confederates went up into Rugiland, the country north of Vienna, and destroyed the Rugians, and Fava their king, then the Lombards went down into the waste land of the Rugians, because it was fertile, and abode there certain years.

Then they moved on again, we know not why, and dwelt in the open plains, which are called feld. One says 'Moravia;' but that they had surely left behind. Rather it is the western plain of Hungary about Comorn. Be that as it may, they quarrelled there with the Heruli. Eutropius says that they paid the Herules tribute for the land, and offered to pay more, if the Herules would not attack them. Paul tells a wild saga, or story, of the Lombard king's daughter insulting a Herule prince, because he was short of stature: he answered by some counter-insult; and she, furious, had him stabbed from behind through a window as he sat with his back to it. Then war came. The Herules, old and practised warriors, trained in the Roman armies, despised the wild Lombards, and disdained to use armour against them, fighting with no clothes save girdles. Rodulf their king, too certain of victory, sat playing at tables, and sent a man up a tree to see how the fight went, telling him that he would cut his head off if he said that the Herules fled; and then, touched by some secret anxiety as to the end, spoke the fatal words himself; and a madness from God came on the Herules; and when they came to a field of flax, they took the blue flowers for water, and spread out their arms to swim through, and were all slaughtered defencelessly.

Then they fought with the Suevi; and their kings' daughters married with the kings of the Franks; and then ruled Aldwin (a name which Dr. Latham identifies with our English Eadwin, or Edwin, 'the noble conqueror,' though Grotius translates it Audwin, 'the old or auld conqueror'), who brought them over the Danube into Pannonia, between the Danube and the Drave, about the year 526. Procopius says, that they came by a grant from the Emperor Justinian, who gave as wife to Aldwin a great niece of Dietrich the Good, carried captive with Witigis to Byzant.

Thus at last they too have reached the forecourt of the Roman Empire, and are waiting for their turn at the Nibelungen hoard. They have one more struggle, the most terrible of all; and then they will be for a while the most important people of the then world.

The Gepidæ are in Hungary before them, now a great people. Ever since they helped to beat the Huns at Netad, they have been holding Attila's old kingdom for themselves and not attempting to move southward into the Empire; so fulfilling their name.

There is continual desultory war; Justinian, according to Procopius' account, playing false with each, in order to make them destroy each other. Then, once (this is Procopius' story, not Paul's) they meet for a great fight; and both armies run away by a panic terror; and Aldwin the Lombard and Thorisend the Gepid are left alone, face to face.—It is the hand of God, say the two wild kings—God does not mean these two peoples to destroy each other. So they make a truce for two years. Then the Gepidæ call in Cutuguri, a Hunnic tribe, to help them; then, says Procopius, Aldwin, helped by Roman mercenaries, under Amalfrid the Goth, Theodoric's great nephew, and brother-in-law of Aldwin, has a great fight with the Gepidæ. But Paul knows naught of all this: with him it is not Aldwin, but Alboin his son, who destroys the Gepidæ. Alboin, Grotius translates as Albe-win, 'he who wins all:' but Dr. Latham, true to his opinion that the Lombards and the Angles were closely connected, identifies it with our Ælfwine, 'the fairy conqueror.'

Aldwin, Paul says, and Thorisend fought in the Asfeld,—wherever that may be,—and Alboin the Lombard prince slew Thorisend the Gepid prince, and the Gepidæ were defeated with a great slaughter.

Then young Alboin asked his father to let him sit at the table with him. No, he could not do that, by Lombard custom, till he has become son-at-arms to some neighbouring king.

Young Alboin takes forty thanes, and goes off to Thorisend's court, as the guest of his enemy. The rites of hospitality are sacred. The king receives him, feasts him, seats him, the slayer of his son, in his dead son's place. And as he looks on him he sighs; and at last he can contain no longer. The seat, he says, I like right well: but not the man who sits in it. One of his sons takes fire, and begins to insult the Lombards and their white gaiters. You Lombards have white legs like so many brood mares. A Lombard flashes up. Go to the Asfeld, and you will see how Lombard mares can kick. Your brother's bones are lying about there like any sorry nag's. This is too much; swords are drawn; but old Thorisend leaps up. He will punish the first man who strikes. Guests are sacred. Let them sit down again, and drink their liquor in peace. And after they have drunk, he gives Alboin his dead son's weapons, and lets them go in peace, like a noble gentleman.

This grand old King dies in peace. Aldwin dies likewise, and to them succeed their sons, Alboin and Cunimund—the latter probably the prince who made the jest about the brood-mares—and they two will fight the quarrel out. Cunimund, says Paul, began the war—of course that is his story. Alboin is growing a great man; he has married a daughter of Clotaire, king of the Franks: and now he takes to his alliance the Avars, who have just burst into the Empire, wild people who afterwards founded a great kingdom in the Danube lands, and they ravage Cunimund's lands. He will fight the Lombards first, nevertheless: he can settle the Avars after. He and his, says Paul, are slain to a man. Alboin makes a drinking-cup of his skull, carries off his daughter Rosamund ('Rosy-mouth'), and a vast multitude of captives and immense wealth. The Gepidæ vanish from history; to this day (says Paul) slaves either of the Lombards or the Huns (by whom he rather means Avars); and Alboin becomes the hero of his time, praised even to Paul's days in sagas, Saxon and Bavarian as well as Lombard, for his liberality and his glory. We shall see now how he has his chance at the Nibelungen hoard.

He has heard enough (as all Teutons have) of Italy, its beauty, and its weakness. He has sent five thousand chosen warriors to Narses, to help him against Totila and the Ostrogoths; and they have told him of the fair land and large, with its vineyards, olive-groves, and orchards, waste by war and pestilence, and crying out for human beings to come and till it once more.

There is no force left in Italy now, which can oppose him. Hardly any left in the Roman world. The plague is come; to add its horrors to all the other horrors of the time—the true old plague, as far as I can ascertain; bred, men say, from the Serbonian bog; the plague which visited Athens in the time of Socrates, and England in the seventeenth century: and after the plague a famine; woe on woe, through all the dark days of Justinian the demon-emperor. The Ostrogoths, as you know, were extinct as a nation. The two deluges of Franks and Allmen, which, under the two brothers Buccelin and Lothaire, all on foot (for the French, as now, were no horsemen), had rolled into Italy during the Gothic war, had been swallowed up, as all things were, in the fatal gulf of Italy. Lothaire and his army, returning laden with plunder, had rotted away like sheep by Lake Benacus (Garda now) of drink, and of the plague. Buccelin, entrenched among his plunder-waggons by the Volturno stream in the far south, had waited in vain for that dead brother and his dead host, till Narses came on him, with his army of trained Herules and Goths; the Francisc axe and barbed pike had proved useless before the arrows and the cavalry of the Romans; and no more than five Allmen, says one, remained of all that mighty host. Awful to think of: 75,000 men, they say, in one column, 100,000 in the other: and like water they flowed over the land; and like water they sank into the ground, and left no trace.

And now Narses, established as exarch of Ravenna, a sort of satrap, like those of the Persian Emperors, and representing the Emperor of Constantinople, was rewarded for all his conquests and labours by disgrace. Eunuch-like, he loved money, they said; and eunuch-like, he was harsh and cruel. The Empress Sophia, listening too readily to court-slanders, bade him 'leave to men the use of arms, and come back to the palace, to spin among the maids.'—'Tell her,' said the terrible old imp, 'I will spin her such a thread as she shall not unravel.'

He went, superseded by Longinus; but not to Constantinople. From Naples he sent (so says Paul the Deacon) to Alboin, and bade him come and try his fortune as king of Italy. He sent, too, (so says old Paul) presents to tempt the simple Lombard men—such presents as children would like—all fruits which grew in Italian orchards. Though the gold was gone, those were still left. Great babies they were, these Teutons, as I told you at the first; and Narses knew it well, and had used them for his ends for many a year.

Then were terrible signs seen in Italy by night; fiery armies fighting in the sky, and streams of blood aloft, foreshadowing the blood which should be shed.

Sent for or not, King Alboin came; and with him all his army, and a mighty multitude, women, and children, and slaves; Bavarians, Gepidæ, Bulgars, Sarmatæ, Pannonians, Sueves, and Noricans; whose names (says Paul) remain unto this day in the names of the villages where they settled. With Alboin, too, came Saxons, twenty thousand of them at the least, with wife and child. And Sigebert king of the Franks put Suevic settlers into the lands which the Saxons had left.

Alboin gave up his own Hungarian land to his friends the Avars, on the condition that he should have them back if he had to return. But return he never did, he nor his Lombard host. This is the end. The last invasion of Italy. The sowing, once for all, of an Italian people. Fresh nations were still pressing down to the rear of the Alps, waiting for their turn to enter the Fairy Land—not knowing, perhaps, that nothing was left therein, but ashes and blood:—but their chance was over now: a people were going into Italy who could hold what they got.

On Easter Tuesday, in the year of grace 568, they came, seemingly by the old road; the path of Alaric and Dietrich and the rest; the pass from Carniola, through which the rail runs now from Laybach to Trieste. It must have been white, in those days, with the bones of nigh 200 years. And they found bisons, aurochsen, in the mountains, Paul says, and is not surprised thereat, because there are plenty of them in Hungary near by. An old man told him he had seen a skin in which fifteen men might lie side by side. None, you must know, are left now, save a very few in the Lithuanian forests. Paul goes out of his way to note this fact, and so shall I.

Alboin left a strong guard in Friuli, and Paul's ancestor among them, under Gisulf his nephew, and Marphrais or master of the horse, who now became duke of Friuli and warden of the marches, bound to prevent the Avars following them into their new abode. Then the human deluge spread itself slowly over the Lombard plains.  None fought with them, and none gainsaid; for all the land was waste.  The plague of three years before, and the famine which followed it had, says Paul, reduced the world into primæval silence.  The villages had no inhabitants but dogs; the sheep were pasturing without a shepherd; the wild birds swarmed unhurt about the fields.  The corn was springing self-sown under the April sun, the vines sprouting unpruned, the lucerne fields unmown, when the great Lombard people flowed into that waste land, and gave to it their own undying name.

The scanty population, worn out with misery, fled to rocks and islands in the lakes, and to the seaport towns; but they seem to have found the Lombards merciful masters, and bowed their necks meekly to the inevitable yoke.  The towns alone seem to have offered resistance.  Pavia Alboin besieged three years, and could not take.  He swore some wild oath of utter destruction to all within, and would have kept it.  At last they capitulated.  As Alboin rode in at St. John's gate, his horse slipped up; and could not rise, though the grooms beat him with their lance-butts.  A ghostly fear came on the Lombards.  'Remember, lord king, thy cruel oath, and cancel it; for there are Christian folk in the city.'  Alboin cancelled his oath, and the horse rose at once.  So Alboin spared the people of Pavia, and entered the palace of old Dietrich the Ostrogoth, as king of Italy, as far as the gates of Rome and Ravenna.

And what was his end?  Such an end as he deserved; earned and worked out for himself.  A great warrior, he had destroyed many nations, and won a fair land.  A just and wise governor, he had settled North Italy on some rough feudal system, without bloodshed or cruelty. A passionate savage, he died as savages deserve to die. You recollect Rosamund his Gepid bride? In some mad drinking-bout (perhaps cherishing still his old hatred of her family) he sent her her father's skull full of wine, and bade her drink before all. She drank, and had her revenge.

The story has become world-famous from its horror: but I suppose I must tell it you in its place.—How she went to Helmichis the shield-bearer, and he bade her get Peredeo the Kemper-man to do the deed: and how Peredeo intrigued with one of her bower-maidens, and how Rosamund did a deed of darkness, and deceived Peredeo; and then said to him, I am thy mistress; thou must slay thy master, or thy master thee. And how he, like Gyges in old Herodotus's tale, preferred to survive; and how Rosamund bound the king's sword to his bedstead as he slept his mid-day sleep, and Peredeo did the deed; and how Alboin leapt up, and fought with his footstool, but in vain. And how, after he was dead, Rosamund became Helmichis' leman, as she had been Peredeo's, and fled with him to Ravenna, with all the treasure and Alpswintha, Alboin's daughter by the Frankish wife; and how Longinus the exarch persuaded her to poison Helmichis, and marry him; and how she gave Helmichis the poisoned cup as he came out of the bath, and he saw by the light of her wicked eyes that it was poison, and made her drink the rest; and so they both fell dead. And then how Peredeo and the treasure were sent to the Emperor at Constantinople; and how Peredeo slew a great lion in the theatre; and how Tiberius, when he saw that he was so mighty a man of his hands, bade put his eyes out; and how he hid two knives in his sleeves, and slew with them two great chamberlains of the Emperor; and so died, like Samson, says old Paul, having got good were-geld for the loss of his eyes—a man for either eye.

And old Narses died at Rome, at a great age; and they wrapt him in lead, and sent him to Byzant with all his wealth. But some say that while he was still alive, he hid his wealth in a great cistern, and slew all who knew of it save one old man, and swore him never to reveal the place. But after Narses' death that old man went to Constantinople to Tiberius the Cæsar, and told him how he could not die with that secret on his mind; and so Tiberius got all the money, so much that it took many days to carry away, and gave it all to the poor, as was his wont.

A myth—a fable: but significant, as one more attempt to answer the question of all questions in a Teuton's mind—What had become of the Nibelungen hoard? What had become of all the wealth of Rome?

# THE CLERGY & THE HEATHEN

I asked in my first lecture, 'What would become of the forest children, unless some kind saint or hermit took pity on them?'

I used the words saint and hermit with a special purpose. It was by the influence, actual or imaginary, of such, that the Teutons, after the destruction of the Roman empire, were saved from becoming hordes of savages, destroying each other by continual warfare.

What our race owes, for good and for evil, to the Roman clergy, I shall now try to set before you.

To mete out to them their due share of praise and blame is, I confess, a very difficult task. It can only be fulfilled by putting oneself, as far as possible, in their place, and making human allowance for the circumstances, utterly novel and unexpected, in which they found themselves during the Teutonic invasions. Thus, perhaps, we may find it true of some of them, as of others, that 'Wisdom is justified of all her children.'

That is a hard saying for human nature. Justified of her children she may be, after we have settled which are to be her children and which not: but of all her children? That is a hard saying. And yet was not every man from the beginning of the world, who tried with his whole soul to be right, and to do good, a child of wisdom, of whom she at least will be justified, whether he is justified or not? He may have had his ignorances, follies, weaknesses, possibly crimes: but he served the purpose of his mighty mother.  He did, even by his follies, just what she wanted done; and she is justified of all her children.

This may sound like optimism: but it also sounds like truth to any one who has fairly studied that fantastic page of history, the contrast between the old monks and our own heathen forefathers.  The more one studies the facts, the less one is inclined to ask, 'Why was it not done better?'—the more inclined to ask, 'Could it have been done better?'  Were not the celibate clergy, from the fifth to the eighth centuries, exceptional agents fitted for an exceptional time, and set to do a work which in the then state of the European races, none else could have done?  At least, so one suspects, after experience of their chronicles and legends, sufficient to make one thoroughly detest the evil which was in their system: but sufficient also to make one thoroughly love many of the men themselves.

A few desultory sketches, some carefully historical, the rest as carefully compiled from common facts, may serve best to illustrate my meaning.

The monk and clergyman, whether celibate or not, worked on the heathen generally in one of three capacities: As tribune of the people; as hermit or solitary prophet; as colonizer; and in all three worked as well as frail human beings are wont to do, in this most piecemeal world.

Let us look first at the Hermits.  All know what an important part they play in old romances and ballads. All are not aware that they played as important a part in actual history.  Scattered through all wildernesses from the cliffs of the Hebrides to the Sclavonian marches, they put forth a power, uniformly, it must be said, for good.

Every one knows how they appear in the old romances.—How some Sir Bertrand or other, wearied with the burden of his sins, stumbles on one of these Einsiedler, 'settlers alone,' and talks with him; and goes on a wiser and a better man. How he crawls, perhaps, out of some wild scuffle, 'all-to bebled,' and reeling to his saddlebow; and 'ever he went through a waste land, and rocks rough and strait, so that it him seemed he must surely starve; and anon he heard a little bell, whereat he marvelled; and betwixt the water and the wood he was aware of a chapel, and an hermitage; and there a holy man said mass, for he was a priest, and a great leech, and cunning withal. And Sir Bertrand went in to him and told him all his case—how he fought Sir Marculf for love of the fair Ellinore, and how the king bade part them, and how Marculf did him open shame at the wineboard, and how he went about to have slain him privily, but could not; and then how he went and wasted Marculf's lands, house with byre, kine with corn, till a strong woman smote him over the head with a quernstone, and all-to broke his brain-pan;' and so forth—the usual story of mad passion, drink, pride, revenge.

'And there the holy man a-read him right godly doctrine, and shrived him, and gave him an oath upon the blessed Gospels, that fight he should not, save in his liege lord's quarrel, for a year and a day. And there he abode till he was well healed, he and his horse.'

Must not that wild fighting Bertrand have gone away from that place a wiser and a better man?  Is it a matter to be regretted, or otherwise, that such men as the hermit were to be found in that forest, to mend Bertrand's head and his morals, at the same time?  Is it a matter to be regretted, or otherwise, that after twenty or thirty years more of fighting and quarrelling and drinking, this same Sir Bertrand—finding that on the whole the lust of the flesh, the lust of the eye, and the pride of life, were poor paymasters, and having very sufficient proof, in the ends of many a friend and foe, that the wages of sin are death—'fell to religion likewise, and was a hermit in that same place, after the holy man was dead; and was made priest of that same chapel; and died in honour, having succoured many good knights, and wayfaring men'?

One knows very well that it would not be right now; that it is not needed now.  It is childish to repeat that, when the question is, was it right then—or, at least, as right as was possible then?  Was it needed then—or, at least, the nearest thing to that which was needed?

If it was, why should not wisdom be justified of all her children?

One hopes that she was; for certainly, if any men ever needed to be in the right, lest they should be of all men most miserable, it was these same old hermits. Praying and preaching continually, they lived on food which dogs would not eat, in dens in which dogs ought not to live.  They had their reasons.  Possibly they knew their own business best.  Possibly also they knew their neighbour's business somewhat; they knew that such generations as they lived in could not be taught, save by some extravagant example of this kind, some caricature, as it were, of the doctrines which were to be enforced. Nothing less startling, perhaps, could have touched the dull hearts, have convinced the dull brains, of fierce, ignorant, and unreasoning men.

Ferocity, lawlessness, rapine, cruelty, and—when they were glutted and debauched by the spoils of the Roman empire—sensuality, were the evils which were making Europe uninhabitable for decent folk, and history—as Milton called it—a mere battle of kites and crows. What less than the example of the hermit—especially when that hermit was a delicate and high-born woman—could have taught men the absolute superiority of soul to body, of spiritual to physical force, of spiritual to physical pleasure, and have said to them, not in vain words, but solid acts—'All that you follow is not the way of life. The very opposite to it is the way of life. The wages of sin are death; and you will find them so,—in this life the victims of your own passions, and of the foes whom your crimes arouse, and in life to come of hell for ever. But I tell you I have no mind to go to hell. I have a mind to go to heaven; and I know my mind right well. If the world is to be such as this, and the rulers thereof such as you, I will flee from you. I will not enter into the congregation of sinners, neither will I cast in my lot with the bloodthirsty. I will be alone with God and His universe. I will go to the mountain cave or to the ocean cliff, and there, while the salt wind whistles through my hair, I will be stronger than you, safer than you, richer than you, happier than you. Richer than you, for I shall have for my companion the beatific vision of God, and of all things and beings God-like, fair, noble, just, and merciful. Stronger than you, because virtue will give me a power over the hearts of men such as your force cannot give you; and you will have to come to my lonely cell, and ask me to advise you, and teach you, and help you against the consequences of your own sins. Safer than you, because God in whom I trust will protect me: and if not, I have still the everlasting life of heaven, which this world cannot give or take away. So go your ways, fight and devour one another, the victims of your own lusts. I am minded to be a good man; and to be that, I will give up—as you have made all other methods impossible for me—all which seems to make life worth having'? Oh! instead of finding fault with such men; instead of, with vulturine beak, picking out the elements of Manichæism, of conceit, of discontent, of what not human frailty and ignorance, which may have been in them, let us honour the enormous moral force which enabled them so to bear witness that not the mortal animal, but the immortal spirit, is the Man; and that when all which outward circumstance can give is cast away, the Man still lives for ever, by God, and in God.

And they did teach that lesson. They were good, while other men were bad; and men saw the beauty of goodness, and felt the strength of it, and worshipped it in blind savage admiration. Read Roswede's Vitæ Patrum Eremiticorum; read the legends of the hermits of the German forests; read Colgan's Lives of the Irish Saints; and see whether, amid all fantastic, incredible, sometimes immoral myths, the goodness of life of some one or other is not the historic nucleus, round which the myths, and the worship of the saint, have crystallized and developed.

Take, for instance, the exquisite hymn of St. Bridget, which Colgan attributes to the sixth century: though it is probably much later; that has nothing to do with the argument:—

'Bridget, the victorious, she loved not the world;
She sat on it as a gull sits on the ocean;
She slept the sleep of a captive mother,
Mourning after her absent child.

She suffered not much from evil tongues;
She held the blessed faith of the Trinity;
Bridget, the mother of my Lord of Heaven,
The best among the sons of the Lord.

She was not querulous, nor malevolent;
She loved not the fierce wrangling of women;
She was not a backbiting serpent, or a liar;
She sold not the Son of God for that which passes away.

She was not greedy of the goods of this life;
She gave away without gall, without slackness;
She was not rough to wayfaring men;
She handled gently the wretched lepers.

She built her a town in the plains (of Kildare);
And dead, she is the patroness of many peoples.'

I might comment much on this quotation. I might point out how St. Bridget is called the mother of the Lord, and by others, the Mary of the Irish, the 'Automata coeli regina,' and seems to have been considered at times as an avatar or incarnation of the blessed Virgin. I might more than hint how that appellation, as well as the calling of Christ 'the best of the sons of the Lord,' in an orthodox Catholic hymn, seems to point to the remnants of an older creed, possibly Buddhist, the transition whence towards Catholic Christianity was slow and imperfect. I might make merry over the fact that there are many Bridgets, some say eleven; even as there are three or four St. Patricks; and raise learned doubts as to whether such persons ever existed, after that Straussian method of pseudo-criticism which cometh not from above, from the Spirit of God, nor yet indeed from below, from the sound region of fact, but from within, out of the naughtiness of the heart, defiling a man. I might weaken, too, the effect of the hymn by going on with the rest of it, and making you smile at its childish miracles and portents; but I should only do a foolish thing, by turning your minds away from the broad fact that St. Bridget, or various persons who got, in the lapse of time, massed together under the name of St. Bridget, were eminently good women.

It matters little whether these legends are historically correct. Their value lies in the moral of them. And as for their real historical correctness, the Straussian argument that no such persons existed, because lies are told of them, is, I hold, most irrational. The falsehood would not have been invented unless it had started in a truth.

The high moral character ascribed to them would never have been dreamed of by persons who had not seen living instances of that character. Man's imagination does not create; it only reproduces and recombines its own experience. It does so in dreams. It does so, as far as the moral character of the saint is concerned, in the legend; and if there had not been persons like St. Bridget in Ireland, the wild Irish could never have imagined them.

Therefore it matters little to a wise man, standing on the top of Croagh Patrick, the grandest mountain perhaps, with the grandest outlook, in these British isles, as he looks on the wild Irish there on pattern days, up among the Atlantic clouds, crawling on bare and bleeding knees round St. Patrick's cell,—it matters little, I say, to the wise man, whether St. Patrick himself owned the ancient image which is worshipped on that mountain peak, or the ancient bell which till late years hung in the sanctuary,—such a strange oblong bell as the Irish saints carried with them to keep off the demons—the magic bells which appear (as far as I am aware) in the legends of no country till you get to Tartary and the Buddhists;—such a bell as came (or did not come) down from heaven to St. Senan; such a bell as St. Fursey sent flying through the air to greet St. Cuanady at his devotions when he could not come himself; such a bell as another saint, wandering in the woods, rang till a stag came out of the covert, and carried his burden for him on his horns. It matters as little to the wise man whether that bell belonged to St. Patrick, as whether all these child's dreams are dreams. It matters little to him, too, whether St. Patrick did, or did not stand on that mountain peak, 'in the spirit and power of Elias' (after whom it was long named), fasting, like Elias, forty days and forty nights, wrestling with the demons of the storm, and the snakes of the fen, and the Peishta-more (the monstrous Python of the lakes), which assembled at the magic ringing of his bell, till he conquered not by the brute force of a Hercules and Theseus, and the monster-quellers of old Greece, but by the spiritual force of which (so the text was then applied) it is written, 'This kind cometh not out but by prayer and fasting,' till he smote the evil things with 'the golden rod of Jesus,' and they rolled over the cliff, in hideous rout, and perished in the Atlantic far below. But it matters much to a wise man that under all these symbols (not childish at all, but most grand, to the man who knows the grand place of which they are told), there is set forth the victory of a good and beneficent man over evil, whether of matter or of spirit. It matters much to him that that cell, that bell, that image are tokens that if not St. Patrick, some one else, at least, did live and worship on that mountain top, in remote primæval times, in a place in which we would not, perhaps could not, endure life a week. It matters much to him that the man who so dwelt there, gained such a power over the minds of the heathen round him, that five millions of their Christian descendants worship him, and God on account of him, at this day.

St. Ita, again. It matters little that she did not—because she could not—perform the miracles imputed to her. It matters little whether she had or not—as I do not believe her to have had—a regularly organized convent of nuns in Ireland during the sixth century. It matters little if the story which follows is a mere invention of the nuns in some after-century, in order to make a good title for the lands which they held—a trick but too common in those days.  But it matters much that she should have been such a person, that such a story as this, when told of her, should have gained belief:—How the tribes of Hy-Connell, hearing of her great holiness, came to her with their chiefs, and offered her all the land about her cell.  But she, not wishing to be entangled with earthly cares, accepted but four acres round her cell, for a garden of herbs for her and her nuns.  And the simple wild Irish were sad and angry, and said, 'If thou wilt not take it alive, thou shalt take it when thou art dead.  So they chose her then and there for their patroness, and she blessed them with many blessings, which are fulfilled unto this day; and when she migrated to the Lord they gave her all the land, and her nuns hold it to this day, the land of Hy-Connell on the east Shannon bank, at the roots of Luachra mountain.'

What a picture!  One hopes that it may be true, for the sake of its beauty and its pathos.  The poor, savage, half-naked, and, I fear, on the authority of St. Jerome and others, now and then cannibal Celts, with their saffron scarfs, and skenes, and darts, and glibs of long hair hanging over their hypo-gorillaceous visages, coming to the prophet maiden, and asking her to take their land, for they could make no decent use of it themselves; and look after them, body and soul, for they could not look after themselves; and pray for them to her God, for they did not know how to pray to Him themselves.  If any man shall regret that such an event happened to any savages on this earth, I am, I confess, sorry for him.

St. Severinus, again, whom I have mentioned to you more than once:—none of us can believe that he made a dead corpse (Silvinus the priest, by name) sit up and talk with him on its road to burial. None of us need believe that he stopped the plague at Vienna by his prayers. None of us need attribute to anything but his sagacity the Divine revelations whereby he predicted the destruction of a town for its wickedness, and escaped thence, like Lot, alone; or by which he discovered, during the famine of Vienna, that a certain rich widow had much corn hidden in her cellars: but there are facts enough, credible and undoubted, concerning St. Severinus, the apostle of Austria, to make us trust that in him, too, wisdom was justified of all her children.

You may remark, among the few words which have been as yet said of St. Severinus, a destruction, a plague, and a famine. Those words are a fair sample of St. Severinus's times, and of the circumstances into which he voluntarily threw himself. About the middle of the fifth century there appears in the dying Roman province of Noricum (Austria we now call it) a strange gentleman, eloquent and learned beyond all, and with the strangest power of melting and ruling the hearts of men. Who he is he will not tell, save that his name is Severinus, a right noble name without doubt. Gradually it oozes out that he has been in the far East, through long travels and strange dangers, through many cities and many lands; but he will tell nothing. He is the servant of God, come hither to try to be of use. He certainly could have come for no other reason, unless to buy slaves; for Austria was at that time the very highway of the nations, the centre of the human Mâhlstrom, in which Huns, Gepiden, Allmannen, Rugen, and a dozen wild tribes more, wrestled up and down round the starving and beleaguered Roman towns of that once fertile and happy province. A man who went there for his own pleasure, or even devotion, would have been as wise as one who had built himself last summer a villa on the Rappahannock, or retired for private meditation to the orchard of Hougoumont during the battle of Waterloo.

Nevertheless, there Severinus stayed till men began to appreciate him; and called him, and not unjustly, Saint. Why not? He preached, he taught, he succoured, he advised, he fed, he governed; he turned aside the raids of the wild German kings; he gained a divine power over their hearts; he taught them something of God and of Christ, something of justice and mercy; something of peace and unity among themselves; till the fame ran through all the Alps, and far away into the Hungarian marches, that there was a prophet of God arisen in the land; and before the unarmed man, fasting and praying in his solitary cell on the mountain above Vienna, ten thousand knights and champions trembled, who never had trembled at the sight of armed hosts.

Who would deny that man the name of saint? And who, if by that sagacity which comes from the combination of intellect and virtue, he sometimes seemed miraculously to foretell coming events, would deny him the name of prophet also?

If St. Severinus be the type of the monk as prophet, St. Columba may stand as the type of the missionary monk; the good man strengthened by lonely meditation; but using that strength not for selfish fanaticism, but for the good of men; going forth unwillingly out of his beloved solitude, that he may save souls. Round him, too, cluster the usual myths. He drives away with the sign of the cross a monster which attacks him at a ford. He expels from a fountain the devils who smote with palsy and madness all who bathed therein. He sees by a prophetic spirit, he sitting in his cell in Ireland, a great Italian town destroyed by a volcano. His friends behold a column of light rising from his head as he celebrates mass. Yes; but they also tell of him, 'that he was angelical in look, brilliant in speech, holy in work, clear in intellect, great in council.' That he 'never passed an hour without prayer, or a holy deed, or reading of the Scriptures (for these old monks had Bibles, and knew them by heart too, in spite of all that has been written to the contrary), that he was of so excellent a humility and charity, bathing his disciples' feet when they came home from labour, and carrying corn from the mill on his own back, that he fulfilled the precept of his Master, 'He that will be the greatest among you, let him be as your servant.'

They also tell of him (and this is fact and history) how he left his monastery of Derm Each, 'the field of oaks,' which we call Derry, and went away at the risk of his life to preach to the wild Picts of Galloway, and founded the great monastery of Iona, and that succession of abbots from whom Christianity spread over the south of Scotland and north of England, under his great successor Aidan.

Aidan has his myths likewise. They tell of him how he stilled the sea-waves with holy oil; how he turned back on Penda and his Saxons the flames with which the heathen king was trying to burn down Bamborough walls. But they tell, too (and Bede had heard it from those who had known Aidan in the flesh) of 'his love of peace and charity, his purity and humility, his mind superior to avarice or pride, his authority, becoming a minister of Christ, in reproving the haughty and power-ful, and his tenderness in relieving the afflicted, and de-fending the poor.' Who, save one who rejoiceth in evil, instead of rejoicing in the truth, will care to fix his eyes for a moment upon the fairy tales which surround such a story, as long as there shines out from among them clear and pure, in spite of all doctrinal errors, the grace of God, the likeness of Jesus Christ our Lord?

Let us look next at the priest as Tribune of the peo-ple, supported usually by the invisible, but most potent presence of the saint, whose relics he kept. One may see that side of his power in Raphael's immortal design of Attila's meeting with the Pope at the gates of Rome, and recoiling as he sees St. Peter and St. Paul floating terri-ble and threatening above the Holy City. Is it a myth, a falsehood? Not altogether. Such a man as Attila probably would have seen them, with his strong savage imagination, as incapable as that of a child from distin-guishing between dreams and facts, between the subjec-tive and the objective world. And it was on the whole well for him and for mankind, that he should think that he saw them, and tremble before the spiritual and the invisible; confessing a higher law than that of his own ambition and self-will; a higher power than that of his brute Tartar hordes.

Raphael's design is but a famous instance of an influence which wrought through the length and breadth of the down-trodden and dying Roman Empire, through the four fearful centuries which followed the battle of Adrianople.  The wild licence, the boyish audacity, of the invading Teutons was never really checked, save by the priest and the monk who worshipped over the bones of some old saint or martyr, whose name the Teutons had never heard.

Then, as the wild King, Earl, or Comes, with his wild reiters at his heels, galloped through the land, fighting indiscriminately his Roman enemies, and his Teutonic rivals—harrying, slaughtering, burning by field and wild—he was aware at last of something which made him pause.  Some little walled town, built on the ruins of a great Roman city, with its Byzantine minster towering over the thatched roofs, sheltering them as the oak shelters the last night's fungus at its base.  More than once in the last century or two, has that same town been sacked.  More than once has the surviving priest crawled out of his hiding-place when the sound of war was past, called the surviving poor around him, dug the dead out of the burning ruins for Christian burial, built up a few sheds, fed a few widows and orphans, organized some form of orderly life out of the chaos of blood and ashes, in the name of God and St. Quemdeusvult whose bones he guards; and so he has established a temporary theocracy, and become a sort of tribune of the people, magistrate and father—the only one they have.  And now he

will try the might of St. Quemdeusvult against the wild
king, and see if he can save the town from being sacked
once more.  So out he comes—a bishop perhaps, with
priests, monks, crucifixes, banners, litanies.  The wild
king must come no further.  That land belongs to no
mortal man, but to St. Quemdeusvult, martyred here by
the heathen five hundred years ago.  Some old Kaiser of
Rome, or it may be some former Gothic king, gave that
place to the saint for ever, and the saint will avenge his
rights.  He is very merciful to those who duly honour
him: but very terrible in his wrath if he be aroused.  Has
not the king heard how the Count of such a place, only
forty years before, would have carried off a maiden from
St. Quemdeusvult's town; and when the bishop with-
stood him, he answered that he cared no more for the
relics of the saint than for the relics of a dead ass, and so
took the maiden and went?  But within a year and a day,
he fell down dead in his drink, and when they came to
lay out the corpse, behold the devils had carried it away,
and put a dead ass in its place.

All which the bishop would fully believe.  Why not?
He had no physical science to tell him that it was impossible.  Morally, it was in his eyes just, and therefore prob-
able; while as for testimony, men were content with very
little in those days, simply because they could get very
little.  News progressed slowly in countries desolate and
roadless, and grew as it passed from mouth to mouth, as
it did in the Highlands a century ago, as it did but lately
in the Indian Mutiny; till after a fact had taken ten years
in crossing a few mountains and forests, it had assumed
proportions utterly fantastic and gigantic.

So the wild king and his wild knights pause. They can face flesh and blood: but who can face the quite infinite terrors of an unseen world? They are men of blood too, men of evil lives; and conscience makes them cowards. They begin to think that they have gone too far. Could they see the saint, and make it up with him somewhat?

No. The saint they cannot see. To open his shrine would be to commit the sin of Uzzah. Palsy and blindness would be the least that would follow. But the dome under which he lies all men may see; and perhaps the saint may listen, if they speak him fair.

They feel more and more uncomfortable. This saint, in heaven at God's right hand, and yet there in the dom-church—is clearly a mysterious, ubiquitous person, who may take them in the rear very unexpectedly. And his priests, with their book-learning, and their sciences, and their strange dresses and chants—who knows what secret powers, magical or other, they may not possess?

They bluster at first: being (as I have said) much of the temper and habits, for good and evil, of English navvies. But they grow more and more uneasy, full of childish curiosity, and undefined dread. So into the town they go, on promise (which they will honourably keep, being German men) of doing no harm to the plebs, the half Roman artisans and burghers who are keeping themselves alive here—the last dying remnants of the civilization, and luxury, and cruelty, and wickedness, of a great Roman colonial city; and they stare at arts and handicrafts new to them; and are hospitably fed by bishops and priests; and then they go, trembling and awkward, into the great dom-church; and gaze wondering at the frescoes, and the carvings of the arcades—marbles from Italy, porphyries from Egypt, all patched together out of the ruins of Roman baths, and temples, and theatres; and at last they arrive at the saint's shrine itself—some marble sarcophagus, most probably covered with vine and ivy leaves, with nymphs and satyrs, long since consecrated with holy water to a new and better use. Inside that lies the saint, asleep, yet ever awake. So they had best consider in whose presence they are, and fear God and St. Quemdeusvult, and cast away the seven deadly sins wherewith they are defiled; for the saint is a righteous man, and died for righteousness' sake; and those who rob the orphan and the widow, and put the fatherless to death, them he cannot abide; and them he will watch like an eagle of the sky, and track like a wolf of the wood, fill he punishes them with a great destruction. In short, the bishop preaches to the king and his men a right noble and valiant sermon, calling things by their true names without fear or favour, and assuming, on the mere strength of being in the right, a tone of calm superiority which makes the strong armed men blush and tremble before the weak and helpless one.

Yes. Spirit is stronger than flesh. 'Meekly bend thy neck, Sicamber!' said St. Remigius to the great conquering King Clovis, when he stept into the baptismal font—(not 'Most Gracious Majesty,' or 'Illustrious Cæsar,' or 'by the grace of God Lord of the Franks,' but Sicamber, as a missionary might now say Maori, or Caffre,—and yet St. Remigius's life was in Clovis's hand then and always),—'Burn what thou hast adored, and adore what thou hast burned!' And the terrible Clovis trembled and obeyed.

So does the wild king at the shrine of St. Quemdeusvult. He takes his bracelet, or his jewel, and offers it civilly enough. Will the bishop be so good as to inform the great Earl St. Quemdeusvult, that he was not aware of his rights, or even of his name; that perhaps he will deign to accept this jewel, which he took off the neck of a Roman General—that—that on the whole he is willing to make the amende honorable, as far as is consistent with the feelings of a nobleman; and trusts that the saint, being a nobleman too, will be satisfied therewith.

After which, probably, it will appear to the wild king that this bishop is the very man that he wants, the very opposite to himself and his wild riders; a man pure, peaceable, just, and brave; possessed, too, of boundless learning; who can read, write, cipher, and cast nativities; who has a whole room full of books and parchments, and a map of the whole world; who can talk Latin, and perhaps Greek, as well as one of those accursed man-eating Grendels, a Roman lawyer, or a logothete from Ravenna; possessed, too, of boundless supernatural power;—Would the bishop be so good as to help him in his dispute with the Count Boso, about their respective marches in such and such a forest? If the bishop could only settle that without more fighting, of course he should have his reward. He would confirm to the saint and his burg all the rights granted by Constantine the Kaiser; and give him moreover all the meadow land in such and such a place, with the mills and fisheries, on service of a dish of trout from the bishop and his successors, whenever he came that way: for the trout there were exceeding good, that he knew.  And so a bargain would be struck, and one of those curious compromises between the spiritual and temporal authorities take root, of which one may read at length in the pages of M. Guizot, or Sir James Stephen.

And after a few years, most probably, the king would express a wish to be baptized, at the instance of his queen who had been won over by the bishop, and had gone down into the font some years before; and he would bid his riders be baptized also; and they would obey, seeing that it could do them no harm, and might do them some good; and they would agree to live more or less according to the laws of God and common humanity; and so one more Christian state would be formed; one more living stone (as it was phrased in those days) built into the great temple of God which was called Christendom.

So the work was done.  Can we devise any better method of doing it?  If not, let us be content that it was done somehow, and believe that wisdom is justified of all her children.

We may object to the fact, that the dom-church and its organization grew up (as was the case in the vast majority of instances) round the body of a saint or martyr; we may smile at the notion of an invisible owner and protector of the soil: but we must not overlook the broad fact, that without that prestige the barbarians would never have been awed into humanity; without that prestige the place would have been swept off the face of the earth, till not one stone stood on another: and he who does not see what a disaster for humanity that would have been, must be ignorant that the civilization of Europe is the child of the towns; and also that our Teutonic forefathers were by profession destroyers of towns, and settlers apart from each other on country freeholds.  Lonely barbarism would have been the fate of Europe, but for the monk who guarded the relics of the saint within the walled burg.

This good work of the Church, in the preservation and even resuscitation of the municipal institutions of the towns, has been discust so well and fully by M. Guizot, M. Sismondi, and Sir James Stephen, that I shall say no more about it, save to recommend you to read what they have written.  I go on to point out to you some other very important facts, which my ideal sketch exemplifies.

The difference between the Clergy and the Teuton conquerors was more than a difference of creed, or of civilization.  It was an actual difference of race.  They were Romans, to whom the Teuton was a savage, speaking a different tongue, obeying different laws, his whole theory of the universe different from the Roman.  And he was, moreover, an enemy and a destroyer.  The Teuton was to them as a Hindoo is to us, with the terrible exception, that the positions were reversed; that the Teuton was not the conquered, but the conqueror.  It is easy for us to feel humanity and Christian charity toward races which we have mastered.  It was not so easy for the Roman priest to feel them toward a race which had mastered him.  His repugnance to the 'Barbarian' must have been at first intense.  He never would have conquered it; he never would have become the willing

converter of the heathen, had there not been in him the
Spirit of God, and firm belief in a Catholic Church, to
which all men of all races ought alike to belong. This
true and glorious idea, the only one which has ever been
or ever will be able to break down the barriers of race,
and the animal antipathy which the natural man has to
all who are not of his own kin: this idea was the sole possession of the Roman clergy; and by it they conquered,
because it was true, and came from God.

But this very difference of race exposed the clergy
to great temptations. They were the only civilized men
left, west of Constantinople. They looked on the Teuton not as a man, but as a child; to be ruled; to be petted
when he did right, punished when he did wrong; and
too often cajoled into doing right, and avoiding wrong.
Craft became more and more their usual weapon. There
were great excuses for them. Their lives and property
were in continual danger. Craft is the natural weapon of
the weak against the strong. It seemed to them, too often, to be not only natural, but spiritual also, and therefore just and right.

Again, the clergy were the only organic remnants of
the Roman Empire. They claimed their privileges and
lands as granted to them by past Roman Emperors, under the Roman law. This fact made it their interest, of
course, to perpetuate that Roman law, and to introduce
it as far as they could among their conquerors, to the ex-
pulsion of the old Teutonic laws; and they succeeded on
the whole. Of that more hereafter. Observe now, that
as their rights dated from times which to the Teutons
were pre-historic, their statements could not be checked

by conquerors who could not even read. Thence rose the temptation to forge; to forge legends, charters, donations, ecclesiastical history of all kinds—an ugly and world-famous instance of which you will hear of hereafter. To that temptation they yielded more and more as the years rolled on, till their statements on ecclesiastical history became such as no historian can trust, without the most plentiful corroboration.

There were great excuses for them, in this matter, as in others. They could not but look on the Teuton as—what in fact and law he was—an unjust and intrusive usurper. They could not but look on their Roman congregations, and on themselves, as what in fact and law they were, the rightful owners of the soil. They were but defending or recovering their original rights. Would not the end justify the means?

But more. Out of this singular position grew a doctrine, which looks to us irrational now, but was by no means so then. If the Church derived her rights from the extinct Roman Cæsars, how could the Teuton conquerors interfere with those rights? If she had owed allegiance to Constantine or Theodosius, she certainly owed none to Dietrich, Alboin, or Clovis. She did not hold their lands of them; and would pay them, if she could avoid it, neither tax nor toll. She did not recognize the sovereignty of these Teutons as 'ordained by God.'

Out of this simple political fact grew up vast consequences. The Teuton king was a heathen or Arian usurper. He was not a king de jure, in the eyes of the clergy, till he was baptized into the Church, and then

lawfully anointed king by the clergy. Thus the clergy
gradually became the makers of kings; and the power of
making involved a corresponding power of unmaking,
if the king rebelled against the Church, and so cut himself off from Christendom. At best, he was one of 'the
Princes of this world,' from whom the Church was free,
absolutely in spiritual matters, and in temporal matters,
also de jure, and therefore de facto as far as she could be
made free. To keep the possessions of the Church from
being touched by profane hands, even that they might
contribute to the common needs of the nation, became
a sacred duty, a fixed idea, for which the clergy must
struggle, anathematize, forge if need be: but also—to
do them justice—die if need be as martyrs. The nations
of this world were nothing to them. The wars of the nations were nothing. They were the people of God, 'who
dwelt alone, and were not reckoned among the nations;'
their possessions were the inheritance of God: and from
this idea, growing (as I have shewn) out of a political
fact, arose the extra-national, and too often anti-nation-
al position, which the Roman clergy held for many ages,
and of which the instinct, at least, lingers among them
in many countries. Out of it arose, too, all after struggles between the temporal and ecclesiastical powers.
Becket, fighting to the death against Henry II., was not,
as M. Thierry thinks, the Anglo-Saxon defying the Nor-
man. He was the representative of the Christian Roman
defying the Teuton, on the ground of rights which he
believed to have existed while the Teuton was a heathen
in the German forests. Gradually, as the nations of Europe became really nations, within fixed boundaries,

and separate Christian organizations, these demands of the Church became intolerable in reason, because unnecessary in fact. But had there not been in them at the first an instinct of right and justice, they would never have become the fixed idea of the clerical mind; the violation of them the one inexpiable sin; and the defence of them (as may be seen by looking through the Romish Calendar) the most potent qualification for saintship.

Yes. The clergy believed that idea deeply enough to die for it. St. Alphege at Canterbury had been, it is said, one of the first advisers of the ignominious payment of the Danegeld: but there was one thing which he would not do. He would advise the giving up of the money of the nation: but the money of his church he would not give up. The Danes might thrust him into a filthy dungeon: he would not take the children's bread and cast it unto the dogs. They might drag him out into their husting, and threaten him with torture: but to the drunken cry of 'Gold! Bishop! Gold!' his only answer would be—Not a penny. He could not rob the poor of Christ. And when he fell, beaten to death with the bones and horns of the slaughtered oxen, he died in faith; a martyr to the great idea of that day, that the gold of the Church did not belong to the conquerors of this world.

But St. Alphege was an Englishman, and not a Roman. True in the letter: but not in the spirit. The priest or monk, by becoming such, more or less renounced his nationality. It was the object of the Church to make him renounce it utterly; to make him regard himself no longer as Englishman, Frank, Lombard, or Goth: but as the representatives by an hereditary descent, considered all the more real because it was spiritual and not carnal, of the Roman Church; to prevent his being entangled, whether by marriage or otherwise, in the business of this life; out of which would flow nepotism, Simony, and Erastian submission to those sovereigns who ought to be the servants, not the lords of the Church.  For this end no means were too costly.  St. Dunstan, in order to expel the married secular priests, and replace them by Benedictine monks of the Italian order of Monte Casino, convulsed England, drove her into civil war, paralysed her monarchs one after the other, and finally left her exhausted and imbecile, a prey to the invading Northmen: but he had at least done his best to make the royal House of Cerdic, and the nations which obeyed that House, understand that the Church derived its rights not from them, but from Rome.

This hereditary sense of superiority on the part of the clergy may explain and excuse much of their seeming flattery.  The most vicious kings are lauded, if only they have been 'erga servos Dei benevoli;' if they have founded monasteries; if they have respected the rights of the Church.  The clergy too often looked on the secular princes as more or less wild beasts, of whom neither common decency, justice, or mercy was to be expected; and they had too often reason enough to do so.  All that could be expected of the kings was, that if they would not regard man, they should at least fear God; which if they did, the proof of 'divine grace' on their part was so unexpected, as well as important, that the monk chroniclers praised them heartily and honestly, judging them by what they had, not by what they had not.

Thus alone can one explain such a case as that of the monastic opinion of Dagobert the Second, king of the Franks.  We are told in the same narrative, seemingly without any great sense of incongruity, how he murdered his own relations and guests, and who not?—how he massacred 9000 Bulgars to whom he had given hospitality; how he kept a harem of three queens, and other women so numerous that Fredegarius cannot mention them; and also how, accompanied by his harem, he chanted among the monks of St. Denis; how he founded many rich convents; how he was the friend, or rather pupil, of St. Arnulf of Metz, St. Omer, and above all of St. Eloi—whose story I recommend you to read, charmingly told, in Mr. Maitland's 'Dark Ages,' pp. 81–122. The three saints were no hypocrites—God forbid! They were good men and true, to whom had been entrusted the keeping of a wild beast, to be petted and praised whenever it shewed any signs of humanity or obedience.

But woe to the prince, however useful or virtuous in other respects, who laid sacrilegious hands on the goods of the Church.  He might, like Charles Martel, have delivered France from the Pagans on the east, and from the Mussulmen on the south, and have saved Christendom once and for all from the dominion of the Crescent, in that great battle on the plains of Poitiers, where the Arab cavalry (says Isidore of Beja) broke against the immoveable line of Franks, like 'waves against a wall of ice.'

But if, like Charles Martel, he had dared to demand of the Church taxes and contributions toward the support of his troops, and the salvation both of Church and commonweal, then all his prowess was in vain.  Some monk would surely see him in a vision, as St. Eucherius, Bishop of Orleans, saw Charles Martel (according to the Council of Kiersy), 'with Cain, Judas, and Caiaphas, thrust into the Stygian whirlpools and Acherontic combustion of the sempiternal Tartarus.'

Those words, which, with slight variations, are a common formula of cursing appended to monastic charters against all who should infringe them, remind us rather of the sixth book of Virgil's Æneid than of the Holy Scriptures; and explain why Dante naturally chooses that poet as a guide through his Inferno.

The cosmogony from which such an idea was derived was simple enough.  I give, of course, no theological opinion on its correctness: but as professor of Modern History, I am bound to set before you opinions which had the most enormous influence on the history of early Europe.  Unless you keep them in mind, as the fixed and absolute background of all human thought and action for more than 1000 years, you will never be able to understand the doings of European men.

This earth, then, or at least the habitable part of it, was considered as most probably a flat plane.  Below that plane, or in the centre of the earth, was the realm of endless fire.  It could be entered (as by the Welsh knight who went down into St. Patrick's Purgatory) by certain caves.  By listening at the craters of volcanoes, which were its mouths, the cries of the tortured might be heard in the depths of the earth.

In that 'Tartarus' every human being born into the world was doomed to be endlessly burnt alive: only in the Church, 'extra quam nulla salus,' was there escape from the common doom.  But to that doom, excommunication, which thrust a man from the pale of the Church, condemned the sinner afresh, with curses the most explicit and most horrible.

The superior clergy, therefore, with whom the anathematizing power lay, believed firmly that they could, proprio motu, upon due cause shewn, cause any man or woman to be burned alive through endless ages.  And what was more, the Teutonic laity, with that intense awe of the unseen which they had brought with them out of the wilderness, believed it likewise, and trembled.  It paralysed the wisest, as well as the fiercest, that belief.  Instead of disgusting the kings of the earth, it gave them over, bound hand and foot by their own guilty consciences, into the dominion of the clergy; and the belief that Charles Martel was damned, only knit (as M. Sismondi well remarks) his descendants the Carlovingians more closely to the Church which possest so terrible a weapon.

Whether they were right or wrong in these beliefs is a question not to be discussed in this chair.  My duty is only to point out to you the universal existence of those beliefs, and the historic fact that they gave the clergy a character supernatural, magical, divine, with a reserve of power before which all trembled, from the beggar to the king; and also, that all struggles between the temporal and spiritual powers, like that between Henry and Becket, can only be seen justly in the light of the practical meaning of that excommunication which Becket so freely employed.  I must also point out to you that so enormous a power (too great for the shoulders of mortal man) was certain to be, and actually was, fearfully abused, not only by its direct exercise, but also by bargaining with men, through indulgences and otherwise, for the remission of that punishment, which the clergy could, if they would, inflict; and worst of all, that out of the whole theory sprang up that system of persecution, in which the worst cruelties of heathen Rome were imitated by Christian priests, on the seemingly irrefragable ground that it was merciful to offenders to save them, or, if not, at least to save others through them, by making them feel for a few hours in this world what they would feel for endless ages in the next.

# THE MONK A CIVILIZER

Historians are often blamed for writing as if the History of Kings and Princes were the whole history of the world. 'Why do you tell us,' is said, 'of nothing but the marriages, successions, wars, characters, of a few Royal Races? We want to know what the people, and not the princes, were like. History ought to be the history of the masses, and not of kings.'

The only answer to this complaint seems to be, that the defect is unavoidable. The history of the masses cannot be written, while they have no history; and none will they have, as long as they remain a mass; ere their history begins, individuals, few at first, and more and more numerous as they progress, must rise out of the mass, and become persons, with fixed ideas, determination, conscience, more or less different from their fellows, and thereby leavening and elevating their fellows, that they too may become persons, and men indeed. Then they will begin to have a common history, issuing out of each man's struggle to assert his own personality and his own convictions. Till that point is reached, the history of the masses will be mere statistic concerning their physical well-being or ill-being, which (for the early ages of our race) is unwritten, and therefore undiscoverable.

The early history of the Teutonic race, therefore, is, and must always remain, simply the history of a few great figures. Of the many of the masses, nothing is said;

because there was nothing to say.  They all ate, drank, married, tilled, fought, and died, not altogether brutally, we will hope, but still in a dull monotony, unbroken by any struggle of principles or ideas.  We know that large masses of human beings have so lived in every age, and are living so now—the Tartar hordes, for instance, or the thriving negroes of central Africa: comfortable folk, getting a tolerable living, son after father, for many generations, but certainly not developed enough, or afflicted enough, to have any history.

I believe that the masses, during the early middle age, were very well off; quite as well off as they deserved; that is, earned for themselves.  They lived in a rough way, certainly: but roughness is not discomfort, where the taste has not been educated.  A Red Indian sleeps as well in a wigwam as we in a spring bed; and the Irish babies thrive as well among the peat ashes as on a Brussels carpet.  Man is a very well constructed being, and can live and multiply anywhere, provided he can keep warm, and get pure water and enough to eat. Indeed, our Teutonic fathers must have been comfortably off, or they could not have multiplied as they did. Even though their numbers may have been overstated, the fact is patent, that howsoever they were slaughtered down, by the Romans or by each other, they rose again as out of the soil, more numerous than ever.  Again and again you read of a tribe being all but exterminated by the Romans, and in a few years find it bursting over the Pfalzgrab or the Danube, more numerous and terrible than before. Never believe that a people deprest by cold, ill-feeding, and ill-training, could have conquered Europe in the face of centuries of destructive war. Those very wars, again, may have helped in the long run the increase of population, and for a reason simple enough, though often overlooked. War throws land out of cultivation; and when peace returns, the new settlers find the land fallow, and more or less restored to its original fertility; and so begins a period of rapid and prosperous increase. In no other way can I explain the rate at which nations after the most desolating wars spring up, young and strong again, like the phoenix, from their own funeral pile. They begin afresh as the tillers of a virgin soil, fattened too often with the ashes of burnt homesteads, and the blood of the slain.

Another element of comfort may have been the fact, that in the rough education of the forest, only the strong and healthy children lived, while the weakly died off young, and so the labour-market, as we should say now, was never overstocked. This is the case with our own gipsies, and with many savage tribes—the Red Indians, for instance—and accounts for their general healthiness: the unhealthy being all dead, in the first struggle for existence. But then these gipsies, and the Red Indians, do not increase in numbers, but the contrary; while our forefathers increased rapidly. On the other hand, we have, at least throughout the middle ages, accounts of such swarms of cripples, lepers, deformed, and other incapable persons, as to make some men believe that there were more of them, in proportion to the population, than there are now. And it may have been so. The strongest and healthiest men always going off to be killed in war, the weakliest only would be left at home to breed; and so an unhealthy population might spring up. And again—and this is a curious fact—as law and order enter a country, so will the proportion of incapables, in body and mind, increase. In times of war and anarchy, when every one is shifting for himself, only the strongest and shrewdest can stand. Woe to those who cannot take care of themselves. The fools and cowards, the weakly and sickly, are killed, starved, neglected, or in other ways brought to grief. But when law and order come, they protect those who cannot protect themselves, and the fools and cowards, the weakly and sickly, are supported at the public expense, and allowed to increase and multiply as public burdens. I do not say that this is wrong, Heaven forbid! I only state the fact. A government is quite right in defending all alike from the brute competition of nature, whose motto is—Woe to the weak. To the Church of the middle age is due the preaching and the practice of the great Christian doctrine, that society is bound to protect the weak. So far the middle age saw: but no further. For our own times has been reserved the higher and deeper doctrine, that it is the duty of society to make the weak strong; to reform, to cure, and above all, to prevent by education, by sanitary science, by all and every means, the necessity of reforming and of curing.

Science could not do that in the middle age. But if Science could not do it, Religion would at least try to do the next best thing to it. The monasteries were the refuges, whither the weak escaped from the competition of the strong. Thither flocked the poor, the crippled, the orphan, and the widow, all, in fact, who could not fight for themselves. There they found something like justice, order, pity, help. Even the fool and the coward, when they went to the convent-door, were not turned away. The poor half-witted rascal, who had not sense enough to serve the king, might still serve the abbot. He would be set to drive, plough, or hew wood—possibly by the side of a gentleman, a nobleman, or even a prince—and live under equal law with them; and under, too, a discipline more strict than that of any modern army; and if he would not hew the wood, or drive the bullocks, as he ought, then the abbot would have him flogged soundly till he did; which was better for him, after all, than wandering about to be hooted by the boys, and dying in a ditch at last.

The coward, too—the abbot could make him of use, even though the king could not. There were, no doubt, in those days, though fewer in number than now, men who could not face physical danger, and the storm of the evil world,—delicate, nervous, imaginative, feminine characters; who, when sent out to battle, would be very likely to run away. Our forefathers, having no use for such persons, used to put such into a bog-hole, and lay a hurdle over them, in the belief that they would sink to the lowest pool of Hela for ever more. But the abbot had great use for such. They could learn to read, write, sing, think; they were often very clever; they might make great scholars; at all events they might make saints. Whatever they could not do, they could pray. And the united prayer of those monks, it was then believed, could take heaven by storm, alter the course of the elements, overcome Divine justice, avert from mankind the anger of an offended God. Whether that belief were right or wrong, people held it; and the man who could not fight with carnal weapons, regained his self-respect, and therefore his virtue, when he found himself fighting, as he held, with spiritual weapons against all the powers of darkness[1]. The first light in which I wish you to look at the old monasteries, is as defences for the weak against the strong.

But what has this to do with what I said at first, as to the masses having no history? This:—that through these monasteries the masses began first to have a history; because through them they ceased to be masses, and became first, persons and men, and then, gradually, a people. That last the monasteries could not make them: but they educated them for becoming a people; and in this way. They brought out, in each man, the sense of individual responsibility. They taught him, whether warrior or cripple, prince or beggar, that he had an immortal soul, for which each must give like account to God.

Do you not see the effect of that new thought? Treated as slaves, as things and animals, the many had learnt to consider themselves as things and animals. And so they had become 'a mass,' that is, a mere heap of inorganic units, each of which has no spring of life in itself as distinguished from a whole, a people, which has one bond, uniting each to all. The 'masses' of the French had fallen into that state, before the Revolution of 1793. The 'masses' of our agricultural labourers,—the 'masses' of our manufacturing workmen, were fast falling into that state in the days of our grandfathers. Whether the

---

1 Cf. Montalembert. 'Moines d'Occident.'

French masses have risen out of it, remains to be seen. The English masses, thanks to Almighty God, have risen out of it; and by the very same factor by which the middle-age masses rose—by Religion. The great Methodist movement of the last century did for our masses, what the monks did for our forefathers in the middle age. Wesley and Whitfield, and many another noble soul, said to Nailsea colliers, Cornish miners, and all manner of drunken brutalized fellows, living like the beasts that perish,—'Each of you—thou—and thou—and thou—stand apart and alone before God. Each has an immortal soul in him, which will be happy or miserable for ever, according to the deeds done in the body. A whole eternity of shame or of glory lies in you—and you are living like a beast.' And in proportion as each man heard that word, and took it home to himself, he became a new man, and a true man. The preachers may have mixed up words with their message with which we may disagree, have appealed to low hopes and fears which we should be ashamed to bring into our calculations;—so did the monks: but they got their work done somehow; and let us thank them, and the old Methodists, and any man who will tell men, in whatever clumsy and rough fashion, that they are not things, and pieces of a mass, but persons, with an everlasting duty, an everlasting right and wrong, an everlasting God in whose presence they stand, and who will judge them according to their works. True, that is not all that men need to learn. After they are taught, each apart, that he is a man, they must be taught, how to be an united people: but the individual teaching must come first; and before we hastily blame the individualizing tendencies of the old Evangelical movement, or that of the middle-age monks, let us remember, that if they had not laid the foundation, others could not build thereon.

Besides, they built themselves, as well as they could, on their own foundation. As soon as men begin to be really men, the desire of corporate life springs up in them. They must unite; they must organize themselves. If they possess duties, they must be duties to their fellow-men; if they possess virtues and graces, they must mix with their fellow-men in order to exercise them.

The solitaries of the Thebaid found that they became selfish wild beasts, or went mad, if they remained alone; and they formed themselves into lauras, 'lanes' of huts, convents, under a common abbot or father. The evangelical converts of the last century formed themselves into powerful and highly organized sects. The middle-age monasteries organized themselves into highly artificial communities round some sacred spot, generally under the supposed protection of some saint or martyr, whose bones lay there. Each method was good, though not the highest. None of them rises to the idea of a people, having one national life, under one monarch, the representative to each and all of that national life, and the dispenser and executor of its laws. Indeed, the artificial organization, whether monastic or sectarian, may become so strong as to interfere with national life, and make men forget their real duty to their king and country, in their self-imposed duty to the sect or order to which they belong. The monastic organization indeed had to die, in many countries, in order that national life might develop itself; and the dissolution of the monasteries marks the birth of an united and powerful England. They or Britain must have died. An imperium in imperio—much more many separate imperia—was an element of national weakness, which might be allowed in times of peace and safety, but not in times of convulsion and of danger.

You may ask, however, how these monasteries became so powerful, if they were merely refuges for the weak? Even if they were (and they were) the homes of an equal justice and order, mercy and beneficence, which had few or no standing-places outside their walls, still, how, if governed by weak men, could they survive in the great battle of life? The sheep would have but a poor life of it, if they set up hurdles against the wolves, and agreed at all events not to eat each other.

The answer is, that the monasteries were not altogether tenanted by incapables. The same causes which brought the low-born into the monasteries, brought the high-born, many of the very highest. The same cause which brought the weak into the monasteries, brought the strong, many of the very strongest.

The middle-age records give us a long list of kings, princes, nobles, who having done (as they held) their work in the world outside, went into those convents to try their hands at what seemed to them (and often was) better work than the perpetual coil of war, intrigue, and ambition, which was not the crime, but the necessary fate, of a ruler in the middle ages. Tired of work, and tired of life; tired too, of vain luxury and vain wealth, they fled to the convent, as to the only place where a man could get a little peace, and think of God, and his own soul; and recollected, as they worked with their own hands by the side of the lowest-born of their subjects, that they had a human flesh and blood, a human immortal soul, like those whom they had ruled.  Thank God that the great have other methods now of learning that great truth; that the work of life, if but well done, will teach it to them: but those were hard times, and wild times; and fighting men could hardly learn, save in the convent, that there was a God above who watched the widows' and the orphans' tears, and when he made inquisition for blood, forgot not the cause of the poor.

Such men and women of rank brought into the convent, meanwhile, all the prestige of their rank, all their superior knowledge of the world; and became the patrons and protectors of the society; while they submitted, generally with peculiar humility and devotion, to its most severe and degrading rules.  Their higher sensibilities, instead of making them shrink from hardship, made them strong to endure self-sacrifices, and often self-tortures, which seem to us all but incredible; and the lives, or rather living deaths, of the noble and princely penitents of the early middle age, are among the most beautiful tragedies of humanity.

To these monasteries, too, came the men of the very highest intellect, of whatsoever class.  I say, of the very highest intellect.  Tolerably talented men might find it worth while to stay in the world, and use their wits in struggling upward there.  The most talented of all would be the very men to see a better 'carrière ouverte aux talens' than the world could give; to long for deeper

and loftier meditation than could be found in the court;
for a more divine life, a more blessed death, than could
be found in the camp and the battle-field.

And so it befals, that in the early middle age the
cleverest men were generally inside the convent, trying,
by moral influence and superior intellect, to keep those
outside from tearing each other to pieces.

But these intellects could not remain locked up in
the monasteries. The daily routine of devotion, even of
silent study and contemplation, was not sufficient for
them, as it was for the average monk. There was still a
reserve of force in them, which must be up and doing;
and which, in a man inspired by that Spirit which is the
Spirit of love to man as well as to God, must needs expand outwards in all directions, to Christianize, to civ-
ilize, to colonize.

To colonize. When people talk loosely of founding
an abbey for superstitious uses, they cannot surely be
aware of the state of the countries in which those ab-
beys were founded; either primæval forest, hardly-tilled
common, or to be described by that terrible epithet of
Domesday-book, 'wasta'—wasted by war. A knowledge
of that fact would lead them to guess that there were almost certainly uses for the abbey which had nothing to
do with superstition; which were as thoroughly practical
as those of a company for draining the bog of Allen, or
running a railroad through an American forest. Such, at
least, was the case, at least for the first seven centuries after the fall of Rome; and to these missionary colonizers
Europe owes, I verily believe, among a hundred benefits,
this which all Englishmen will appreciate; that Roman

agriculture not only revived in the countries which were once the Empire, but spread from thence eastward and northward, into the principal wilderness of the Teuton and Sclavonic races.

I cannot, I think, shew you better what manner of men these monk-colonizers were, and what sort of work they did, than by giving you the biography of one of them; and out of many I have chosen that of St. Sturmi, founder whilome of the great abbey of Fulda, which lies on the central watershed of Germany, about equidistant, to speak roughly, from Frankfort, Cassel, Gotha, and Coburg.

His life is matter of history, written by one Eigils (sainted like himself), who was his disciple and his friend.  Naturally told it is, and lovingly; but if I recollect right, without a single miracle or myth; the living contemporaneous picture of such a man, living in such a state of society, as we shall never (and happily need never) see again, but which is for that very reason worthy to be preserved, for a token that wisdom is justified of all her children.

It stands at length in Pertz's admirable 'Monumenta Historica,' among many another like biography, and if I tell it here somewhat at length, readers must forgive me.

Every one has heard of little king Pepin, and many may have heard also how he was a mighty man of valour, and cut off a lion's head at one blow; and how he was a crafty statesman, and first consolidated the temporal power of the Popes, and helped them in that detestable crime of overthrowing the noble Lombard kingdom, which cost Italy centuries of slavery and shame, and which has to be expiated even yet, it would seem, by some fearful punishment.

But every one may not know that Pepin had great excuses—if not for helping to destroy the Lombards—yet still for supporting the power of the Popes. It seemed to him—and perhaps it was—the only practical method of uniting the German tribes into one common people, and stopping the internecine wars by which they were tearing themselves to pieces. It seemed to him—and perhaps it was—the only practical method for civilizing and Christianizing the still wild tribes, Frisians, Saxons, and Sclaves, who pressed upon the German marches, from the mouth of the Elbe to the very Alps. Be that as it may, he began the work; and his son Charlemagne finished it; somewhat well, and again somewhat ill—as most work, alas! is done on earth. Now in the days of little king Pepin there was a nobleman of Bavaria, and his wife, who had a son called Sturmi; and they brought him to St. Boniface, that he might make him a priest. And the child loved St. Boniface's noble English face, and went with him willingly, and was to him as a son. And who was St. Boniface? That is a long story. Suffice it that he was a man of Devon, brought up in a cloister at Exeter; and that he had crossed over into Frankenland, upon the lower Rhine, and become a missionary of the widest and loftiest aims; not merely a preacher and winner of souls, though that, it is said, in perfection; but a civilizer, a colonizer, a statesman. He, and many another noble Englishman and Scot (whether Irish or Caledonian) were working under the Frank kings to convert the heathens of the marches, and carry the Cross into the far East.  They led lives of poverty and danger; they were martyred, half of them, as St. Boniface was at last. But they did their work; and doubtless they have their reward.  They did their best, according to their light. God grant that we, to whom so much more light has been given, may do our best likewise.  Under this great genius was young Sturmi trained.  Trained (as was perhaps needed for those who had to do such work in such a time) to have neither wife, nor child, nor home, nor penny in his purse; but to do all that he was bid, learn all that he could, and work for his living with his own hands; a life of bitter self-sacrifice.  Such a life is not needed now.  Possibly, nevertheless, it was needed then.

So St. Boniface took Sturmi about with him in his travels, and at last handed him over to Wigbert, the priest, to prepare him for the ministry.  'Under whom,' says his old chronicler, 'the boy began to know the Psalms thoroughly by heart; to understand the Holy Scriptures of Christ with spiritual sense; took care to learn most studiously the mysteries of the four Gospels, and to bury in his heart, by assiduous reading, the treasures of the Old and New Testament.  For his meditation was in the Law of the Lord day and night; profound in understanding, shrewd of thought, prudent of speech, fair of face, sober of carriage, honourable in morals, spotless in life, by sweetness, humility, and alacrity, he drew to him the love of all.'

He grew to be a man; and in due time he was ordained priest, 'by the will and consent of all;' and he 'began to preach the words of Christ earnestly to the people;' and his preaching wrought wonders among them.

Three years he preached in his Rhineland parish, winning love from all. But in the third year 'a heavenly thought' came into his mind that he would turn hermit and dwell in the wild forest. And why? Who can tell? He may, likely enough, have found celibacy a fearful temptation for a young and eloquent man, and longed to flee from the sight of that which must not be his. And that, in his circumstances, was not a foolish wish. He may have wished to escape, if but once, from the noise and crowd of outward things, and be alone with God and Christ, and his own soul. And that was not a foolish wish. John Bunyan so longed, and found what he wanted in Bedford Jail, and set it down and printed it in a Pilgrim's Progress, which will live as long as man is man. George Fox longed for it, and made himself clothes of leather which would not wear out, and lived in a hollow tree, till he, too, set down the fruit of his solitude in a diary which will live likewise as long as man is man. Perhaps, again, young Sturmi longed to try for once in a way what he was worth upon God's earth; how much he could endure; what power he had of helping himself, what courage to live by his own wits, and God's mercy, on roots and fruits, as wild things live. And surely that was not altogether a foolish wish. At least, he longed to be a hermit; but he kept his longing to himself, however, till St. Boniface, his bishop, appeared; and then he told him all his heart.

And St. Boniface said: 'Go; in the name of God;' and gave him two comrades, and sent him into 'the wilderness which is called Buchonia, the Beech Forest, to find a place fit for the servants of the Lord to dwell in.

For the Lord is able to provide his people a home in the desert.'

So those three went into the wild forest. And 'for three days they saw nought but earth and sky and mighty trees. And they went on, praying Christ that He would guide their feet into the way of peace. And on the third day they came to the place which is called Hersfelt (the hart's down?), and searched it round, and prayed that Christ would bless the place for them to dwell in; and then they built themselves little huts of beech-bark, and abode there many days, serving God with holy fastings, and watchings, and prayers.'

Is it not a strange story? so utterly unlike anything which we see now;—so utterly unlike anything which we ought to see now? And yet it may have been good in its time. It looks out on us from the dim ages, like the fossil bone of some old monster cropping out of a quarry. But the old monster was good in his place and time. God made him and had need of him. It may be that God made those three poor monks, and had need of them likewise.

As for their purposes being superstitious, we shall be better able to judge of that when we have seen what they were—what sort of a house they meant to build to God. As for their having self-interest in view, no doubt they thought that they should benefit their own souls in this life, and in the life to come. But one would hardly blame them for that, surely?

One would not blame them as selfish and sordid if they had gone out on a commercial speculation? Why, then, if on a religious one? The merchant adventurer is often a noble type of man, and one to whom the world owes much, though his hands are not always clean, nor his eye single. The monk adventurer of the middle age is, perhaps, a still nobler type of man, and one to whom the world owes more, though his eye, too, was not always single, nor his hands clean.

As for selfishness, one must really bear in mind that men who walked away into that doleful 'urwarld' had need to pray very literally 'that Christ would guide their feet into the way of peace;' and must have cared as much for their wordly interests as those who march up to the cannon's mouth. Their lives in that forest were not worth twenty-four hours' purchase, and they knew it. It is an ugly thing for an unarmed man, without a compass, to traverse the bush of Australia or New Zealand, where there are no wild beasts. But it was uglier still to start out under the dark roof of that primæval wood. Knights, when they rode it, went armed cap-à-pie, like Sintram through the dark valley, trusting in God and their good sword. Chapmen and merchants stole through it by a few tracks in great companies, armed with bill and bow. Peasants ventured into it a few miles, to cut timber, and find pannage for their swine, and whispered wild legends of the ugly things therein—and sometimes, too, never came home. Away it stretched from the fair Rhineland, wave after wave of oak and alder, beech and pine, God alone knew how far, into the land of night and wonder, and the infinite unknown; full of elk and bison, bear and wolf, lynx and glutton, and perhaps of worse beasts still. Worse beasts, certainly, Sturmi and his comrades would have met, if they had met them in human form.  For there were waifs and strays of barbarism there, uglier far than any waif and stray of civilization, border ruffian of the far west, buccaneer of the Tropic keys, Cimaroon of the Panama forests; men verbiesterte, turned into the likeness of beasts, wildfanger, hüner, ogres, wehr-wolves, strong thieves and outlaws, many of them possibly mere brutal maniacs; naked, living in caves and coverts, knowing no law but their own hunger, rage, and lust; feeding often on human flesh; and woe to the woman or child or unarmed man who fell into their ruthless clutch.  Orson, and such like human brutes of the wilderness, serve now to amuse children in fairy tales; they were then ugly facts of flesh and blood.  There were heathens there, too, in small colonies: heathen Saxons, cruelest of all the tribes; who worshipped at the Irmensul, and had an old blood-feud against the Franks; heathen Thuringer, who had murdered St. Kilian the Irishman at Wurzburg; heathen Slaves, of different tribes, who had introduced into Europe the custom of impaling their captives: and woe to the Christian priest who fell into any of their hands.  To be knocked on the head before some ugly idol was the gentlest death which they were like to have. They would have called that martyrdom, and the gate of eternal bliss; but they were none the less brave men for going out to face it.

And beside all these, and worse than all these, there were the terrors of the unseen world; very real in those poor monks' eyes, though not in ours.  There were Nixes in the streams, and Kobolds in the caves, and Tannhäuser in the dark pine-glades, who hated the Christian man, and would lure him to his death. There were fair swan-maidens and elf-maidens; nay, dame Venus herself, and Herodias the dancer, with all their rout of revellers; who would tempt him to sin, and having made him sell his soul, destroy both body and soul in hell. There was Satan and all the devils, too, plotting to stop the Christian man from building the house of the Lord, and preaching the gospel to the heathen; ready to call up storms, and floods, and forest fires; to hurl the crag down from the cliffs, or drop the rotting tree on their defenceless heads—all real and terrible in those poor monks' eyes, as they walked on, singing their psalms, and reading their Gospels, and praying to God to save them, for they could not save themselves; and to guide them, for they knew not, like Abraham, whither they went; and to show them the place where they should build the house of the Lord, and preach righteousness, peace, and joy in the Holy Spirit to the heathen round. We talk still, thank heaven, of heroes, and understand what that great word should mean. But were not these poor monks heroes? Knights-errant of God, doing his work as they best knew how. We have a purer gospel than they: we understand our Bibles better. But if they had not done what they did, where would have been now our gospel, and our Bible? We cannot tell. It was a wise old saw of our forefathers—'Do not speak ill of the bridge which carries you over.'

If Sturmi had had a 'holy longing' to get into the wild wood, now he had a 'holy longing' to go back; and to find St. Boniface, and tell him what a pleasant place Hersfelt was, and the quality of the soil, and the direction of the watershed, and the meadows, and springs, and so forth, in a very practical way.  And St. Boniface answered, that the place seemed good enough; but that he was afraid for them, on account of the savage heathen Saxons.  They must go deeper into the forest, and then they would be safe.  So he went back to his fellow-hermits, and they made to themselves a canoe; and went paddling up and down the Fulda stream, beneath the alder boughs, 'trying the mouths of the mountain-streams, and landing to survey the hills and ridges,'—pioneers of civilization none the less because they pioneered in the name of Him who made earth and heaven: but they found nothing which they thought would suit the blessed St. Boniface, save that they stayed a little at the place which is called Ruohen-bah, 'the rough brook,' to see if it would suit; but it would not.  So they went back to their birch huts to fast and pray once more.

St. Boniface sent for Sturmi after awhile, probably to Maintz, to ask of his success; and Sturmi threw himself on his face before him; and Boniface raised him up, and kissed him, and made him sit by his side—which was a mighty honour; for St. Boniface, the penniless monk, was at that moment one of the most powerful men of Europe; and he gave Sturmi a good dinner, of which, no doubt, he stood in need; and bade him keep up heart, and seek again for the place which God had surely prepared, and would reveal in His good time.

And this time Sturmi, probably wiser from experience, determined to go alone; but not on foot.  So he took to him a trusty ass, and as much food as he could pack on it; and, axe in hand, rode away into the wild

wood, singing his psalms. And every night, before he
lay down to sleep, he cut boughs, and stuck them up for
a ring fence round him and the ass, to the discomfiture
of the wolves, which had, and have still, a great hanker-
ing after asses' flesh. It is a quaint picture, no doubt; but
let us respect it, while we smile at it; if we, too, be brave
men.

Then one day he fell into a great peril. He came to
the old road (a Roman one, I presume; for the Teutons, whether in England or elsewhere, never dreamed
of making roads till three hundred years ago, but used
the old Roman ones), which led out of the Thuringen
land to Maintz. And at the ford over the Fulda he met
a great multitude bathing, of Sclavonian heathens, going to the fair at Maintz. And they smelt so strong, the
foul miscreants, that Sturmi's donkey backed, and refused to face them; and Sturmi himself was much of the
donkey's mind, for they began to mock him (possibly
he nearly went over the donkey's head), and went about
to hurt him.

'But,' says the chronicler, 'the power of the Lord held
them back.'

Then he went on, right thankful at having escaped
with his life, up and down, round and round, exploring
and surveying—for what purpose we shall see hereafter.
And at last he lost himself in the place which is called
Aihen-loh, 'the glade of oaks;' and at night-fall he heard
the plash of water, and knew not whether man or wild
beast made it. And not daring to call out, he tapped
a tree-trunk with his axe (some backwoodsman's sign
of those days, we may presume), and he was answered.

And a forester came to him, leading his lord's horse; a man from the Wetterau, who knew the woods far and wide, and told him all that he wanted to know. And they slept side by side that night; and in the morning they blest each other, and each went his way.

Yes, there were not merely kings and wars, popes and councils, in those old days;—there were real human beings, just such as we might meet by the wayside any hour, with human hearts and histories within them. And we will be thankful if but one of them, now and then, starts up out of the darkness of twelve hundred years, like that good forester, and looks at us with human eyes, and goes his way again, blessing, and not unblest.

And now Sturmi knew all that he needed to know; and after awhile, following the counsel of the forester, he came to 'the blessed place, long ago prepared of the Lord. And when he saw it, he was filled with immense joy, and went on exulting; for he felt that by the merits and prayers of the holy Bishop Boniface that place had been revealed to him. And he went about it, and about it, half the day; and the more he looked on it the more he gave God thanks;' and those who know Fulda say, that Sturmi had reason to give God thanks, and must have had a keen eye, moreover, for that which man needs for wealth and prosperity, in soil and water, meadow and wood. So he blessed the place, and signed it with the sign of the Cross (in token that it belonged thenceforth neither to devils nor fairies, but to his rightful Lord and Maker), and went back to his cell, and thence a weary journey to St. Boniface, to tell him of the fair place which he had found at last.

And St. Boniface went his weary way, either to Paris or to Aix, to Pepin and Carloman, kings of the Franks; and begged of them a grant of the Aihen-loh, and all the land for four miles round, and had it.  And the nobles about gave up to him their rights of venison, and vert, and pasture, and pannage of swine; and Sturmi and seven brethren set out thither, 'in the year of our Lord 744, in the first month (April, presumably), in the twelfth day of the month, unto the place prepared of the Lord,' that they might do what?

That they might build an abbey.  Yes; but the question is, what building an abbey meant, not three hundred, nor five hundred, but eleven hundred years ago— for centuries are long matters, and men and their works change in them.

And then it meant this: Clearing the back woods for a Christian settlement; an industrial colony, in which every man was expected to spend his life in doing good—all and every good which he could for his fellow-men.  Whatever talent he had he threw into the common stock; and worked, as he was found fit to work, at farming, gardening, carpentering, writing, doctoring, teaching in the schools, or preaching to the heathen round.  In their common church they met to worship God; but also to ask for grace and strength to do their work, as Christianizers and civilizers of mankind.  What Christianity and civilization they knew (and they knew more than we are apt now to believe) they taught it freely; and therefore they were loved, and looked up to as superior beings, as modern missionaries, wherever they do their work even decently well, are looked up to now.

So because the work could be done in that way, and (as far as men then, or now, can see) in no other way, Pepin and Carloman gave Boniface the glade of oaks, that they might clear the virgin forest, and extend cultivation, and win fresh souls to Christ, instead of fighting, like the kings of this world, for the land which was already cleared, and the people who were already Christian.

In two months' time they had cut down much of the forest; and then came St. Boniface himself to see them, and with him a great company of workmen, and chose a place for a church. And St. Boniface went up to the hill which is yet called Bishop's Mount, that he might read his Bible in peace, away from kings and courts, and the noise of the wicked world; and his workmen felled trees innumerable, and dug peat to burn lime withal; and then all went back again, and left the settlers to thrive and work.

And thrive and work they did, clearing more land, building their church, ploughing up their farm, drawing to them more and more heathen converts, more and more heathen school-children; and St. Boniface came to see them from time to time, whenever he could get a holiday, and spent happy days in prayer and study, with his pupil and friend. And ten years after, when St. Boniface was martyred at last by the Friesland heathens, and died, as he had lived, like an apostle of God, then all the folk of Maintz wanted to bring his corpse home to their town, because he had been Archbishop there. But he 'appeared in a dream to a certain deacon, and said: "Why delay ye to take me home to Fulda, to my rest in the wilderness which God bath prepared for me?"'

So St. Boniface sleeps at Fulda,—unless the French Republican armies dug up his bones, and scattered them, as they scattered holier things, to the winds of heaven. And all men came to worship at his tomb, after the fashion of those days. And Fulda became a noble abbey, with its dom-church, library, schools, workshops, farmsteads, almshouses, and all the appanages of such a place, in the days when monks were monks indeed. And Sturmi became a great man, and went through many troubles and slanders, and conquered in them all, because there was no fault found in him, as in Daniel of old; and died in a good old age, bewept by thousands, who, but for him, would have been heathens still. And the Aihen-loh became rich corn-land and garden, and Fulda an abbey borough and a principality, where men lived in peace under mild rule, while the feudal princes quarrelled and fought outside; and a great literary centre, whose old records are now precious to the diggers among the bones of bygone times; and at last St. Sturmi and the Aihen-lob had so developed themselves, that the latest record of the Abbots of Fulda which I have seen is this, bearing date about 1710:—

'The arms of the most illustrious Lord and Prince, Abbot of Fulda, Archchancellor of the most Serene Empress, Primate of all Germany and Gaul, and Prince of the Holy Roman Empire.' Developed, certainly: and not altogether in the right direction. For instead of the small beer, which they had promised St. Boniface to drink to the end of the world, the abbots of Fulda had the best wine in Germany, and the best table too.

Be that as it may, to have cleared the timber off the Ai-hen-lob, and planted a Christian colony instead, was enough to make St. Sturmi hope that he had not read his Bible altogether in vain.

Surely such men as St. Sturmi were children of wisdom, put what sense on the word you will. In a dark, confused, lawless, cut-throat age, while everything was decided by the sword, they found that they could do no good to themselves, or any man, by throwing their swords into either scale. They would be men of peace, and see what could be done so. Was that not wise? So they set to work. They feared God exceedingly, and walked with God. Was not that wise? They wrought righteousness, and were merciful and kind, while kings and nobles were murdering around them; pure and temperate, while other men were lustful and drunken; just and equal in all their ways, while other men were unjust and capricious; serving God faithfully, according to their light, while the people round them were half or wholly heathen; content to do their work well on earth, and look for their reward in heaven, while the kings and nobles, the holders of the land, were full of insane ambition, every man trying to seize a scrap of ground from his neighbour, as if that would make them happier. Was that not wise? Which was the wiser, the chief killing human beings, to take from them some few square miles which men had brought into cultivation already, or the monk, leaving the cultivated land, and going out into the backwoods to clear the forest, and till the virgin soil? Which was the child of wisdom, I ask again? And do not tell me that the old monk worked only for fanatical and superstitious ends. It is not so. I know well his fanaticism and his superstition, and the depths of its ignorance and silliness: but he had more in him than that. Had he not, he would have worked no lasting work. He was not only the pioneer of civilization, but he knew that he was such. He believed that all knowledge came from God, even that which taught a man to clear the forest, and plant corn instead; and he determined to spread such knowledge as he had wherever he could. He was a wiser man than the heathen Saxons, even than the Christian Franks, around him; a better scholar, a better thinker, better handicraftsman, better farmer; and he did not keep his knowledge to himself. He did not, as some tell you, keep the Bible to himself. It is not so; and those who say so, in this generation, ought to be ashamed of themselves. The monk knew his Bible well himself, and he taught it. Those who learnt from him to read, learnt to read their Bibles. Those who did not learn (of course the vast majority, in days when there was no printing), he taught by sermons, by pictures, afterward by mystery and miracle plays. The Bible was not forbidden to the laity till centuries afterwards—and forbidden then, why? Because the laity throughout Europe knew too much about the Bible, and not too little. Because the early monks had so ingrained the mind of the masses, throughout Christendom, with Bible stories, Bible personages, the great facts, and the great doctrines, of our Lord's life, that the masses knew too much; that they could contrast too easily, and too freely, the fallen and profligate monks of the 15th and 16th centuries, with those Bible examples, which the old monks of centuries before had taught their forefathers. Then the clergy tried to keep from the laity, because it testified against themselves, the very book which centuries before they had taught them to love and know too well. In a word, the old monk missionary taught all he knew to all who would learn, just as our best modern missionaries do; and was loved, and obeyed, and looked on as a superior being, as they are.

Of course he did not know how far civilization would extend. He could not foretell railroads and electric telegraphs, any more than he could political economy, or sanitary science. But the best that he knew, he taught—and did also, working with his own hands. He was faithful in a few things, and God made him ruler over many things. For out of those monasteries sprang—what did not spring? They restored again and again sound law and just government, when the good old Teutonic laws, and the Roman law also, was trampled underfoot amid the lawless strife of ambition and fury. Under their shadow sprang up the towns with their corporate rights, their middle classes, their artizan classes. They were the physicians, the alms-givers, the relieving officers, the schoolmasters of the middle-age world. They first taught us the great principle of the division of labour, to which we owe, at this moment, that England is what she is, instead of being covered with a horde of peasants, each making and producing everything for himself, and starving each upon his rood of ground. They transcribed or composed all the books of the then world; many of them spent their lives in doing nothing but writing; and the number of books, even of those to be found in single monasteries, considering the tedious labour of copying, is altogether astonishing. They preserved to us the treasures of classical antiquity. They discovered for us the germs of all our modern inventions. They brought in from abroad arts and new knowledge; and while they taught men to know that they had a common humanity, a common Father in heaven taught them also to profit by each other's wisdom instead of remaining in isolated ignorance. They, too, were the great witnesses against feudal caste. With them was neither high-born nor low-born, rich nor poor: worth was their only test; the meanest serf entering there might become the lord of knights and vassals, the counsellor of kings and princes. Men may talk of democracy—those old monasteries were the most democratic institutions the world had ever till then seen. 'A man's a man for a' that,' was not only talked of in them, but carried out in practice—only not in anarchy, and as a cloak for licentiousness: but under those safeguards of strict discipline, and almost military order, without which men may call themselves free, and yet be really only slaves to their own passions. Yes, paradoxical as it may seem, in those monasteries was preserved the sacred fire of modern liberty, through those feudal centuries when all the outside world was doing its best to trample it out. Remember, as a single instance, that in the Abbot's lodging at Bury St. Edmunds, the Magna Charta was drawn out, before being presented to John at Runymede. I know what they became afterwards, better than most do here; too well to defile my lips, or your ears, with tales too true. They had done their work, and they went. Like all things born in time, they died; and decayed in time; and the old order changed, giving place to the new; and God fulfilled himself in many ways. But in them, too, he fulfilled himself. They were the best things the world had seen; the only method of Christianizing and civilizing semi-barbarous Europe. Like all human plans and conceptions, they contained in themselves original sin; idolatry, celibacy, inhuman fanaticism; these were their three roots of bitterness; and when they bore the natural fruit of immorality, the monasteries fell with a great and just destruction. But had not those monasteries been good at first, and noble at first; had not the men in them been better and more useful men than the men outside, do you think they would have endured for centuries? They would not even have established themselves at all. They would soon, in those stormy times, have been swept off the face of the earth. Ill used they often were, plundered and burnt down. But men found that they were good. Their own plunderers found that they could not do without them; and repented, and humbled themselves, and built them up again, to be centres of justice and mercy and peace, amid the wild weltering sea of war and misery. For all things endure, even for a generation, only by virtue of the good which is in them. By the Spirit of God in them they live, as do all created things; and when he taketh away their breath they die, and return again to their dust.

And what was the original sin of them? We can hardly say that it was their superstitious and partially false creed: because that they held in common with all Europe. It was rather that they had identified themselves with, and tried to realize on earth, one of the worst falsehoods of that creed—celibacy.  Not being founded on the true and only ground of all society, family life, they were merely artificial and self-willed arrangements of man's invention, which could not develop to any higher form.  And when the sanctity of marriage was re-vindicated at the Reformation, the monasteries, having identified themselves with celibacy, naturally fell.  They could not partake in the Reformation movement, and rise with it into some higher form of life, as the laity out-side did.  I say, they were altogether artificial things.  The Abbot might be called the Abba, Father, of his monks: but he was not their father—just as when young ladies now play at being nuns, they call their superior, Mother: but all the calling in the world will not make that sacred name a fact and a reality, as they too often find out.

And celibacy brought serious evils from the first.  It induced an excited, hysterical tone of mind, which is most remarkable in the best men; violent, querulous, suspicious, irritable, credulous, visionary; at best more womanly than manly; alternately in tears and in rap-tures.  You never get in their writings anything of that manly calmness, which we so deservedly honour, and at which we all aim for ourselves.  They are bombastic; excited; perpetually mistaking virulence for strength, putting us in mind for ever of the allocutions of the Popes.  Read the writings of one of the best of monks, and of men, who ever lived, the great St. Bernard, and you will be painfully struck by this hysterical element.  The fact is, that their rule of life, from the earliest to the latest,—from that of St. Benedict of Casino, 'father of all monks,' to that of Loyola the Jesuit, was pitched not too low, but too high. It was an ideal which, for good or for evil, could only be carried out by new converts, by people in a state of high religious excitement, and therefore the history of the monastic orders is just that of the protestant sects. We hear of continual fallings off from their first purity; of continual excitements, revivals, and startings of new orders, which hoped to realize the perfection which the old orders could not. You must bear this in mind, as you read mediæval history. You will be puzzled to know why continual new rules and new orders sprung up. They were so many revivals, so many purist attempts at new sects. You will see this very clearly in the three great revivals which exercised such enormous influence on the history of the 13th, the 16th and the 17th centuries,—I mean the rise first of the Franciscans and Dominicans, next of the Jesuits, and lastly of the Port Royalists. They each professed to restore monachism to what it had been at first; to realize the unnatural and impossible ideal.

Another serious fault of these monasteries may be traced to their artificial celibate system. I mean their avarice. Only one generation after St. Sturmi, Charlemagne had to make indignant laws against Abbots who tried to get into their hands the property of everybody around them: but in vain. The Abbots became more and more the great landholders, till their power was intolerable. The reasons are simple enough. An abbey had no children between whom to divide its wealth, and therefore more land was always flowing in and concentrating, and never breaking up again; while almost every

Abbot left his personalities, all his private savings and purchases, to his successor.

Then again, in an unhappy hour, they discovered that the easiest way of getting rich was by persuading sinners, and weak persons, to secure the safety of their souls by leaving land to the Church, in return for the prayers and masses of monks; and that shameful mine of wealth was worked by them for centuries, in spite of statutes of mortmain, and other checks which the civil power laid on them, very often by most detestable means. One is shocked to find good men lending themselves to such base tricks: but we must recollect, that there has always been among men a public and a private conscience, and that these two, alas! have generally been very different. It is an old saying, that 'committees have no consciences;' and it is too true. A body of men acting in concert for a public purpose will do things which they would shrink from with disgust, if the same trick would merely put money into their private purses; and this is too often the case when the public object is a good one. Then the end seems to sanctify the means, to almost any amount of chicanery.

So it was with those old monks. An abbey had no conscience. An order of monks had no conscience. A Benedictine, a Dominican, a Franciscan, who had not himself a penny in the world, and never intended to have one, would play tricks, lie, cheat, slander, forge, for the honour and the wealth of his order; when for himself, and in himself, he may have been an honest God-fearing man enough. So it was; one more ugly fruit of an unnatural attempt to be not good men, but something more than men; by trying to be more than men, they ended by being less than men.  That was their sin, and that sin, when it had conceived, brought forth death.

# THE LOMBARD LAWS

I have tried to shew you how the Teutonic nations were Christianized. I have tried to explain to you why the clergy who converted them were, nevertheless, more or less permanently antagonistic to them. I shall have, hereafter, to tell you something of one of the most famous instances of that antagonism: of the destruction of the liberties of the Lombards by that Latin clergy. But at first you ought to know something of the manners of these Lombards; and that you may learn best by studying their Code.

They are valuable to you, as giving you a fair specimen of the laws of an old Teutonic people. You may profitably compare them with the old Gothic, Franco-Salic, Burgundian, Anglo-Saxon, and Scandinavian laws, all formed on the same primæval model, agreeing often in minute details, and betokening one primæval origin, of awful antiquity. By studying them, moreover, you may gain some notion of that primæval liberty and self-government, common at first to all the race, but preserved alone by England;—to which the descendants of these very Lombards are at this very moment so manfully working their way back.

These laws were collected and published in writing by king Rothar, A.D. 643, 76 years after Alboin came into Italy. The cause, he says, was the continual wearying of the poor, and the superfluous exactions, and even violence, of the strong against those who were weak. They are the 'laws of our fathers, as far as we have learnt them from ancient men, and are published with the counsel and consent of our princes, judges, and all our most prosperous army,' i.e. the barons, or freemen capable of bearing arms; 'and are confirmed according to the custom of our nation by garathinx,' that is, as far as I can ascertain from Grimm's German Law, by giving an earnest, garant, or warrant of the bargain.

Among these Lombards, as among our English forefathers, when a man thingavit, i.e. donavit, a gift or bequest to any one, it was necessary, according to law CLXXII., to do it before gisiles, witnesses, and to give a garathinx, or earnest, of his bequest—a halm of straw, a turf, a cup of drink, a piece of money—as to this day a drover seals his bargain with a shilling, and a commercial traveller with a glass of liquor. Whether Rothar gave the garathinx to his barons, or his barons to him, I do not understand: but at least it is clear from the use of this one word that the publication of these laws was a 'social contract'—a distinct compact between king and people. From all which you will perceive at once that these Lombards, like all Teutons, were a free people, under a rough kind of constitutional monarchy. They would have greeted with laughter the modern fable of the divine right of kings, if by that they were expected to understand that the will of the king was law, or that the eldest son of a certain family had any God-given ipso-facto right to succeed his father. Sixteen kings, says the preface, had reigned from Agilmund to Rothar; and seven times had the royal race been changed. That the king should belong to one of the families who derived their pedigree from Wodin, and that a son should, as natural, succeed his father, were old rules: but the barons would, as all history shews, make little of crowning a younger son instead of an elder, if the younger were a hero, and the elder an 'arga'—a lazy loon; and little, also, would they make of setting aside the whole royal family, and crowning the man who would do their business best. The king was, as this preface and these laws shew, the commander in chief of the exercitus, the militia, and therefore of every free man in the state; (for all were bound to fight when required). He was also the supreme judge, the head of the executive, dispenser and fountain of law: but with no more power of making the law, of breaking the law, or of arbitrarily depriving a man of his property, than an English sovereign has now; and his power was quamdiu se bene gesserit, and no longer, as history proves in every page.

The doctrine of the divine right of kings as understood in England in the seventeenth century, and still in some continental countries, was, as far as I can ascertain, invented by the early popes, not for the purpose of exalting the kings, but of enslaving them, and through them the nations. A king and his son's sons had divine 'right to govern wrong' not from God, but from the vicar of God and the successor of St. Peter, to whom God had given the dominion of the whole earth, and who had the right to anoint, or to depose, whomsoever he would. Even in these old laws, we see that new idea obtruding itself. 'The king's heart,' says one of them 'is in the hand of God.' That is a text of Scripture. What it was meant to mean, one cannot doubt, or by whom it was inserted.

The 'Chancellor,' or whoever else transcribed those laws in Latin, was, of course, a cleric, priest or monk. From his hand comes the first hint of arbitrary power; the first small blot of a long dark stain of absolutism, which was to darken and deepen through centuries of tyranny and shame.

But to plead the divine right of kings, in a country which has thrown off its allegiance to the pope, is to assert the conclusion of a syllogism, the major and minor premiss of which are both denied by the assertor. The arguments for such a right drawn from the Old Testament, which were common among the high-church party from James I. to James II. and the Nonjurors, are really too inconsequent to require more than a passing smile. How can you prove that a king has the power to make laws, from the history of the Jewish nation, when that very history represents it all through as bound by a primæval and divinely revealed law, to which kings and people were alike subject? How can you prove that the eldest son's eldest son has a divine right to wear the crown as 'God's anointed,' when the very persons to whom that title is given are generally either not eldest sons, or not of royal race at all? The rule that the eldest son's eldest son should succeed, has been proved by experience to be in practice a most excellent one: but it rests, as in England, so in Lombardy, or Spain, or Frankreich of old time, simply upon the consent of the barons, and the will of the thing or parliament.

There is a sentimental admiration of 'Imperialism' growing up now-a-days, under the pretentious titles of 'hero-worship,' and 'strong government;' and the British constitution is represented as a clumsy and artificial arrangement of the year 1688. 1688 after Christ? 1688 before Christ would be nearer the mark. It is as old, in its essentials, as the time when not only all the Teutons formed one tribe, but when Teutons and Scandinavians were still united—and when that was, who dare say? We at least brought the British constitution with us out of the bogs and moors of Jutland, along with our smock-frocks and leather gaiters, brown bills and stone axes; and it has done us good service, and will do, till we have carried it right round the world.

As for these Lombard kings, they arose on this wise. After Alboin's death the Lombards were for ten years under dukes, and evil times came, every man doing what was right in his own eyes; enlarging their frontier by kill-ing the Roman landholders, and making the survivors give them up a portion of their lands, as Odoacer first, and the Ostrogoths next, had done. At last, tired of law-lessness, dissension and weakness, and seemingly dread-ing an invasion from Childebert, king of the Franks, they chose a king, Autharis the son of Cleph, and called him Flavius, by which Roman title the Lombard kings were afterwards known. Moreover, they agreed to give him (I conclude only once for all) the half of all their substance, to support the kingdom. There were certain tributes afterwards paid into the king's treasury every three years; and certain fines, and also certain portions of the property of those who died without direct heirs, seem to have made up the revenue. Whereon, Paul says, perfect peace and justice followed.

Now for the laws, which were reduced into writing

about sixty years afterwards. The first thing that you will remark about these laws, is that duel, wager of battle under shield, 'diremptio causæ per pugnam sub uno scuto,' is the earliest form of settling a lawsuit. If you cannot agree, fight it out fairly, either by yourself or per campionem, a champion or kemper man, and God defend the right. Then follows 'faida,' blood-feud, from generation to generation. To stop which a man is allowed to purge himself by oath; his own and that of certain neighbours, twelve in general, who will swear their belief in his innocence. This was common to the northern nations, and was the origin of our trial by jury. If guilty, the offender has to pay the weregeld, or legal price, set upon the injury he has inflicted. When the composition is paid, there is an end of the feud; if after taking the composition the plaintiff avenges himself, he has to pay it back. Hence our system of fines.

This method of composition by fines runs through all the Teutonic laws; and makes the punishment of death, at least among freemen, very rare.

Punishments by stripes, by imprisonment, or by cruel or degrading methods, there are none. The person of a freeman is sacred, 'Vincire et verberare nefas,' as Tacitus said of these Germans 600 years before.

The offences absolutely punishable by death seem to be, treason against the king's life; cowardice in battle; concealment of robbers; mutinies and attempts to escape out of the realm; and therefore (under the then military organization) to escape from the duty of every freeman, to bear arms in defence of the land.

More than a hundred of these laws define the dif-

ferent fines, or 'weregelds,' by which each offence is to
be compounded for, from 900 solidi aurei, gold pieces,
for a murder, downwards to the smallest breach of the
peace. Each limb has its special price. For the loss of
an eye, half the price of the whole man is to be paid. A
front tooth is worth 16s., solidi aurei; their loss being
a disfigurement; but a back tooth is worth only 8s. A
slave's tooth, on the other hand, is worth but 4s.; and in
every case, the weregeld of a slave is much less than that
of a freeman.

The sacredness of the household, and the strong
sense of the individual rights of property, are to be remarked. One found in a 'court,' courtledge (or homestead), by night (as we say in old English), may be killed.
You know, I dare say, that in many Teutonic and Scandinavian nations the principle that a man's house is his
castle was so strongly held that men were not allowed
to enter a condemned man's house to carry him off to
execution; but if he would not come out, could only
burn the house over his head. Shooting, or throwing
a lance into any man's homestead, costs 20s. 'Oberos,'
or 'curtis ruptura,' that is, making violent entry into a
man's homestead, costs 20s. also. Nay, merely to fetch
your own goods out of another man's house secretly, and
without asking leave, was likewise punished as oberos.

So of personal honour. 'Schelte' or insult, for instance, to call a man arga, i.e. a lazy loon, is a serious
offence. If the defendant will confess that he said it in a
passion, and will take oath that he never knew the plaintiff to be arga, he must still pay 12s.; but if he will stand
to his word, then he must fight it out by duel, sub uno

scuto.

The person, for the same reason, was sacred.  If a man had lain in wait for a freeman, 'cum virtute et solatio,' with valour and comfort, i.e. with armed men to back him, and had found him standing or walking simply, and had shamefully held him, or 'battiderit,' committed assault and battery on him, he must pay half the man's weregeld; the 'turpiter et ridiculum' being considered for a freeman as half as bad as death.  Here you find in private life, as well as in public, the vincire et verberare nefas.

If, again, one had a mind to lose 80 shillings of gold, he need but to commit the offence of 'meerworphin,' a word which will puzzle you somewhat, till you find it to signify 'mare warping,' to warp, or throw one's neighbour off his mare or horse.

A blow with the closed fist, again, costs three shillings: but one with the open hand, six.  The latter is an insult as well as an injury.  A freeman is struck with the fist, but a slave with the palm of the hand.  Breaking a man's head costs six solidi.  But if one had broken his skull, then (as in the Alemannic laws) one must pay twelve shillings, and twelve more for each fracture up to three—after which they are not counted.  But a piece of bone must come out which will make a sound when thrown into a shield twelve feet off; which feet are to be measured by that of a man of middle stature. From which strange law may be deduced, not only the toughness of the Lombard brain-pan, but the extreme necessity of defining each particular, in order to prevent subsequent disputes, followed up by a blood-feud, which might be handed down from father to son. For by accepting the legal fine, the injured man expressly renounced his primæval right of feud.

Then follow some curious laws in favour of the masters of Como, Magistri Comacenes, who seem to have been a guild of architects, perhaps the original germ of the great society of free-masons—belonging, no doubt, to the Roman population—who were settled about the lake of Como, and were hired, on contract, (as the laws themselves express,) to build for the Lombards, who of course had no skill to make anything beyond a skin-tent or a log-hall.

Then follow laws against incendiaries; a fine for damage by accidental house-fire, if the offender have carried fire more than nine feet from the hearth; a law against leaving a fire alight on a journey, as in the Australian colonies now. Then laws to protect mills; important matters in those days, being unknown to the Lombards before their entrance into Italy.

Then laws of inheritance; on which I shall remark, that natural sons, if free, are to have a portion of their father's inheritance; but less than the legitimate sons: but that a natural son born of a slave remains a slave, 'nisi pater liberum thingaverit.' This cruel law was the law of Rome and of the Church; our Anglo-Saxon forefathers, to their honour, held the reverse rule. 'Semper a patre, non a matre, generationis ordo texitur.' Next, it is to be remarked, that no free woman can live in Lombardy, or, I believe, in any Teutonic state, save under the 'mundium' of some one. You should understand this word 'mund.' Among most of the Teutonic races, women, slaves, and youths, at least not of age to carry arms, were under the mund of some one. Of course, primarily the father, head of the family, and if he died, an uncle, elder brother, &c. The married woman was, of course, under the mund of her husband. He was answerable for the good conduct of all under his mund; he had to pay their fines if they offended; and he was bound, on the other hand, to protect them by all lawful means.

This system still lingers in the legal status of women in England, for good and evil; the husband is more or less answerable for the wife's debts; the wife, till lately, was unable to gain property apart from her husband's control; the wife is supposed, in certain cases of law, to act under the husband's compulsion. All these, and many others, are relics of the old system of mund for women; and that system has, I verily believe, succeeded. It has called out, as no other system could have done, chivalry in the man. It has made him feel it a duty and an honour to protect the physically weaker sex. It has made the woman feel that her influence, whether in the state or in the family, is to be not physical and legal, but moral and spiritual; and that it therefore rests on a ground really nobler and deeper than that of the man. The modern experiments for emancipating women from all mund, and placing them on a physical and legal equality with the man, may be right, and may be ultimately successful. We must not hastily prejudge them. But of this we may be almost certain; that if they succeed, they will cause a wide-spread revolution in society, of which the patent danger will be, the destruction of the feeling of chivalry, and the consequent brutalization of the male sex.

Then follow laws relating to marriage and women, of which I may remark, that (as in Tacitus' time), the woman brings her dowry, or 'fader fee,' to her husband; and that the morning after the wedding she receives from him, if he be content with her, her morgen gap, or morning gift; which remains her own private property, unless she misbehaves.

The honour of women, whether in fact or merely in fame, is protected by many severe laws, among which I shall only notice, that the calling a free woman 'striga' (witch) is severely punishable. If any one does so who has the mund of her, except her father or brother, he loses his mund.

On the whole, woman's condition seems inferior to man's on some points: but superior on others. e.g. A woman's weregeld—the price of her life—is 1200 solidi; while the man's is only 900. For he can defend himself, but she cannot. On the other hand, if a man kill his wife, he pays only the 1200 solidi, and loses her dowry: but if she kill him, she dies.

Again. If a free man be caught thieving, up to the amount of 20 siliquæ, beans, *i.e.* one gold piece—though Pope Gregory makes the solidus (aureus) 24 siliquæ—he replaces the theft, and pays 80 solidi, or dies; and a slave one half, or dies.

But if a free woman is taken in theft, she only replaces it; for she has suffered for her wrong-doing, and must lay it to her own shame, that she has tried to do 'operam indecentem,' a foul deed. And if an aldia or slave-woman steals, her master replaces the theft, and pays 40 solidi, minus the value of the stolen goods—and beats her afterwards, I presume, if he chooses.

And now concerning slaves, who seem to have been divided into three classes.

The Aldius and Aldia, masculine and feminine, who were of a higher rank than other slaves.

The Aldius could marry a free woman, while the slave marrying a free woman is punishable by death; and, as experimentum crucis, if an Aldius married an Aldia or a free woman, the children followed the father. If he married a slave, the children followed the mother, and became slaves of his lord.

The Aldius, again, may not sell his lord's land or slaves, which indicates that he held land and slaves under his lord.

What the word means, Grimm does not seem to know. He thinks it synonymous with 'litus,' of whom we hear as early as Tacitus' time, as one of the four classes, nobles, freemen, liti, slaves; and therefore libertus, a freedman. But the word does not merely mean, it appears, a slave half freed by his master; but one rather hereditarily half free, and holding a farm under his lord.

Dió, however, is said to be an old German word for a slave; and it is possible that aldius (a word only known, seemingly, in Lombardy) may have signified originally an old slave, an old Roman colonus, or peasant of some sort, found by the conquerors in possession of land, and allowed to retain, and till it, from father to son. We, in England, had the same distinction between 'Læt,' or 'villains' settled on the land, glebæ adscripti, and mere thralls or theows, slaves pure and simple. No doubt such would have better terms than the mere mancipia—

slaves taken in war, or bought—for the simple reason, that they would be agriculturists, practised in the Roman tillage, understanding the mysteries of irrigation, artificial grasses, and rotation of crops, as well as the culture of vines, fruit, and olives.

Next to them you have different sorts of slaves; Servus massarius, who seems to be also rusticanus, one who takes care of his lord's 'massa' or farm, and is allowed a peculium, it seems, some animals of his own, which he may not sell, though he may give them away. And again, servus doctus, an educated household slave, whose weregeld is higher than that of others.

The laws relating to fugitive slaves seem as merciful as such things can be; and the Lombards have always had the credit of being kind and easy masters.

Connected with fugitive slaves are laws about portunarii, ferrymen, who appear, as you know, in the old ballads as very important, and generally formidable men. The fight between Von Troneg Hagen and the old ferryman in the Nibelungen Lied, is a famous instance of the ancient ferrymen's prowess. One can easily understand how necessary strict laws were, to prevent these ferrymen carrying over fugitive slaves, outlaws, and indeed any one without due caution; for each man was bound to remain in his own province, that he might be ready when called on for military service; and a traveller to foreign parts was looked on as a deserter from his liege-lord and country.

Then follow a great number of laws, to me both amusing and instructive, as giving us some glimpse of the country life of those Lombards in the 8th century.

Scattered in the vast woodlands and marshes lie small farms, enclosed by ditches and posts and rails, from which if you steal a rail, you are fined 1s., if you steal a post, 3s. There were stake fences, which you must be careful in making, for if a horse stakes himself by leaping in, you pay nothing; but if he does so by leaping out, you pay the price of the horse. Moreover, you must leave no sharp stakes standing out of the hedge; for if a man or beast wounds himself thereby in passing, you have to pay full weregeld.

Walking over sown land, or sending a woman of your mundium to do so, in accordance with an ancient superstition, is a severe offence; so is injuring a vineyard, or taking more than tres uvæ (bunches of grapes, I presume) from the vine. Injuring landmarks cut on the trees (theclaturas and signaturas) or any other boundary mark, is severely punishable either in a slave, or in a freeman.

In the vast woods range herds of swine, and in the pastures, horses, cared for by law; for to take a herd of swine or brood mares as pledge, without the king's leave, is punishable by death, or a fine of 900s. Oxen or horses used to the yoke can be taken as pledge; but only by leave of the king, or of the schuldhais (local magistrate), on proof that the debtor has no other property; for by them he gets his living. If, however, you find pigs routing in your enclosure, you may kill one, under certain restrictions, but not the 'sornpair,' sounder boar, who 'battit et vincit' all the other boars in the sounder (old English for herd).

Rival swineherds, as is to be supposed, 'battidunt inter se,' and 'scandalum faciunt,' often enough. Whereon the law advises them to fight it out, and then settle the damage between them.

Horses are cared for.  To ride another man's horse costs 2*s*.; to dock or crop him, eight-fold the damage; and so on of hurting another man's horse.  Moreover, if your neighbour's dog flies at you, you may hit him with a stick or little sword, and kill him, but if you throw a stone after him and kill him, you being then out of danger, you must give the master a new dog.

Then there are quaint laws about hunting; and damage caused by wild beasts caught in snares or brought to bay.  A wounded stag belongs to the man who has wounded it for twenty-four hours: but after that to anyone.  Tame deer, it is observable, are kept; and to kill a doe or fawn costs 6*s*., to kill a buck, 12*s*.  Tame hawks, cranes, and swans, if taken in snares, cost 6*s*.  But any man may take flying hawks out of his neighbour's wood, but not out of the Gaias Regis, the king's gehage, haies, hedges, or enclosed parks.

And now, I have but one more law to mention— would God that it had been in force in later centuries—

'Let no one presume to kill another man's aldia or ancilla, as a striga, witch, which is called masca; because it is not to be believed by Christian minds, that a woman can eat up a live man from within; and if any one does so he shall pay 60*s*. as her price, and for his fault, half to her master, and half to the king.'

This last strange law forces on us a serious question, one which may have been suggesting itself to you throughout my lecture.  If these were the old Teutonic laws, this the old Teutonic liberty, the respect for man as man, for woman as woman, whence came the opposite element?  How is it that these liberties have been lost throughout almost all Europe?  How is it that a system of law prevailed over the whole continent, up to the French revolution, and prevails still in too many countries, the very opposite of all this?

I am afraid that I must answer, Mainly through the influence of the Roman clergy during the middle age.

The original difference of race between the clergy and the Teutonic conquerors, which I have already pointed out to you, had a curious effect, which lingers to this day.  It placed the Church in antagonism, more or less open, to the civil administration of justice.  The criminal was looked on by the priest rather as a sufferer to be delivered, than an offender to be punished.  All who are conversant with the lives of saints must recollect cases in which the saint performs even miracles on behalf of the condemned.  Mediæval tales are full of instances of the same feeling which prompted the Italian brigands, even in our own times, to carry a leaden saint's image in his hat as a safeguard.  In an old French fabliau, for instance, we read how a certain highway-robber was always careful to address his prayers to the Blessed Virgin, before going out to murder and steal; and found the practice pay him well.  For when he was taken and hanged, our Lady put her 'mains blanches' under his feet, and supported him invisibly for a whole day, till the executioner, finding it impossible to kill him, was forced to let him retire peaceably into a monastery, where he lived and died devoutly.  We may laugh at such fancies; or express, if we will, our abhorrence of their immorality: but it will be more useful to examine into the causes which produced them. They seem to have been twofold. In the first place, the Church did not look on the Teutonic laws, whether Frank, Burgund, Goth or Lombard, as law at all. Her law, whether ecclesiastical or civil, was formed on the Roman model; and by it alone she wished herself, and those who were under her protection, to be judged. Next—and this count is altogether to her honour—law, such as it was, was too often administered, especially by the Franks, capriciously and brutally; while the servile population, always the great majority, can hardly be said to have been under the protection of law at all. No one can read the pages of Fredegarius, or Gregory of Tours, without seeing that there must have been cases weekly, even daily, which called on the clergy, in the name of justice and humanity, to deliver if possible, the poor from him that spoiled him; which excused fully the rise of the right of sanctuary, and of benefit of clergy, afterwards so much abused; which made it a pious duty in prelates to work themselves into power at court, and there, as the 'Chancellors' of princes, try to get something like regular justice done; and naturally enough, to remodel the laws of each nation on the time-honoured and scientific Roman form. Nevertheless, the antagonism of the Church to the national and secular law remained for centuries. It died out first perhaps, in England, after the signature of Magna Charta. For then the English prelates began to take up that truly Protestant and national attitude which issued in the great Reformation: but it lingers still in Ireland and in Italy. It lingered in France up to the French revolution, as may be seen notably in the account of the execution of the Marquise de Brinvilliers, by the priest who attended her. Horror at her atrocious crimes is quite swallowed up, in the mind of the good father, by sympathy with her suffering; and the mob snatch her bones from the funeral pile, and keep them as the relics of a saint.

But more. While the Roman clergy did real good to Europe, in preserving the scientific elements of Roman law, they did harm by preserving therewith other elements—Roman chicane, and Roman cruelty. In that respect, as in others, 'Rome conquered her conquerors;' and the descendants of those Roman lawyers, whom the honest Teutons called adders, and as adders killed them down, destroyed, in course of time, Teutonic freedom.

But those descendants were, alas! the clergy. Weak, they began early to adopt those arms of quibbling and craft, which religious men too often fancy are the proper arms of 'the saints' against 'the world.' Holding human nature in suspicion and contempt, they early gave way to the maxim of the savage, that every one is likely to be guilty till proved innocent, and therefore licensed the stupid brutalities of torture to extract confession. Holding self-degradation to be a virtue, and independence as a carnal vice; glorying in being slaves themselves, till to become, under the name of holy obedience, 'perinde ac cadaver,' was the ideal of a good monk; and accustomed, themselves, to degrading corporal punishment; they did not shrink from inflicting, even on boys and women, tortures as dastardly as indecent. Looking on the world, and on the future of the human race, through a medium compared with which the darkest fancies of a modern fanatic are bright and clear, they did not shrink from inflicting penalties, the very mention of which makes the blood run cold.  Suspecting, if not alternately envying and despising, all women who were not nuns; writing openly of the whole sex (until unsexed) as the snare and curse of mankind; and possessed by a Manichæan belief in the power and presence of innumerable demons, whose especial victims were women; they erected witch-hunting into a science; they pandered to, and actually formalized, and justified on scientific grounds, the most cruel and cowardly superstitions of the mob; and again and again raised literal crusades against women, torturing, exposing, burning, young and old, not merely in the witch-mania of the 17th century, but through the whole middle age.  It is a detestable page of history.  I ask those who may think my statement exaggerated, to consult the original authorities.  Let them contrast Rothar's law about the impossibility of witchcraft, with the pages of the Malleus Maleficarum, Nider's Fornicarium, or Delrio the Jesuit, and see for themselves who were the false teachers.  And if they be told, that the cruelties of the Inquisition were only those in vogue according to the secular law of the day, let them recollect that the formulizers of that law were none other than the celibate Roman clergy.

I do not deny that there was in all this a just, though a terrible, Nemesis.  What was the essential fault of these Lombard laws—indeed of all the Teutonic codes? This—that there was one law for the free man, another for the slave. Ecclesiastical dominion was necessary, to make one law for all classes, even though it were a law of common slavery. As the free had done to the slave, even so, and far worse, would the Roman clergy do to them. The Albigense persecutors, burning sixty ladies in one day; Conrad of Marpurg scourging his own sovereign, St. Elizabeth; shaving the Count of Saiym's head; and burning noble ladies almost without trial; Sprenger and his compeers, offering up female hecatombs of the highest blood thoughout Germany; English bishops burning in Smithfield Anne Askew, the hapless court-beauty, and her fellow-courtier Mr. Lascelles, just as if they had been Essex or Berkshire peasants;—all these evildoers were welding the different classes of the European nations, by a community of suffering, into nations; into the belief that free and slave had one blood, one humanity, one conscience, one capacity of suffering; and at last, one capacity of rebelling, and making common cause, high and low alike, against him who reigned in Italy under the 'Romani nominis umbram.'

And if our English law, our English ideas of justice and mercy, have retained, more than most European codes, the freedom, the truthfulness, the kindliness, of the old Teutonic laws, we owe it to the fact, that England escaped, more than any other land, the taint of effete Roman civilization; that she therefore first of the lands, in the 12th century, rebelled against, and first of them, in the 16th century, threw off, the Ultramontane yoke.

And surely it will be so, in due time, with the descendants of these very Lombards. We have seen them in these very years arise out of the dust and shame of centuries, and determine to be Lombards once again.  We have seen a hero arise among them of the true old Teuton stamp, bearing worthily the name which his forefathers brought over the Alps with Alboin—Garibald, the 'bold in war.'  May they succeed in the same noble struggle as that in which we succeeded, and returning, not in letter, but in spirit, to the old laws of Rothar and their free forefathers, become the leading race of a free and united Italy!

# THE POPES & THE LOMBARDS

'Our Lady the Mother of God, even Virgin Maria, together with us, protests to you, adjuring you with great obligations, and admonishes and commands you, and with her the thrones, dominations, all the heavenly angels, the martyrs and confessors of Christ, on behalf of the Roman city, committed to us by the Lord God, and the sheep of the Lord dwelling in it.  Defend and free it speedily from the hands of the persecuting Lombards, lest my body which suffered torments for Christ, and my home in which it rests by the command of God, be contaminated by the people of the Lombards, who are guilty of such iniquitous perjury, and are proud transgressors of the divine scripture.  So will I at the day of judgment reward you with my patronage, and prepare for you in the kingdom of God most shining and glorious tabernacles, promising you the reward of eternal retribution, and the infinite joys of paradise.

'Run, by the true and living God I exhort you, run, and help; before the living fountain, whence you were consecrated and born again, shall dry up: before the little spark remaining of that brilliant flame, from which you knew the light, be extinguished; before your spiritual mother, the holy Church of God, in which you hope to receive eternal life, shall be humiliated, invaded, violated, and defiled by the impious.

'But if not, may your provinces in return, and your possessions, be invaded by people whom you know not.

Separate not yourselves from my Roman people; so you will not be aliens, and separate from the kingdom of God, and eternal life. For whatever you shall ask of me, I will surely give you, and be your patron. Assist my Roman people, your brothers; and strive more perfectly; for it is written, No man receiveth the crown, unless he strive lawfully.

'I conjure you, most beloved, by the living God, leave not this my city of Rome to be any longer torn by the Lombards, lest your bodies and souls be torn and tormented for ever, in inextinguishable and Tartarian fire with the devil and his pestiferous angels; and let not the sheep of the Lord's flock, which are the Roman people, be dispersed any more, lest the Lord disperse you, and cast you forth as the people of Israel was dispersed.'

You will conclude, doubtless, that this curious document can be nothing but a papal allocution. Its peculiar scriptural style (wrongly supposed to have been invented by the Puritans, who merely learnt it from the old Roman clergy), as well as the self-conceit, which fancies the fate of the whole world to depend on the prosperity of a small half-ruined city in Italy, will be to you sufficient marks of the Roman hand. But you will be somewhat mistaken. It is hardly an epistle from the successor of St. Peter. It professes to be an epistle from St. Peter himself, and sent by him through the hands of Pope Stephen III. to Pepin the king of the Franks, in the year 755. You will have concluded also from it, that Catholic Christianity is in its extreme agony; that the worship and name of our Lord, and the fountains of sacramental grace are about to be extinguished for ever,

and that nothing but heresy or heathendom can follow.
Then you will be quite mistaken.  These Lombards are
pious Catholics.  Builders of churches and monasteries,
they are taking up the relics of the Roman martyrs, to
transfer them to the churches of Milan and Pavia.  They
have just given Pope Stephen the most striking proof of
their awe of his person and office.  But they are quarrelling with him about the boundaries of his estates for
the patrimony of St. Peter.  They consider that he and
his predecessors have grossly wronged them at different
times; and now last of all, by calling in foreign invaders;
and they are at the gates of Rome laying waste the country, and demanding a poll-tax as ransom.  That is all.

The causes which led to this quarrel must be sought
far back in history.  The original documents in which
you will find the facts will be Paulus Diaconus, as far
as King Luitprand's death; then the Life and Writings
of Gregory the Great; and then Baronius' Annals, especially his quotations from Anastasius' Life of Stephen
III., bearing in mind that, as with the Ostrogoths, we
have only the Roman Papal story; that the Lombards
have never stated their case, not even through Paulus
Diaconus, who, being a clergyman, prudently holds his
tongue about the whole matter.  But by far the best account is to be found in Dean Milman's 'Latin Christianity,' Vols. I. and II.  Rome, you must understand, has
become gradually the patrimony of St. Peter; the Popes
are the practical kings of Rome, possessing, in the name
of the Church, much land round Rome, and many estates scattered throughout Italy, and even in Sicily, Gaul,
Africa, and the East—estates probably bequeathed by

pious people. They have succeeded to this jurisdiction simply by default. They rule Rome, because there is no one else to rule it. We find St. Gregory the Great feeding the pauper-masses of Rome, on the first day of every month, from the fruitful corn-bearing estates in Sicily; keeping up the 'Panem;' but substituting, thank Heaven, for the 'Circenses' at least the services of the Church. Of course, the man who could keep the Roman people alive must needs become, ipso facto, their monarch.

The Pope acknowledges, of course, a certain allegiance to the Emperor at Constantinople, and therefore to his representative, the Exarch of Ravenna: that is to say, he meets them with flattery when they are working on his side; with wrath when they oppose him. He intrigues with them, too, whenever he can safely do so, against the Lombards.

Thus the Pope has become, during the four centuries which followed the destruction of the Western Empire, the sole surviving representative of that Empire. He is the head of the 'gens togata;' of the 'Senatus Populusque Romanus.' In him Rome has risen again out of her grave, to awe the peoples once more by the Romani nominis umbra; and to found a new Empire; not as before, on physical force, and the awe of visible power; but on the deeper and more enduring ground of spiritual force, and the awe of the invisible world.

An Empire, I say. The Popes were becoming, from the 5th to the 8th centuries, not merely the lords of Rome, but the lords of the Western Church. Their spiritual Empire, to do them justice, was not so much deliberately sought by them, as thrust upon them. As the clergy were, all over the Empire, the representatives of the down-trodden Romans, so they naturally gravitated toward the Eternal City, their ancient mistress. Like all disciplined and organized bodies they felt the need of unity, of monarchy. Where could they find it, save at Rome? Rome was still, practically and in fact, the fountain of their doctrine, of their superior civilization; and to submit themselves to the Pope of Rome was their only means of keeping up one faith, one practice, and the strength which comes from union.

To seat the Pope upon the throne of the Cæsars; to attribute to him powers weightier than all which the Cæsars had possest . . . It was a magnificent idea. A politic idea, too; for it would cover the priesthood with all the prestige of ancient Rome, and enable them to face the barbarian in the name of that great people whose very memory still awed him; whose baths, aqueducts, palaces, he looked on as the work of demons; whose sages and poets were to him enchanters; whose very gems, dug out of the ruins by night, in fear and trembling, possest magic influence for healing, for preservation, for good fortune in peace or war.

Politic; and in their eyes, true. Easy enough to be believed honestly, by men who already believed honestly in their own divine mission. They were the representatives of Christ on earth. Of that fact there could be then, or can be now, no doubt whatsoever. Whatsoever truth, light, righteousness, there was in the West, came to it through them. And Christ was the King of kings. But He delayed his coming: at moments, He seemed to have deserted the earth, and left mankind to tear itself in pieces, with wild war and misrule. But it could not be so. If Christ were absent, He must at least have left an authority behind Him to occupy till He came; a head and ruler for his opprest and distracted Church. And who could that be, if not the Pope of Rome?

It ought to be so.—It must be so—thought they. And to men in that mood, proofs that it was so soon came to hand, and accumulated from generation to generation; till the Pope at last found himself proclaiming, and what was more, believing, that God had given the whole world to St. Peter, and through St. Peter to him; and that he was the only source of power, law, kingship, who could set up and pull down whom he would, as the vicegerent of God on earth.

Such pretensions, of course, grew but slowly. It was not, I believe, till the year 875, 180 years after the time of which I am speaking, that Pope John VIII. distinctly asserted his right, as representative of the ancient Roman Empire, to create the Cæsar; and informed the Synod of Pavia that he had 'elected and approved Charles the Bald, with the consent of his brothers the bishops, of the other ministers of the Holy Roman Church, and' (significant, though empty words) 'of the Roman senate and people.'

At the time of which I speak, the power was still in embryo, growing, through many struggles: but growing surely and strongly, and destined speedily to avenge the fall of Rome on the simple barbarians who were tearing each other to pieces over her spoils.

It is not easy to explain the lasting and hereditary hatred of the Popes to the Lombards. Its origin is simple enough: but not so its continuance.  Why they should be nefandissimi in the eyes of Pope Gregory the Great one sees: but why 100 years afterwards, they should be still nefandissimi, and 'non dicenda gens Langobardorum,' not to be called a nation, is puzzling.

At first, of course, the Pope could only look on them as a fresh horde of barbarous conquerors; half heathen, half Arian.  Their virtuous and loyal life within the boundaries of Alboin's conquests—of which Paulus Diaconus says, that violence and treachery were unknown—that no one oppressed, no one plundered—that the traveller went where he would in perfect safety—all this would be hid from the Pope by the plain fact, that they were continually enlarging their frontier toward Rome; that they had founded two half-independent Dukedoms of Beneventum and Spoleto, that Autharis had swept over South Italy, and ridden his horse into the sea at Reggio, to strike with his lance a column in the waves, and cry, 'Here ends the Lombard kingdom.'

The Pope (Gregory the Great I am speaking of) could only recollect, again, that during the lawless interregnum before Autharis' coronation, the independent Lombard dukes had plundered churches and monasteries, slain the clergy, and destroyed the people, who had 'grown up again like corn.'

But as years rolled on, these Arian Lombards had become good Catholics; and that in the lifetime of Gregory the Great.

Theodelinda, the Bavarian princess, she to whom Autharis had gone in disguise to her father's court, and only confessed himself at his departure, by rising in his stirrups, and burying his battle-axe in a tree stem with the cry, 'Thus smites Autharis the Lombard,'—this Theodelinda, I say, had married after his death Agilwulf his cousin, and made him king of the Lombards.

She was a Catholic; and through her Gregory the Great converted Autharis, and the Lombard nation. To her he addressed those famous dialogues of his, full alike of true piety and earnestness, and of childish superstition. But in judging them and him we must bear in mind, that these Lombards became at least by his means Catholics, and that Arians would have believed in the superstitions just as much as Catholics. And it is surely better to believe a great truth, plus certain mistakes which do not affect it in the least, than a great lie, plus the very same mistakes likewise. Which is best, to believe that the road to London lies through Bishopstortford, and that there are dog-headed men on the road: or that it lies through Edinburgh, but that there are dog-headed men on that road too?

Theodelinda had built at Modicæa, twelve miles above Milan, a fair basilica to John the Baptist, enriched by her and the Lombard kings and dukes, 'crowns, crosses, golden tables adorned with emeralds, hyacinths, amber, carbuncles and pearls, gold and silver altar-cloths, and that admirable cup of sapphire,' all which remained till the eighteenth century. There, too, was the famous iron crown of Lombardy, which Austria still claims as her own; so called from a thin ring of iron inserted in it, made from a nail of the true cross which Gregory had sent Agilwulf; just as he sent Childebert, the Frankish king, some filings of St. Peter's chains; which however, he says, did not always allow their sacred selves to be filed.

In return, Agilwulf had restored the church-property which he had plundered, had reinstated the bishops; and why did not all go well? Why are these Lombards still the most wicked of men?

Again, in the beginning of the eighth century came the days of the good Luitprand, 'wise and pious, a lover of peace, and mighty in war; merciful to offenders, chaste and modest, instant in prayer, bountiful in alms, equal to the philosophers, though he knew no letters, a nourisher of his people, an augmenter of the laws.' He it was, who, when he had quarrelled with Pope Gregory II., and marched on Rome, was stopped at the Gates of the Vatican by the Pontiff's prayers and threats. And a sacred awe fell on him; and humbly entering St. Peter's, he worshipped there, and laid on the Apostle's tomb his royal arms, his silver cross and crown of gold, and withdrawing his army, went home again in peace. But why were this great king's good deeds towards the Pope and the Catholic faith rewarded, by what we can only call detestable intrigue and treachery?

Again; Leo the Iconoclast Emperor destroyed the holy images in the East, and sent commands to the Exarch of Ravenna to destroy them in western Italy. Pope Gregory II. replied by renouncing allegiance to the Emperor of Constantinople; and by two famous letters which are still preserved; in which he tells the Iconoclast Emperor, that, 'if he went round the grammar-schools at Rome, the children would throw their horn-books at his head . . . that he implored Christ to send the Emperor a devil, for the destruction of his body and the salvation of his soul . . . that if he attempted to destroy the images in Rome, the pontiff would take refuge with the Lombards, and then he might as well chase the wind that the Popes were the mediators of peace between East and West, and that the eyes of the nations were fixed on the Pope's humility, and adored as a God on earth the apostle St. Peter. And that the pious Barbarians, kindled into rage, thirsted to avenge the persecution of the East.' Then Luitprand took up the cause of the Pope and his images, and of the mob, who were furious at the loss of their idols; and marched on Ravenna, which opened her gates to him, so that he became master of the whole Pentapolis; and image-worship, to which some plain-spoken people give a harsher name, was saved for ever and a day in Italy. Why did Gregory II. in return, call in Orso, the first Venetian Doge, to expel from Ravenna the very Luitprand who had fought his battles for him, and to restore that Exarchate of Ravenna, of which it was confessed, that its civil quarrels, misrule, and extortions, made it the most miserable government in Italy? And why did he enter into secret negotiations with the Franks to come and invade Italy?

Again, when Luitprand wanted to reduce the duchies of Beneventum and Spoleto, which he considered as rebels against him, their feudal suzerain; why did the next Pope, Gregory III., again send over the Alps to Charles Martel to come and invade Italy, and deliver the Church and Christ's people from ruin?

And who were these Franks, the ancestors of that

magnificent, but profligate aristocracy whose destruction our grandfathers beheld in 1793? I have purposely abstained from describing them, till they appear upon the stage of Italy, and take part in her fortunes—which were then the fortunes of the world.

They appear first on the Roman frontier in A.D. 241, and from that time are never at rest till they have conquered the north of Gaul. They are supposed (with reason) not to have been a race or tribe at all; but a confederation of warriors, who were simply 'Franken,' 'free;' 'free companions,' or 'free lances,' as they would have been called a few centuries later; who recruited themselves from any and every tribe who would join them in war and plunder. If this was the case; if they had thrown away, as adventurers, much of the old Teutonic respect for law, for the royal races, for family life, for the sacred bonds of kindred, many of their peculiarities are explained. Falsehood, brutality, lawlessness, ignorance, and cruelty to the conquered Romans, were their special sins; while their special, and indeed only virtue, was that indomitable daring which they transmitted to their descendants for so many hundred years. The buccaneers of the young world, they were insensible to all influences save that of superstition. They had become, under Clovis, orthodox Christians: but their conversion, to judge from the notorious facts of history, worked little improvement on their morals. The pages of Gregory of Tours are comparable, for dreary monotony of horrors, only to those of Johnson's History of the Pyrates.

But, as M. Sismondi well remarks, their very ignorance and brutality made them the more easily the tools of the Roman clergy: 'Cette haute vénération pour l'Église, et leur sévère orthodoxie, d'autant plus facile à conserver que, ne faisant aucune étude, et ne disputant jamais sur la foi, ils ne connaissaient pas même les questions controversées, leur donnèrent dans le clergé de puissants auxiliaires. Les Francs se montrèrent disposés à haïr les Ariens, à les combattres, et les dépouiller sans les entendre; les évêques, en retour, ne se montrèrent pas scrupuleux sur le reste des enseignements moraux de la religion: ils fermèrent les yeux sur les violences, le meurtre, le déréglement des moeurs; ils autorisèrent en quelque sorte publiquement la poligamie, et ils prêchèrent le droit divin des rois et le devoir le l'obéissance pour les peuples.'

A painful picture of the alliance: but, I fear, too true.

The history of these Franks you must read for yourselves. You will find it well told in the pages of Sismondi, and in Mr. Perry's excellent book, 'The Franks.' It suffices now to say, that in the days of Luitprand these Franks, after centuries of confusion and bloodshed, have been united into one great nation, stretching from the Rhine to the Loire and the sea, and encroaching continually to the southward and eastward. The government has long passed out of the hands of their fainéant Meerwing kings into that of the semi-hereditary Majores Domûs, or Mayors of the Palace; and Charles Martel, perhaps the greatest of that race of great men, has just made himself mayor of Austrasia (the real Teutonic centre of Frank life and power), Neustria and Burgundy. He has crushed Eudo, the duke of Romanized Aquitaine, and has finally delivered France and Christendom from the invading Saracens. On his Franks, and on the Lombards of Italy, rest, for the moment, the destinies of Europe.

For meanwhile another portent has appeared, this time out of the far East. Another swarm of destroyers has swept over the earth. The wild Arabs of the desert, awakening into sudden life and civilization under the influence of a new creed, have overwhelmed the whole East, the whole north of Africa, destroying the last relics of Roman and Greek civilization, and with them the effete and semi-idolatrous Christianity of the Empire. All the work of Narses and Belisarius is undone. Arab Emirs rule in the old kingdom of the Vandals. The new human deluge has crossed the Straits into Europe. The Visigoths, enervated by the luxurious climate of Spain, have recoiled before the Mussulman invaders. Roderick, the last king of the Goths, is wandering as an unknown penitent in expiation of his sin against the fair Cava, which brought down (so legends and ballads tell) the scourge of God upon the hapless land; and the remnants of the old Visigoths and Sueves are crushed together into the mountain fastnesses of Asturias and Gallicia, thence to reissue, after long centuries, as the noble Spanish nation, wrought in the forges of adversity into the likeness of tempered steel; and destined to reconquer, foot by foot, their native land from the Moslem invader.

But at present the Crescent was master of the Cross; and beyond the Pyrenees all was slavery and 'miscreance.' The Arabs, invading France in 732, in countless thousands, had been driven back at the great fight of Tours, with a slaughter so great, that the excited imagination of Paulus Diaconus sees 375,000 miscreants dead upon the field, while only 1500 Franks had perished. But home troubles had prevented 'the Hammer of the Moors' from following up his victory. The Saracens had returned in force in 737, and again in 739. They still held Narbonne. The danger was imminent. There was no reason why they should not attempt a third invasion. Why should they not spread along the shores of the Mediterranean, establishing themselves there, as they were already doing in Sicily, and menacing Rome from north as well as south? To unite, therefore, the two great Catholic Teutonic powers, the Frank and the Lombard, for the defence of Christendom, should have been the policy of him who called himself the Chief Pontiff in Christendom. Yet the Pope preferred, in the face of that great danger, to set the Teutonic nations on destroying each other, rather than to unite them against the Moslem.

The bribe offered to the Frank was significant—the title of Roman Consul; beside which he was to have filings of St. Peter's chains, and the key of his tomb, to preserve him body and soul from all evil.

Charles would not come. Frank though he was, he was too honourable to march at a priest's bidding against Luitprand, his old brother in arms, to whom he had sent the boy Pepin, his son, that Luitprand might take him on his knee, and cut his long royal hair, and become his father-in-arms, after the good old Teuton fashion; Luitprand, who with his Lombards had helped him to save Christendom a second time from the Mussulman in 737. The Pope, one would think, should have remembered that good deed of the good Lombard's whereof his epitaph sings,

> 'Deinceps tremuere feroces
> Usque Saraceni, quos dispulit impiger, ipsos
> Cum premerent Gallos, Karolo poscente juvari.'

So Charles Martel took the title of Patrician from the Pope, but sent him no armies; and the quarrel went on; while Charles filled up the measure of his iniquity by meddling with that church-property in Gaul which his sword had saved from the hordes of the Saracens; and is now, as St. Eucherius (or Bishop Hincmar) saw in a vision, writhing therefore in the lowest abyss of hell.

So one generation more passes by; and then Pepin le Bref, grown to manhood, is less scrupulous than his father. He is bound to the Pope by gratitude. The Pope has confirmed him as king, allowing him to depose the royal house of the Merovingians, and so assumed the right of making kings.—A right which future popes will not forget.

Meanwhile the Pope has persuaded the Lombard king Rachis to go into a monastery. Astulf seizes the crown, and attacks Ravenna. The Pope succeeding, Stephen III., opposes him; and he marches on Rome, threatening to assault it, unless the citizens redeem their lives by a poll-tax.

Stephen determines to go himself to Pepin to ask for help: and so awful has the name and person of a Pope become, that he is allowed to do it; allowed to pass safely and unarmed through the very land upon which he is going to let loose all the horrors of invading warfare.

It is a strange, and instructive figure, that. The dread of the unseen, the fear of spiritual power, has fallen on the wild Teutons; on Frank and on Lombard alike. The Pope and his clergy are to them magicians, against whom neither sword nor lance avails; who can heal the sick and blast the sound; who can call to their aid out of the clouds that pantheon of demi-gods, with which, under the name of saints, they have peopled heaven; who can let loose on them the legions of fiends who dwell in every cave, every forest, every ruin, every cloud; who can, by the sentence of excommunication, destroy both body and soul in hell. They were very loth to fear God, these wild Teutons; therefore they had instead, as all men have who will not fear God, to fear the devil.

So Pope Stephen goes to Pepin, the eldest son of the Church. He promises to come with all his Franks. Stephen's conscience seems to have been touched: he tries to have no fighting, only negotiation: but it is too late now. Astolf will hear of no terms; Pepin sweeps over the Alps, and at the gates of Pavia dictates his own terms to the Lombards. The old Lombard spirit seems to have past away.

Pepin goes back again, and Astolf refuses to fulfil his promises. The Pope sends Pepin that letter from St. Peter himself with which this lecture commenced.

Astolf has marched down, as we heard, to the walls of Rome, laying the land waste; cutting down the vines, carrying off consecrated vessels, insulting the sacrament of the altar. The Lombards have violated nuns; and tried to kill them, the Pope says; though, if they had really tried, one cannot see why they should not have succeeded. In fact, Pope Stephen's hysterical orations to Pepin must be received with extreme caution. No Catholic historian of that age cares to examine the truth of a fact which makes for him; nothing is too bad to say of an enemy: and really the man who would forge a letter from St. Peter might dare to tell a few lesser falsehoods into the bargain. Pepin cannot but obey so august a summons; and again he is in Italy, and the Lombards dare not resist him. He seizes not only all that Astolf had taken from the Pope, but the Pentapolis and Exarchate, the property, if of any one, of the Greek Emperors, and bestows them on Stephen, the Pope, and 'the holy Roman Republic.'

The pope's commissioners received the keys of the towns, which were placed upon the altar of St. Peter; and this, the Dotation of Pepin, the Dotation of the Exarchate, was the first legal temporal sovereignty of the Popes:—born in sin, and conceived in iniquity, as you may see.

The Lombard rule now broke up rapidly. The Lombards of Spoleto yielded to the double pressure of Franks and Romans, asked to be 'taken into the service of St. Peter,' and clipt their long German locks after the Roman fashion.

Charlemagne, in his final invasion, had little left to do. He confirmed Pepin's gift, and even, though he hardly kept his promise, enlarged it to include the whole of Italy, from Lombardy to the frontier of Naples, while he himself became king of Lombardy, and won the iron crown.

And so by French armies—not for the last time—

was the Pope propt up on his ill-gotten throne.

But the mere support of French armies was not enough to seat the Pope securely upon the throne of the western Cæsars. Documentary evidence was required to prove that they possessed Rome, not as the vassals of the Frankish Kaisers, or of any barbarian Teutons whatsoever; but in their own right, as hereditary sovereigns of Rome. And the documents, when needed, were forthcoming. Under the name of St. Isidore, some ready scribe produced the too-famous 'Decretals,' and the 'Donation of Constantine,' and Pope Adrian I. saw no reason against publishing them to Charlemagne and to the world.

It was discovered suddenly, by means of these remarkable documents, that Constantine the Great had been healed of leprosy, and afterwards baptized, by Pope Sylvester; that he had, in gratitude for his cure, resigned to the Popes his western throne, and the patrimony of St. Peter, and the sovereignty of Italy and the West; and that this was the true reason of his having founded Constantinople, as a new seat of government for the remnant of his empire.

This astounding falsehood was, of course, accepted humbly by the unlettered Teutons; and did its work well, for centuries to come. It is said—I trust not truly—to be still enrolled among the decrees of the Canon law, though reprobated by all enlightened Roman Catholics. Be that as it may, on the strength of this document the Popes began to assume an all but despotic sovereignty over the western world, and—the Teutonic peoples, and Rome's conquest of her conquerors was at last complete.

What then were the causes of the Papal hatred of a race who were good and devout Catholics for the last 200 years of their rule?

There were deep political reasons (in the strictest, and I am afraid lowest sense of the word); but over and above them there were evidently moral reasons, which lay even deeper still.

A free, plain-spoken, practical race like these Lombards; living by their own laws; disbelieving in witchcraft; and seemingly doing little for monasticism, were not likely to find favour in the eyes of popes. They were not the material which the Papacy could mould into the Neapolitan ideal of 'Little saints,—and little asses.' These Lombards were not a superstitious race; they did not, like the Franks and Anglo-Saxons, crowd into monasteries. I can only find four instances of Lombard sovereigns founding monasteries in all Paulus' history. One of them, strangely enough, is that of the very Astulf against whom the Pope fulminated so loudly the letter from St. Peter which I read you.

Moreover, it must be said in all fairness—the Lombards despised the Romans exceedingly. So did all the Teutons. 'We Lombards,' says Bishop Luitprand, 'Saxons, Franks, Lorrainers, Bavarians, Sueves, Burgunds, consider it a sufficient insult to call our enemy a Roman; comprehending in that one name of Roman, whatever is ignoble, cowardly, avaricious, luxurious, false, in a word, every vice.' If this was—as it very probably was—the feeling of the whole Teutonic race; and if it was repaid—as it certainly was—on the part of the Roman, by contempt for the 'barbarism' and 'ignorance' of the Teuton; what must have been the feeling between Roman and Lombard?  Contact must have embittered mutual contempt into an utter and internecine hatred, in which the Pope, as representative of the Roman people, could not but share.

As for the political reasons, they are clear enough.  It is absurd to say that they wished to free Italy from Lombard tyrants.  What did they do but hand her over to Frankish tyrants instead?  No.  The true reason was this. Gradually there had arisen in the mind of all Popes, from Gregory the Great onward, the idea of a spiritual supremacy, independent of all kings of the earth.  It was a great idea, as the event proved: it was a beneficent one for Europe; but a ruinous one for Italy.  For the Popes were not content with spiritual power.  They could not conceive of it as separated from temporal power, and temporal power meant land.  How early they set their hearts on the Exarchate of Ravenna, we shall never know: the fact is patent, that it was a Naboth's vineyard to them; and that to obtain it they called in the Franks.

Their dread was, evidently, lest the Lombards should become masters of the whole of Italy.  A united Italy suited their views then, no more than it does now.  Not only did they conceive of Rome as still the centre of the western world, but more, their stock in trade was at Rome. The chains of St. Peter, the sepulchres of St. Peter and St. Paul, the catacombs filled with the bones of innumerable martyrs;—these were their stock in trade.  By giving these, selling these, working miracles with these, calling pilgrims from all parts of Christendom to visit these in situ, they kept up their power and their wealth. I do not accuse them of misusing that power and that wealth in those days. They used them, on the contrary, better than power and wealth had been ever used in the world before. But they were dependent on the sanctity attached to a particular spot; and any power, which, like the Lombard, tended to give Italy another centre than Rome, they dreaded and disliked. That Lombard basilica, near Milan, with all its treasures, must have been in their eyes, a formidable rival. Still more frightful must it have been to them to see Astulf, when he encamped before the walls of Rome, searching for martyrs' relics, and carrying them off to Milan. That, as a fact, seems to have been the exciting cause of Stephen's journey to Pepin. This Astulf was a good Catholic. He founded a nunnery, and put his own daughters in it. What could a man do more meritorious in the eyes of the Pope? But he took away the lands of the Church, and worse, the relics, the reserved capital by which the Church purchased lands. This was indeed a crime only to be expiated by the horrors of a Frank invasion.

On the same principle the Popes supported the Exarchs of Ravenna, and the independent duchies of Spoleto and Beneventum. Well or ill ruled, Iconoclast or not, they were necessary to keep Italy divided and weak. And having obtained what they wanted from Pepin and Charlemagne, it was still their interest to pursue the same policy; to compound for their own independence, as they did with Charlemagne and his successors, by defending the pretences of foreign kings to the sovereignty of the rest of Italy. This has been their policy for centuries.  It is their policy still; and that policy has been the curse of Italy.  This fatal gift of the patrimony of St. Peter—as Dante saw—as Machiavelli saw,—as all clear-sighted Italians have seen,—as we are seeing it now in these very days—has kept her divided, torn by civil wars, conquered and reconquered by foreign invaders. Unable, as a celibate ecclesiastic, to form his dominions into a strong hereditary kingdom; unable, as the hierophant of a priestly caste, to unite his people in the bonds of national life; unable, as Borgia tried to do, to conquer the rest of Italy for himself; and form it into a kingdom large enough to have weight in the balance of power; the Pope has been forced, again and again, to keep himself on his throne by intriguing with foreign princes, and calling in foreign arms; and the bane of Italy, from the time of Stephen III. to that of Pius IX., has been the temporal power of the Pope.

But on the popes, also, the Nemesis came.  In building their power on the Roman relics, on the fable that Rome was the patrimony of Peter, they had built on a lie; and that lie avenged itself.

Had they been independent of the locality of Rome; had they been really spiritual emperors, by becoming cosmopolitan, journeying, it may be, from nation to nation in regular progresses, then their power might have been as boundless as they ever desired it should be. Having committed themselves to the false position of being petty kings of a petty kingdom, they had to endure continual treachery and tyranny from their foreign allies; to see not merely Italy, but Rome itself insulted, and even sacked, by faithful Catholics; and to become more and more, as the centuries rolled on, the tools of those very kings whom they had wished to make their tools.

True, they defended themselves long, and with astonishing skill and courage. Their sources of power were two, the moral, and the thaumaturgic; and they used them both: but when the former failed, the latter became useless. As long as their moral power was real; as long as they and their clergy were on the whole, in spite of enormous faults, the best men in Europe; so long the people believed in them, and in their thaumaturgic relics likewise. But they became by no means the best men in Europe. Then they began to think that after all it was more easy to work the material than the moral power— easier to work the bones than to work righteousness. They were deceived. Behold! when the righteousness was gone, the bones refused to work. People began to question the virtues of the bones, and to ask, We can believe that the bones may have worked miracles for good men, but for bad men? We will examine whether they work any miracles at all. And then, behold, it came out that the bones did not work miracles, and that possibly they were not saints' bones at all; and then the storm came: and the lie, as all lies do, punished itself. The salt had lost its savour. The Teutonic intellect appealed from its old masters to God, and to God's universe of facts, and emancipated itself once and for all. They who had been the light of Europe, became its darkness; they who had been first, became last; a warning to mankind until the end of time, that on Truth and Virtue depends the only abiding strength.

# THE STRATEGY OF PROVIDENCE

I no not know whether any of you know much of the theory of war. I know very little myself. But something of it one is bound to know, as Professor of History. For, unfortunately, a large portion of the history of mankind is the history of war; and the historian, as a man who wants to know how things were done—as distinct from the philosopher, the man who wants to know how things ought to have been done—ought to know a little of the first of human arts—the art of killing. What little I know thereof I shall employ to-day, in explaining to you the invasion of the Teutons, from a so-called mechanical point of view. I wish to shew you how it was possible for so small and uncivilized a people to conquer one so vast and so civilized; and what circumstances (which you may attribute to what cause you will: but I to God) enabled our race to conquer in the most vast and important campaign the world has ever seen.

I call it a campaign rather than a war. Though it lasted 200 years and more, it seems to me (it will, I think, seem to you) if you look at the maps, as but one campaign: I had almost said, one battle. There is but one problem to be solved; and therefore the operations of our race take a sort of unity. The question is, how to take Rome, and keep it, by destroying the Roman Empire.

Let us consider the two combatants—their numbers, and their position.

One glance at the map will shew you which are the most numerous. When you cast your eye over the vastness of the Roman Empire from east to west—Italy, Switzerland, half Austria, Turkey and Greece, Asia Minor, Syria, Egypt, North Africa, Spain, France, Britain—and then compare it with the narrow German strip which reaches from the mouth of the Danube to the mouth of the Rhine, the disparity of area is enormous; ten times as great at least; perhaps more, if you accept, as I am inclined to do, the theory of Dr. Latham, that we were always 'Markmen,' men of the Marches, occupying a narrow frontier between the Slavs and the Roman Empire; and that Tacitus has included among Germans, from hearsay, many tribes of the interior of Bohemia, Prussia, and Poland, who were Slavs or others; and that the numbers and area of our race has been, on Tacitus' authority, greatly overrated.

What then were the causes of the success of the Teutons? Native courage and strength?

They had these: but you must recollect what I have told you, that those very qualities were employed against them; that they were hired, in large numbers, into the Roman armies, to fight against their own brothers.

Unanimity? Of that, alas! one can say but little. The great Teutonic army had not only to fight the Romans, but to fight each brigade the brigade before it, to make them move on; and the brigade behind it likewise, to prevent their marching over them; while too often two brigades quarrelled like children, and destroyed each other on the spot.

What, then, was the cause of their success? I think

a great deal of it must be attributed to their admirable military position.

Look at a map of Europe; putting yourself first at the point to be attacked—at Rome, and looking north, follow the German frontier from the Euxine up the Danube and down the Rhine. It is a convex arc: but not nearly as long as the concave arc of the Roman frontier opposed to it. The Roman frontier overlaps it to the north-west by all Britain, to the south-west by part of Turkey and the whole of Asia Minor.

That would seem to make it weak, and liable to be outflanked on either wing. In reality it made it strong.

Both the German wings rested on the sea; one on the Euxine, one on the North Sea. That in itself would not have given strength; for the Roman fleets were masters of the seas. But the lands in the rear, on either flank, were deserts, incapable of supporting an army. What would have been the fate of a force landed at the mouth of the Weser on the north, or at the mouth of the Dnieper at the west? Starvation among wild moors, and bogs, and steppes, if they attempted to leave their base of operations on the coast. The Romans saw this, and never tried the plan. To defend the centre of their position was the safest and easiest plan.

Look at this centre. It is complicated. The Roman position is guarded by the walls of Italy, the gigantic earthwork of the Alps. To storm them, is impossible. But right and left of them, the German position has two remarkable points—strategic points, which decided the fate of the world.

They are two salient angles, promontories of the

German frontier. The one is north-east of Switzerland; the Allman country, between the head-waters of the Danube and the Upper Rhine, Basle is its apex. Mentz its northern point, Ratisbon its southern. That triangle encloses the end of the Schwartzwald; the Black Forest of primæval oak. Those oaks have saved Europe.

The advantages of a salient angle of that kind, in invading an enemy's country, are manifest. You can break out on either side, and return at once into your own country on 'lines of interior operation;' while the enemy has to march round the angle, three feet for your one, on 'lines of exterior operation.' The early German invaders saw that, and burst again and again into Gaul from that angle. The Romans saw it also (admirable strategists as they were) and built Hadrian's wall right across it, from the Maine to the Danube, to keep them back. And why did not Hadrian's wall keep them back? On account of the Black Forest. The Roman never dared to face it; to attempt to break our centre, and to save Italy by carrying the war into the heart of Germany. They knew (what the invaders of England will discover to their cost) that a close woodland is a more formidable barrier than the Alps themselves. The Black Forest, I say, was the key of our position, and saved our race.

From this salient angle, and along the whole Rhine above it, the Western Teutons could throw their masses into Gaul; Franks, Vandals, Alans, Suevi, following each other in échellon. You know what an échellon means? When bodies of troops move in lines parallel to each other, but each somewhat in the rear of the other, so that their whole position resembles an échelle—a flight of steps. This mode of attack has two great advantages. It cannot be outflanked by the enemy; and he dare not concentrate his forces on the foremost division, and beat the divisions in detail. If he tries to do so, he is outflanked himself; and he is liable to be beaten in detail by continually fresh bodies of troops. Thus only a part of his line is engaged at a time. Now it was en échellon, from necessity, that the tribes moved down. They could not follow immediately in each other's track, because two armies following each other would not have found subsistence in the same country. They had to march in parallel lines; those nearest to Italy moving first; and thus forming a vast échellon, whose advanced left rested on, and was protected by, the Alps.

But you must remember (and this is important) that all these western attacks along the Rhine and Rhone were mistakes, in as far as they were aimed at Rome. The Teutons were not aware, I suppose, that the Alps turned to the South between Gaul and Italy, and ran right down to the Mediterranean. There they found themselves still cut off from Rome by them. Hannibal's pass over the Mont Cenis they seem not to have known. They had to range down to the Mediterranean; turn eastward along the Genoese coast at Nice; and then, far away from their base of operations, were cut off again and again, just as the Cimbri and Teutons were cut off by Marius. All attempts to take Rome from the Piedmontese entrance into Italy failed. But these western attacks had immense effects. They cut the Roman position in two.

And then came out the real weakness of that great ill-gotten Empire, conquered for conquering's sake. To the north-west, the Romans had extended their line far beyond what they could defend. The whole of North Gaul was taken by the Franks. Britain was then isolated, and had to be given up to its fate. South Gaul, being nearer to Italy their base, they could defend, and did, like splendid soldiers as they were; but that defence only injured them. It thrust the foremost columns of the enemy on into Spain. Spain was too far from their base of operation to be defended, and was lost likewise, and seized by Vandals and Suevi. The true point of attack was at the other salient angle of our position, on the Roman right centre.

You know that the Danube as you ascend it lies east and west from the Black Sea to Belgrade; but above the point where the Save enters it, it turns north almost at right angles. This is the second salient point; the real key of the whole Roman Empire. For from this point the Germans could menace—equally, Constantinople and Turkey on the right (I speak always as standing at Rome and looking north), and Italy and Rome on the left. The Danube once crossed, between them and Constantinople was nothing but the rich rolling land of Turkey; between them and Rome nothing but the easy passes of the Carnic Alps, Laybach to Trieste. Trieste was the key of the Roman position. It was, and always will be, a most important point. It might be the centre of a great kingdom. The nation which has it ought to spend its last bullet in defending it.

The Teutons did cross the Danube, as you know, in 376, and had a great victory, of which nothing came but moral force. They waited long in Moesia before they found out the important step which they had made. The genius of Alaric first discovered the key of the Roman position, and discovered that it was in his own hands.

I do not say that no Germans had crossed the Laybach pass before him. On the contrary, Markmen, Quadi, Vandals, seem to have come over it as early as 180, and appeared under the walls of Aquileia. Of course, some one must have gone first, or Alaric would not have known of it. There were no maps then, at least among our race. Their great generals had to feel their way foot by foot, trusting to hearsays of old adventurers, deserters, and what not, as to whether a fruitful country or an impassable alp, a great city or the world's end, was twenty miles a-head of them. Yes, they had great generals among them, and Alaric, perhaps, the greatest.

If you consider Alaric's campaigns, from A.D. 400 to A.D. 415, you will see that the eye of a genius planned them. He wanted Rome, as all Teutons did. He was close to Italy, in the angle of which I just spoke; but instead of going hither, he resolved to go south, and destroy Greece, and he did it. Thereby, if you will consider, he cut the Roman Empire in two. He paralysed and destroyed the right wing of its forces, which might, if he had marched straight for Italy, have come up from Greece and Turkey, to take him in flank and rear. He prevented their doing that; he prevented also their succouring Italy by sea by the same destruction. And then he was free to move on Rome, knowing that he leaves no strong place on his left flank, save Constantinople itself; and that the Ostrogoths, and other tribes left behind, would mask it for him. Then he moved into Italy over the Carnic Alps, and was repulsed the first time at Pollentia.  He was not disheartened; he retired upon Hungary, waited five years, tried it again, and succeeded, after a campaign of two years.

Yes.  He was a great general.  To be able to move vast masses of men safely through a hostile country and in face of an enemy's army (beside women and children) requires an amount of talent bestowed on few.  Alaric could do it. Dietrich the Ostrogoth could do it. Alboin the Lombard could do it, though not under such fearful disadvantages.  There were generals before Marlborough or Napoleon.

And do not fancy that the work was easy; that the Romans were degenerate enough to be an easy prey. Alaric had been certainly beaten out of Italy, even though the victory of Pollentia was exaggerated.  And in 405, Radagast with 200,000 men had tried to take Rome by Alaric's route, and had simply, from want of generalship, been forced to capitulate under the walls of Florence, and the remnant of his army sold for slaves.

Why was Alaric more fortunate?  Because he was a great genius.  And why when he died, did the Goths lose all plan, and wander wildly up Italy, and out into Spain? Because the great genius was gone.  Native Teuton courage could ensure no permanent success against Roman discipline and strategy, unless guided by men like Alaric or Dietrich.

You might fancy the campaign over now: but it was not. Along the country of the Danube, from the Euxine to the Alps, the Teutons had still the advantage of interior lines, and vast bodies of men—Herules, Gepids,

Ostrogoths, Lombards—were coming down in an enormous échellon similar to that which forced the Rhine; to force Italy at the same fatal point—Venetia. The party who could command the last reserve would win, as is the rule. And the last reserves were with our race. They must win. But not yet. They had, in the mean time, taken up a concave line; a great arc running round the whole west of the Mediterranean from Italy, France, Spain, Algeria, as far as Carthage. They could not move forces round that length of coast, as fast as the Romans could move them by sea; and they had no fleets. Although they had conquered the Western Empire, they were in a very dangerous position, and were about to be very nearly ruined.

For you see, the Romans in turn had changed front at more than a right angle. They lay at first north-west and south-east. They lay in Justinian's time, north and south. Their right was Constantinople; their left Pentapolis; between those two points they held Greece, Asia Minor, Syria and Egypt; a position of wealth incalculable. Meanwhile, as we must remember always, they were masters of the sea, and therefore of the interior lines of operation. They had been forced into this position; but, like Romans, they had accepted it. With the boundless common sense of the race (however fallen, debauched, pedantic), they worked it out, and with terrible effect.

Their right in Constantinople was so strong that they cared nothing for it, though it was the only exposed point. They would defend it by hiring the Barbarians, and when they could not pay them, setting them on to kill down each other; while they quietly drew into

Constantinople the boundless crops of Asia, Syria and Egypt.

The strength of Constantinople was infinite—commanding two seas and two continents. It is, as the genius of Constantinople saw—as the genius of the Czar Nicholas saw—the strongest spot, perhaps, in the world. That fact was what enabled Justinian's Empire to arise again, and enabled Belisarius and Narses to reconquer Africa and Italy. Remember that, and see how strong the Romans were still.

The Teutons meanwhile had changed their front, by conquering the Western Mediterranean, and were becoming weak, because scattered on exterior lines, to their extreme danger.

I cannot exaggerate the danger of that position. It enabled the Romans by rapid movements of their fleets, to reconquer Africa and Italy. It might have enabled them to do much more.

Belisarius, with great wisdom, began by attacking the Vandals at Carthage on the extreme right. They had put themselves into an isolated position, and were destroyed without help. Then he moved on Italy and the Ostrogoths. He was going to force the positions in detail, and drive them back behind the Alps. What he did not finish, Narses did; and the Teutons were actually driven back behind the Alps for some years.

But Narses had to stop at Italy. Even if not recalled, he could have gone no further. The next move should have been on Spain, if he had really had strength in Italy. But to attack Spain from Constantinople, would have been to go too far from home. The Franks would have

crost the Pyrenees, and fallen on his flank. The Visigoths, even if beaten, would have been only pushed across
the Straits of Gibraltar, to reconquer the Vandal coast
of Africa; while to take troops from Italy for any such
purpose, would have been to let in the Lombards—who
came, let in or not. There were reserves in Germany still,
of which Narses knew full well; for he had seen 5000
Lombards, besides Herules, and Huns, and Avars, fight
for him at Nuceria, and destroy the Ostrogoths; and he
knew well that they could, if they chose, fight against
him.

On the other hand, the Roman Empire had no reserves; while the campaign had just come to that point
at which he who can bring up the last reserve wins.
Ours were so far from being exhausted, that the heavi-
est of them, the Franks, came into action, stronger than
ever, 200 years after.

But the Roman reserves were gone. If Greece, if
Asia Minor, if Egypt, had been the holds of a hardy people, the Romans might have done still—Heaven alone
knows what. At least, they might have extended their
front once more to the line of Carthage, Sicily, Italy.

But the people of Syria and Egypt, were—what they
were. No recruits, as far as I know, were drawn from
them. Had they been, they would have been face to face
with a Frank, or a Lombard, or a Visigoth, much what—
not a Sikh, a Rohilla, or a Ghoorka, but a Bengalee
proper—would be face to face with an Englishman.
One thousand Varangers might have walked from Constantinople to Alexandria without fighting a pitched
battle, if they had had only Greeks and Syrians to face.

Thus the Romans were growing weak.  If we had lost, so had they.  Every wild Teuton who came down to perish, had destroyed a Roman, or more than one, before he died.  Each column which the admirable skill and courage of the Romans had destroyed, had weakened them as much, perhaps more, than its destruction weakened the Teutons; and had, by harrying the country, destroyed the Roman's power of obtaining supplies. Italy and Turkey at last became too poor to be a fighting ground at all.

But now comes in one of the strangest new elements in this strange epic—Mohammed and his Arabs.

Suddenly, these Arab tribes, under the excitement of the new Mussulman creed, burst forth of the unknown East.  They take the Eastern Empire in the rear; by such a rear attack as the world never saw before or since; they cut it in two; devour it up: and save Europe thereby.

That may seem a strange speech.  I must explain it.  I have told you how the Eastern Empire and its military position was immensely strong; that Constantinople was a great maritime base of operations, mistress of the Mediterranean.  What prevented the Romans from reconquering all the shores of that sea, and establishing themselves in strength in the Morea, or in Sicily, or in Carthage, or in any central base of operations?  What forced them to cling to Constantinople, and fight a losing campaign thenceforth.  Simply this; the Mussulman had forced their position from the rear, and deprived them of Syria, Egypt, Africa.

But the Teutons could not have opposed them. During the 7th century the Lombards in Italy were lazy and divided; the Goths in Spain lazier and more divided still; the Franks were tearing themselves in pieces by civil war. The years from A.D. 550 to A.D. 750 and the rise of the Carlovingian dynasty, were a period of exhaustion for our race, such as follows on great victories, and the consequent slaughter and collapse.

This was the critical period of the Teutonic race; little talked of, because little known: but very perilous. Nevertheless, whatever the Eastern Empire might have done, the Saracens prevented its doing; and if you hold (with me) that the welfare of the Teutonic race is the welfare of the world; then, meaning nothing less, the Saracen invasion, by crippling the Eastern Empire, saved Europe and our race.

And now, gentlemen, was this vast campaign fought without a general? If Trafalgar could not be won without the mind of a Nelson, or Waterloo without the mind of a Wellington, was there no one mind to lead those innumerable armies, on whose success depended the future of the whole human race? Did no one marshal them in that impregnable convex front, from the Euxine to the North Sea? No one guide them to the two great strategic centres, of the Black Forest and Trieste? No one cause them, blind barbarians without maps or science, to follow those rules of war, without which victory in a protracted struggle is impossible; and by the pressure of the Huns behind, force on their flagging myriads to an enterprise which their simplicity fancied at first beyond the powers of mortal men? Believe it who will: but I cannot. I may be told that they gravitated into their places, as stones and mud do. Be it so. They obeyed natural laws of course, as all things do on earth, when they obeyed the laws of war: those too are natural laws, explicable on simple mathematical principles. But while I believe that not a stone or a handful of mud gravitates into its place without the will of God; that it was ordained, ages since, into what particular spot each grain of gold should be washed down from an Australian quartz reef, that a certain man might find it at a certain moment and crisis of his life;—if I be superstitious enough (as thank God I am) to hold that creed, shall I not believe that though this great war had no general upon earth, it may have had a general in Heaven? and that in spite of all their sins, the hosts of our forefathers were the hosts of God?

# THE LIMITS OF EXACT SCIENCE AS APPLIED TO HISTORY

It is with a feeling of awe, I had almost said of fear, that I find myself in this place, upon this errand. The responsibility of a teacher of History in Cambridge is in itself very heavy: but doubly heavy in the case of one who sees among his audience many men as fit, it may be some more fit, to fill this Chair: and again, more heavy still, when one succeeds to a man whose learning, like his virtues, one can never hope to equal.

But a Professor, I trust, is like other men, capable of improvement; and the great law, 'docendo disces,' may be fulfilled in him, as in other men. Meanwhile, I can only promise that such small powers as I possess will be honestly devoted to this Professorate; and that I shall endeavour to teach Modern History after a method which shall give satisfaction to the Rulers of this University.

I shall do that best, I believe, by keeping in mind the lessons which I, in common with thousands more, have learnt from my wise and good predecessor. I do not mean merely patience in research, and accuracy in fact. They are required of all men: and they may be learnt from many men. But what Sir James Stephen's life and writings should especially teach us, is the beauty and the value of charity; of that large-hearted humanity, which sympathizes with all noble, generous, earnest thought and endeavour, in whatsoever shape they may have ap-

peared; a charity which, without weakly or lazily con-
founding the eternal laws of right and wrong, can make
allowances for human frailty; can separate the good
from the evil in men and in theories; can understand,
and can forgive, because it loves.  Who can read Sir
James Stephen's works without feeling more kindly toward many a man, and many a form of thought, against
which he has been more or less prejudiced; without a
more genial view of human nature, a more hopeful view
of human destiny, a more full belief in the great saying,
that 'Wisdom is justified of all her children'?  Who,
too, can read those works without seeing how charity
enlightens the intellect, just as bigotry darkens it; how
events, which to the theorist and the pedant are merely monstrous and unmeaning, may explain themselves
easily enough to the man who will put himself in his
fellow-creatures' place; who will give them credit for being men of like passions with himself; who will see with
their eyes, feel with their hearts, and take for his motto,
'Homo sum, nil humani a me alienum puto'?

I entreat gentlemen who may hereafter attend my
lectures to bear in mind this last saying.  If they wish to
understand History, they must first try to understand
men and women.  For History is the history of men and
women, and of nothing else; and he who knows men
and women thoroughly will best understand the past
work of the world, and be best able to carry on its work
now.  The men who, in the long run, have governed the
world, have been those who understood the human
heart; and therefore it is to this day the statesman who
keeps the reins in his hand, and not the mere student.

He is a man of the world; he knows how to manage his fellow-men; and therefore he can get work done which the mere student (it may be) has taught him ought to be done; but which the mere student, much less the mere trader or economist, could not get done; simply because his fellow-men would probably not listen to him, and certainly outwit him.  Of course, in proportion to the depth, width, soundness, of his conception of human nature, will be the greatness and wholesomeness of his power.  He may appeal to the meanest, or to the loftiest motives.  He may be a fox or an eagle; a Borgia, or a Hildebrand; a Talleyrand, or a Napoleon; a Mary Stuart, or an Elizabeth: but however base, however noble, the power which he exercises is the same in essence. He makes History, because he understands men.  And you, if you would understand History, must understand men.

If, therefore, any of you should ask me how to study history, I should answer—Take by all means biographies: wheresoever possible, autobiographies; and study them.  Fill your minds with live human figures; men of like passions with yourselves; see how each lived and worked in the time and place in which God put him. Believe me, that when you have thus made a friend of the dead, and brought him to life again, and let him teach you to see with his eyes, and feel with his heart, you will begin to understand more of his generation and his circumstances, than all the mere history-books of the period would teach you.  In proportion as you understand the man, and only so, will you begin to understand the elements in which he worked.  And not only to understand, but to remember. Names, dates, genealogies, geographical details, costumes, fashions, manners, crabbed scraps of old law, which you used, perhaps, to read up and forget again, because they were not rooted, but stuck into your brain, as pins are into a pincushion, to fall out at the first shake—all these you will remember; because they will arrange and organize themselves around the central human figure: just as, if you have studied a portrait by some great artist, you cannot think of the face in it, without recollecting also the light and shadow, the tone of colouring, the dress, the very details of the background, and all the accessories which the painter's art has grouped around; each with a purpose, and therefore each fixing itself duly in your mind. Who, for instance, has not found that he can learn more French history from French memoirs, than even from all the truly learned and admirable histories of France which have been written of late years? There are those, too, who will say of good old Plutarch's lives (now-a-days, I think, too much neglected), what some great man used to say of Shakspeare and English history—that all the ancient history which they really knew, they had got from Plutarch. I am free to confess that I have learnt what little I know of the middle-ages, what they were like, how they came to be what they were, and how they issued in the Reformation, not so much from the study of the books about them (many and wise though they are), as from the thumbing over, for years, the semi-mythical saints' lives of Surius and the Bollandists.

Without doubt History obeys, and always has

obeyed, in the long run, certain laws. But those laws assert themselves, and are to be discovered, not in things, but in persons; in the actions of human beings; and just in proportion as we understand human beings, shall we understand the laws which they have obeyed, or which have avenged themselves on their disobedience. This may seem a truism: if it be such, it is one which we cannot too often repeat to ourselves just now, when the rapid progress of science is tempting us to look at human beings rather as things than as persons, and at abstractions (under the name of laws) rather as persons than as things. Discovering, to our just delight, order and law all around us, in a thousand events which seemed to our fathers fortuitous and arbitrary, we are dazzled just now by the magnificent prospect opening before us, and fall, too often, into more than one serious mistake.

First; students try to explain too often all the facts which they meet by the very few laws which they know; and especially moral phænomena by physical, or at least economic laws. There is an excuse for this last error. Much which was thought, a few centuries since, to belong to the spiritual world, is now found to belong to the material; and the physician is consulted, where the exorcist used to be called in. But it is a somewhat hasty corollary therefrom, and one not likely to find favour in this University, that moral laws and spiritual agencies have nothing at all to do with the history of the human race. We shall not be inclined here, I trust, to explain (as some one tried to do lately) the Crusades by a hypothesis of over-stocked labour-markets on the Continent.

Neither, again, shall we be inclined to class those

same Crusades among 'popular delusions,' and mere outbursts of folly and madness. This is a very easy, and I am
sorry to say, a very common method of disposing of facts
which will not fit into the theory, too common of late,
that need and greed have been always, and always ought
to be, the chief motives of mankind. Need and greed,
heaven knows, are powerful enough: but I think that
he who has something nobler in himself than need and
greed, will have eyes to discern something nobler than
them, in the most fantastic superstitions, in the most ferocious outbursts, of the most untutored masses. Thank
God, that those who preach the opposite doctrine belie
it so often by a happy inconsistency; that he who de-
clares self-interest to be the mainspring of the world, can
live a life of virtuous self-sacrifice; that he who denies,
with Spinoza, the existence of free-will, can disprove his
own theory, by willing, like Spinoza, amid all the temptations of the world, to live a life worthy of a Roman
Stoic; and that he who represents men as the puppets of
material circumstance, and who therefore has no logical
right either to praise virtue, or to blame vice, can shew,
by a healthy admiration of the former, a healthy scorn of
the latter, how little his heart has been corrupted by the
eidola specus, the phantoms of the study, which have
oppressed his brain. But though men are often, thank
heaven, better than their doctrines, yet the goodness
of the man does not make his doctrine good; and it is
immoral as well as unphilosophical to call a thing hard
names simply because it cannot be fitted into our theory
of the universe. Immoral, because all harsh and hasty
wholesale judgments are immoral; unphilosophical, be-

cause the only philosophical method of looking at the strangest of phænomena is to believe that it too is the result of law, perhaps a healthy result; that it is not to be condemned as a product of disease before it is proven to be such; and that if it be a product of disease, disease has its laws, as much as health; and is a subject, not for cursing, but for induction; so that (to return to my example) if every man who ever took part in the Crusades were proved to have been simply mad, our sole business would be to discover why he went mad upon that special matter, and at that special time. And to do that, we must begin by recollecting that in every man who went forth to the Crusades, or to any other strange adventure of humanity, was a whole human heart and brain, of like strength and weakness, like hopes, like temptations, with our own; and find out what may have driven him mad, by considering what would have driven us mad in his place.

May I be permitted to enlarge somewhat on this topic? There is, as you are aware, a demand just now for philosophies of History. The general spread of Inductive Science has awakened this appetite; the admirable contemporary French historians have quickened it by feeding it; till, the more order and sequence we find in the facts of the past, the more we wish to find. So it should be (or why was man created a rational being?) and so it is; and the requirements of the more educated are becoming so peremptory, that many thinking men would be ready to say (I should be sorry to endorse their opinion), that if History is not studied according to exact scientific method, it need not be studied at all.

A very able anonymous writer has lately expressed this general tendency of modern thought in language so clear and forcible that I must beg leave to quote it:—

'Step by step,' he says, 'the notion of evolution by law is transforming the whole field of our knowledge and opinion. It is not one order of conception which comes under its influence: but it is the whole sphere of our ideas, and with them the whole system of our action and conduct. Not the physical world alone is now the domain of inductive science, but the moral, the intellectual, and the spiritual are being added to its empire. Two co-ordinate ideas pervade the vision of every thinker, physicist or moralist, philosopher or priest. In the physical and the moral world, in the natural and the human, are ever seen two forces—invariable rule, and continual advance; law and action; order and progress; these two powers working harmoniously together, and the result, inevitable sequence, orderly movement, irresistible growth. In the physical world indeed, order is most prominent to our eyes; in the moral world it is progress, but both exist as truly in the one as in the other. In the scale of nature, as we rise from the inorganic to the organic, the idea of change becomes even more distinct; just as when we rise through the gradations of the moral world, the idea of order becomes more difficult to grasp. It was the last task of the astronomer to show eternal change even in the grand order of our Solar System. It is the crown of philosophy to see immutable law even in the complex action of human life. In the latter, indeed, it is but the first germs which are clear. No rational thinker hopes to discover more than some few primary actions of law, and some approximative theory of growth. Much is dark and contradictory. Numerous theories differing in method and degree are offered; nor do we decide between them. We insist now only upon this, that the principle of development in the moral, as in the physical, has been definitely admitted; and something like a conception of one grand analogy through the whole sphere of knowledge, has almost become a part of popular opinion. Most men shrink from any broad statement of the principle, though all in some special instances adopt it. It surrounds every idea of our life, and is diffused in every branch of study. The press, the platform, the lecture-room, and the pulpit ring with it in every variety of form. Unconscious pedants are proving it. It flashes on the statistician through his registers; it guides the hand of simple philanthropy; it is obeyed by the instinct of the statesman. There is not an act of our public life which does not acknowledge it. No man denies that there are certain, and even practical laws of political economy. They are nothing but laws of society. The conferences of social reformers, the congresses for international statistics and for social science bear witness of its force. Everywhere we hear of the development of the constitution, of public law, of public opinion, of institutions, of forms of society, of theories of history. In a word, whatever views of history may be inculcated on the Universities by novelists or epigrammatists, it is certain that the best intellects and spirits of our day are labouring to see more of that invariable order, and of that principle of growth in the life of human societies and of the great society of mankind which nearly all men, more or less, acknowledge, and partially and unconsciously confirm.'

This passage expresses admirably, I think, the tendencies of modern thought for good and evil.

For good. For surely it is good, and a thing to thank God for, that men should be more and more expecting order, searching for order, welcoming order. But for evil also. For young sciences, like young men, have their time of wonder, hope, imagination, and of passion too, and haste, and bigotry. Dazzled, and that pardonably, by the beauty of the few laws they may have discovered, they are too apt to erect them into gods, and to explain by them all matters in heaven and earth; and apt, too, as I think this author does, to patch them where they are weakest, by that most dangerous succedaneum of vague and grand epithets, which very often contain, each of them, an assumption far more important than the law to which they are tacked.

Such surely are the words which so often occur in this passage—'Invariable, continual, immutable, inevitable, irresistible.' There is an ambiguity in these words, which may lead—which I believe does lead—to most unphilosophical conclusions. They are used very much as synonyms; not merely in this passage, but in the mouths of men. Are you aware that those who carelessly do so, blink the whole of the world-old arguments between necessity and free-will? Whatever may be the rights of that quarrel, they are certainly not to be assumed in a passing epithet. But what else does the writer do, who tells us that an inevitable sequence, an irresistible growth, exists in the moral as well as in the physical world; and then says, as a seemingly identical statement, that it is the crown of philosophy to see immutable law, even in the complex action of human life?

The crown of philosophy? Doubtless it is so. But not a crown, I should have thought, which has been reserved as the special glory of these latter days. Very early, at least in the known history of mankind, did Philosophy (under the humble names of Religion and Common Sense) see most immutable, and even eternal, laws, in the complex action of human life, even the laws of right and wrong; and called them The Everlasting Judgments of God, to which a confused and hard-worked man was to look; and take comfort, for all would be well at last. By fair induction (as I believe) did man discover, more or less clearly, those eternal laws: by repeated verifications of them in every age, man has been rising, and will yet rise, to clearer insight into their essence, their limits, their practical results. And if it be these, the old laws of right and wrong, which this author and his school call invariable and immutable, we shall, I trust, most heartily agree with them; only wondering why a moral government of the world seems to them so very recent a discovery.

But we shall not agree with them, I trust, when they represent these invariable and immutable laws as resulting in any inevitable sequence, or irresistible growth. We shall not deny a sequence—Reason forbids that; or again, a growth—Experience forbids that: but we shall be puzzled to see why a law, because it is immutable itself, should produce inevitable results; and if they quote the facts of material nature against us, we shall be ready to meet them on that very ground, and ask:—You say that as the laws of matter are inevitable, so probably are the laws of human life? Be it so: but in what sense are the laws of matter inevitable? Potentially, or actually? Even in the seemingly most uniform and universal law, where do we find the inevitable or the irresistible? Is there not in nature a perpetual competition of law against law, force against force, producing the most endless and un-expected variety of results? Cannot each law be inter-fered with at any moment by some other law, so that the first law, though it may struggle for the mastery, shall be for an indefinite time utterly defeated? The law of grav-ity is immutable enough: but do all stones inevitably fall to the ground? Certainly not, if I choose to catch one, and keep it in my hand. It remains there by laws; and the law of gravity is there too, making it feel heavy in my hand: but it has not fallen to the ground, and will not, till I let it. So much for the inevitable action of the laws of gravity, as of others. Potentially, it is immutable; but actually it can be conquered by other laws.

I really beg your pardon for occupying you here with such truisms: but I must put the students of this Uni-versity in mind of them, as long as too many modern thinkers shall choose to ignore them.

Even if then, as it seems to me, the history of man-kind depended merely on physical laws, analogous to those which govern the rest of nature, it would be a hopeless task for us to discover an inevitable sequence in History, even though we might suppose that such ex-isted. But as long as man has the mysterious power of breaking the laws of his own being, such a sequence not only cannot be discovered, but it cannot exist. For man can break the laws of his own being, whether physical, intellectual, or moral. He breaks them every day, and has always been breaking them.

The greater number of them he cannot obey till he knows them. And too many of them he cannot know, alas, till he has broken them; and paid the penalty of his ignorance. He does not, like the brute or the vegetable, thrive by laws of which he is not conscious: but by laws of which he becomes gradually conscious; and which he can disobey after all. And therefore it seems to me very like a juggle of words to draw analogies from the physical and irrational world, and apply them to the moral and rational world; and most unwise to bridge over the gulf between the two by such adjectives as 'irresistible' or 'inevitable,' such nouns as 'order, sequence, law'—which must bear an utterly different meaning, according as they are applied to physical beings or to moral ones.

Indeed, so patent is the ambiguity, that I cannot fancy that it has escaped the author and his school; and am driven, by mere respect for their logical powers, to suppose that they mean no ambiguity at all; that they do not conceive of irrational beings as differing from rational beings, or the physical from the moral, or the body of man from his spirit, in kind and property; and that the immutable laws which they represent as governing human life and history have nothing at all to do with those laws of right and wrong, which I intend to set forth to you, as the 'everlasting judgments of God.'

In which case, I fear, they must go their way; while

we go ours; confessing that there is an order, and there
is a law, for man; and that if he disturb that order, or
break that law in anywise, they will prove themselves
too strong for him, and reassert themselves, and go
forward, grinding him to powder if he stubbornly try
to stop their way. But we must assert too, that his disobedience to them, even for a moment, has disturbed
the natural course of events, and broken that inevitable
sequence, which we may find indeed, in our own imaginations, as long as we sit with a book in our studies: but
which vanishes the moment that we step outside into
practical contact with life; and, instead of talking cheerfully of a necessary and orderly progress, find ourselves
more inclined to cry with the cynical man of the world:

> 'All the windy ways of men,
> Are but dust that rises up;
> And is lightly laid again.'

The usual rejoinder to this argument is to fall back
upon man's weakness and ignorance, and to take refuge
in the infinite unknown. Man, it is said, may of course
interfere a little with some of the less important laws of
his being: but who is he, to grapple with the more vast
and remote ones? Because he can prevent a pebble from
falling, is he to suppose that he can alter the destiny of
nations, and grapple forsooth with 'the eternities and
the immensities,' and so forth? The argument is very
powerful: but addrest rather to the imagination than
the reason. It is, after all, another form of the old omne
ignotum pro magnifico; and we may answer, I think

fairly—About the eternities and immensities we know nothing, not having been there as yet; but it is a mere assumption to suppose, without proof, that the more remote and impalpable laws are more vast, in the sense of being more powerful (the only sense which really bears upon the argument), than the laws which are palpably at work around us all day long; and if we are capable of interfering with almost every law of human life which we know of already, it is more philosophical to believe (till disproved by actual failure) that we can interfere with those laws of our life which we may know hereafter. Whether it will pay us to interfere with them, is a different question. It is not prudent to interfere with the laws of health, and it may not be with other laws, hereafter to be discovered. I am only pleading that man can disobey the laws of his being; that such power has always been a disturbing force in the progress of the human race, which modern theories too hastily overlook; and that the science of history (unless the existence of the human will be denied) must belong rather to the moral sciences, than to that 'positive science' which seems to me inclined to reduce all human phænomena under physical laws, hastily assumed, by the old fallacy of εἰς ἄλλο γένος, to apply where there is no proof whatsoever that they do or even can apply.

As for the question of the existence of the human will—I am not here, I hope, to argue that. I shall only beg leave to assume its existence, for practical purposes. I may be told (though I trust not in this University), that it is, like the undulatory theory of light, an unphilosophical 'hypothesis.' Be that as it may, it is very convenient (and may be for a few centuries to come) to retain the said 'hypothesis,' as one retains the undulatory theory; and for the simple reason, that with it one can explain the phænomena tolerably; and without it cannot explain them at all.

A dread (half-unconscious, it may be) of this last practical result, seems to have crossed the mind of the author on whom I have been commenting; for he confesses, honestly enough (and he writes throughout like an honest man) that in human life 'no rational thinker hopes to discover more than some few primary actions of law, and some approximative theory of growth.' I have higher hopes of a possible science of history; because I fall back on those old moral laws, which I think he wishes to ignore: but I can conceive that he will not; because he cannot, on his own definitions of law and growth. They are (if I understand him aright) to be irresistible and inevitable. I say that they are not so, even in the case of trees and stones; much more in the world of man. Facts, when he goes on to verify his theories, will leave him with a very few primary actions of law, a very faint approximative theory; because his theories, in plain English, will not work. At the first step, at every step, they are stopped short by those disturbing forces, or at least disturbed phænomena, which have been as yet, and probably will be hereafter, attributed (as the only explanation of them) to the existence, for good and evil, of a human will.

Let us look in detail at a few of these disturbances of anything like inevitable or irresistible movement. Shall we not, at the very first glance, confess—I am afraid only too soon—that there always have been fools therein; fools of whom no man could guess, or can yet, what they were going to do next or why they were going to do it? And how, pray, can we talk of the inevitable, in the face of that one miserable fact of human folly, whether of ignorance or of passion, folly still? There may be laws of folly, as there are laws of disease; and whether there are or not, we may learn much wisdom from folly; we may see what the true laws of humanity are, by seeing the penalties which come from breaking them: but as for laws which work of themselves, by an irresistible movement,—how can we discover such in a past in which every law which we know has been outraged again and again? Take one of the highest instances—the progress of the human intellect—I do not mean just now the spread of conscious science, but of that unconscious science which we call common sense. What hope have we of laying down exact laws for its growth, in a world wherein it has been ignored, insulted, crushed, a thousand times, sometimes in whole nations and for whole generations, by the stupidity, tyranny, greed, caprice of a single ruler; or if not so, yet by the mere superstition, laziness, sensuality, anarchy of the mob? How, again, are we to arrive at any exact laws of the increase of population, in a race which has had, from the beginning, the abnormal and truly monstrous habit of slaughtering each other, not for food—for in a race of normal cannibals, the ratio of increase or decrease might easily be calculated—but uselessly, from rage, hate, fanaticism, or even mere wantonness? No man is less inclined than I to undervalue vital statistics, and their already admirable results: but how can they help us, and how can we help them, in looking at such a past as that of three-fourths of the nations of the world? Look—as a single instance among too many—at that most noble nation of Germany, swept and stunned, by peasant wars, thirty years' wars, French wars, and after each hurricane, blossoming up again into brave industry and brave thought, to be in its turn cut off by a fresh storm ere it could bear full fruit: doing nevertheless such work, against such fearful disadvantages, as nation never did before; and proving thereby what she might have done for humanity, had not she, the mother of all European life, been devoured, generation after generation, by her own unnatural children. Nevertheless, she is their mother still; and her history, as I believe, the root-history of Europe: but it is hard to read—the sibylline leaves are so fantastically torn, the characters so blotted out by tears and blood.

And if such be the history of not one nation only, but of the average, how, I ask, are we to make calculations about such a species as man? Many modern men of science wish to draw the normal laws of human life from the average of humanity: I question whether they can do so; because I do not believe the average man to be the normal man, exhibiting the normal laws: but a very abnormal man, diseased and crippled, but even if their method were correct, it could work in practice, only if the destinies of men were always decided by majorities: and granting that the majority of men have common sense, are the minority of fools to count for nothing? Are they powerless? Have they had no influence on History? Have they even been always a minority, and not at times a terrible majority, doing each that which was right in the sight of his own eyes? You can surely answer that question for yourselves. As far as my small knowledge of History goes, I think it may be proved from facts, that any given people, down to the lowest savages, has, at any period of its life, known far more than it has done; known quite enough to have enabled it to have got on comfortably, thriven, and developed; if it had only done, what no man does, all that it knew it ought to do, and could do. St. Paul's experience of himself is true of all mankind—'The good which I would, I do not; and the evil which I would not, that I do.' The discrepancy between the amount of knowledge and the amount of work, is one of the most patent and most painful facts which strikes us in the history of man; and one not certainly to be explained on any theory of man's progress being the effect of inevitable laws, or one which gives us much hope of ascertaining fixed laws for that progress.

And bear in mind, that fools are not always merely imbecile and obstructive; they are at times ferocious, dangerous, mad. There is in human nature what Goethe used to call a demoniac element, defying all law, and all induction; and we can, I fear, from that one cause, as easily calculate the progress of the human race, as we can calculate that of the vines upon the slopes of Ætna, with the lava ready to boil up and overwhelm them at any and every moment. Let us learn, in God's name, all we can, from the short intervals of average peace and common sense: let us, or rather our grandchildren, get precious lessons from them for the next period of sanity.

But let us not be surprised, much less disheartened, if after learning a very little, some unexpected and truly demoniac factor, Anabaptist war, French revolution, or other, should toss all our calculations to the winds, and set us to begin afresh, sadder and wiser men. We may learn, doubtless, even more of the real facts of human nature, the real laws of human history, from these critical periods, when the root-fibres of the human heart are laid bare, for good and evil, than from any smooth and respectable periods of peace and plenty: nevertheless their lessons are not statistical, but moral.

But if human folly has been a disturbing force for evil, surely human reason has been a disturbing force for good. Man can not only disobey the laws of his being, he can also choose between them, to an extent which science widens every day, and so become, what he was meant to be, an artificial being; artificial in his manufactures, habits, society, polity—what not? All day long he has a free choice between even physical laws, which mere things have not, and which make the laws of mere things inapplicable to him. Take the simplest case. If he falls into the water, he has his choice whether he will obey the laws of gravity and sink, or by other laws perform the (to him) artificial process of swimming, and get ashore. True, both would happen by law: but he has his choice which law shall conquer, sink or swim. We have yet to learn why whole nations, why all mankind may not use the same prudential power as to which law they shall obey,—which, without breaking it, they shall conquer and repress, as long as seems good to them.

It is true, nature must be obeyed in order that she may he conquered: but then she is to be conquered. It has been too much the fashion of late to travestie that great dictum of Bacon's into a very different one, and say, Nature must be obeyed because she cannot be conquered; thus proclaiming the impotence of science to discover anything save her own impotence—a result as contrary to fact, as to Bacon's own hopes of what science would do for the welfare of the human race. For what is all human invention, but the transcending and conquering one natural law by another? What is the practical answer which all mankind has been making to nature and her pretensions, whenever it has progressed one step since the foundation of the world: by which all discoverers have discovered, all teachers taught: by which all polities, kingdoms, civilizations, arts, manufactures, have established themselves; all who have raised themselves above the mob have faced the mob, and conquered the mob, crucified by them first and worshipped by them afterwards: by which the first savage conquered the natural law which put wild beasts in the forest, by killing them; conquered the natural law which makes raw meat wholesome, by cooking it; conquered the natural law which made weeds grow at his hut door, by rooting them up, and planting corn instead; and won his first spurs in the great battle of man against nature, proving thereby that he was a man, and not an ape? What but this?—'Nature is strong, but I am stronger. I know her worth, but I know my own. I trust her and her laws, but my trusty servant she shall be, and not my tyrant; and if she interfere with my ideal, even with my personal comfort, then Nature and I will fight it out to the last gasp, and Heaven defend the right!'

In forgetting this, in my humble opinion, lay the error of the early, or laissez faire School of Political Economy. It was too much inclined to say to men: 'You are the puppets of certain natural laws. Your own freewill and choice, if they really exist, exist merely as a dangerous disease. All you can do is to submit to the laws, and drift whithersoever they may carry you, for good or evil.' But not less certainly was the same blame to be attached to the French Socialist School. It, though based on a revolt from the Philosophie du neant, philosophie de la misère, as it used to term the laissez faire School, yet retained the worst fallacy of its foe, namely, that man was the creature of circumstances; and denied him just as much as its antagonist the possession of freewill, or at least the right to use freewill on any large scale.

The laissez faire School was certainly the more logical of the two. With them, if man was the creature of circumstances, those circumstances were at least defined for him by external laws which he had not created: while the Socialists, with Fourier at their head (as it has always seemed to me), fell into the extraordinary paradox of supposing that though man was the creature of circumstances, he was to become happy by creating the very circumstances which were afterwards to create him. But both of them erred, surely, in ignoring that self-arbitrating power of man, by which he can, for good or for evil, rebel against and conquer circumstance.

I am not, surely, overstepping my province as Professor of History, in alluding to this subject. Just notions of Political Economy are absolutely necessary to just notions of History; and I should wish those young gentlemen who may attend my Lectures, to go first, were it possible, to my more learned brother, the Professor of Political Economy, and get from him not merely exact habits of thought, but a knowledge which I cannot give, and yet which they ought to possess.  For to take the very lowest ground, the first fact of history is, Bouche va toujours; whatever men have or have not done, they have always eaten, or tried to eat; and the laws which regulate the supply of the first necessaries of life are, after all, the first which should be learnt, and the last which should be ignored.

The more modern school, however, of Political Economy while giving due weight to circumstance, has refused to acknowledge it as the force which ought to determine all human life; and our greatest living political economist has, in his Essay on Liberty, put in a plea unequalled since the Areopagitica of Milton, for the self-determining power of the individual, and for his right to use that power.

But my business is not with rights, so much as with facts; and as a fact, surely, one may say, that this inventive reason of man has been, in all ages, interfering with any thing like an inevitable sequence or orderly progress of humanity.  Some of those writers, indeed, who are most anxious to discover an exact order, are most loud in their complaints that it has been interfered with by over-legislation; and rejoice that mankind is returning to a healthier frame of mind, and leaving nature alone to her own work in her own way.  I do not altogether agree with their complaints; but of that I hope to speak in subsequent lectures. Meanwhile, I must ask, if (as is said) most good legislation now-a-days consists in repealing old laws which ought never to have been passed; if (as is said) the great fault of our forefathers was that they were continually setting things wrong, by intermeddling in matters political, economic, religious, which should have been let alone, to develop themselves in their own way, what becomes of the inevitable laws, and the continuous progress, of the human mind?

Look again at the disturbing power, not merely of the general reason of the many, but of the genius of the few. I am not sure, but that the one fact, that genius is occasionally present in the world, is not enough to prevent our ever discovering any regular sequence in human progress, past or future.

Let me explain myself. In addition to the infinite variety of individual characters continually born (in it-self a cause of perpetual disturbance), man alone of all species has the faculty of producing, from time to time, individuals immeasurably superior to the average in some point or other, whom we call men of genius. Like Mr. Babbage's calculating machine, human nature gives millions of orderly respectable common-place results, which any statistician can classify, and enables hasty philosophers to say—It always has gone on thus; it must go on thus always; when behold, after many millions of orderly results, there turns up a seemingly disorderly, a certainly unexpected, result, and the law seems broken (being really superseded by some deeper law) for that once, and perhaps never again for centuries. Even so it is with man, and the physiological laws which determine the earthly appearance of men. Laws there are, doubt it not; but they are beyond us: and let our induction be as wide as it may, they will baffle it; and great nature, just as we fancy we have found out her secret, will smile in our faces as she brings into the world a man, the like of whom we have never seen, and cannot explain, define, classify—in one word, a genius. Such do, as a fact, become leaders of men into quite new and unexpected paths, and, for good or evil, leave their stamp upon whole generations and races. Notorious as this may be, it is just, I think, what most modern theories of human progress ignore. They take the actions and the tendencies of the average many, and from them construct their scheme: a method not perhaps quite safe were they dealing with plants or animals; but what if it be the very peculiarity of this fantastic and altogether unique creature called man, not only that he develops, from time to time, these exceptional individuals, but that they are the most important individuals of all? that his course is decided for him not by the average many, but by the extraordinary few; that one Mahommed, one Luther, one Bacon, one Napoleon, shall change the thoughts and habits of millions?—So that instead of saying that the history of mankind is the history of the masses, it would be much more true to say, that the history of mankind is the history of its great men; and that a true philosophy of history ought to declare the laws—call them physical, spiritual, biological, or what we choose—by which great minds have been produced into the world, as necessary results, each in his place and time.

That would be a science indeed; how far we are as yet from any such, you know as well as I. As yet, the appearance of great minds is as inexplicable to us as if they had dropped among us from another planet. Who will tell us why they have arisen when they did, and why they did what they did, and nothing else? I do not deny that such a science is conceivable; because each mind, however great or strange, may be the result of fixed and unerring laws of life: and it is conceivable, too, that such a science may so perfectly explain the past, as to be able to predict the future; and tell men when a fresh genius is likely to arise and of what form his intellect will be. Conceivable: but I fear only conceivable; if for no other reason, at least for this one. We may grant safely that the mind of Luther was the necessary result of a combination of natural laws. We may go further, and grant, but by no means safely, that Luther, was the creature of circumstances, that there was no self-moving originality in him, but that his age made him what he was. To some modern minds these concessions remove all difficulty and mystery: but not, I trust, to our minds. For does not the very puzzle de quo agitur remain equally real; namely, why the average of Augustine monks, the average of German men, did not, by being exposed to the same average circumstances as Luther, become what Luther was? But whether we allow Luther to have been a person with an originally different character from all others, or whether we hold him to have been the mere puppet of outside influences, the first step towards discovering how he became what he was, will be to find out what he was. It will be more easy, and, I am sorry to say, more common to settle beforehand our theory, and explain by it such parts of Luther as will fit it; and call those which will not fit it hard names. History is often so taught, and the method is popular and lucrative. But we here shall be of opinion, I am sure, that we only can learn causes through their effects; we can only learn the laws which produced Luther, by learning Luther himself; by analyzing his whole character; by gauging all his powers; and that—unless the less can comprehend the greater—we cannot do till we are more than Luther himself. I repeat it. None can comprehend a man, unless he be greater than that man. He must be not merely equal to him, because none can see in another elements of character which he has not already seen in himself: he must be greater; because to comprehend him thoroughly, he must be able to judge the man's failings as well as his excellencies; to see not only why he did what he did, but why he did not do more: in a word, he must be nearer than his object is to the ideal man.

And if it be assumed that I am quibbling on the words 'comprehend' and 'greater,' that the observer need be greater only potentially, and not in act; that all the comprehension required of him, is to have in himself the germs of other men's faculties, without having developed those germs in life; I must still stand to my assertion. For such a rejoinder ignores the most mysterious element of all character, which we call strength: by virtue of which, of two seemingly similar characters, while one does nothing, the other shall do great things; while in one the germs of intellect and virtue remain comparatively embryonic, passive, and weak, in the other these same germs shall develop into manhood, action, success. And in what that same strength consists, not even the dramatic imagination of a Shakespeare could discover. What are those heart-rending sonnets of his, but the confession that over and above all his powers he lacked one thing, and knew not what it was, or where to find it—and that was—to be strong?

And yet he who will give us a science of great men, must begin by having a larger heart, a keener insight, a more varying human experience, than Shakespeare's own; while those who offer us a science of little men, and attempt to explain history and progress by laws drawn from the average of mankind, are utterly at sea the moment they come in contact with the very men whose actions make the history, to whose thought the progress is due. And why? Because (so at least I think) the new science of little men can be no science at all: because the average man is not the normal man, and never yet has been; because the great man is rather the normal man, as approaching more nearly than his fellows to the true 'norma' and standard of a complete human character; and therefore to pass him by as a mere irregular sport of nature, an accidental giant with six fingers and six toes, and to turn to the mob for your theory of humanity, is (I think) about as wise as to ignore the Apollo and the Theseus, and to determine the proportions of the human figure from a crowd of dwarfs and cripples.

No, let us not weary ourselves with narrow theories, with hasty inductions, which will, a century hence, furnish mere matter for a smile. Let us confine ourselves, at least in the present infantile state of the anthropologic sciences, to facts; to ascertaining honestly and patiently the thing which has been done; trusting that if we make ourselves masters of them, some rays of inductive light will be vouchsafed to us from Him who truly comprehends mankind, and knows what is in man, because He is the Son of Man; who has His own true theory of human progress, His own sound method of educating the human race, perfectly good, and perfectly wise, and at last, perfectly victorious; which nevertheless, were it revealed to us to-morrow, we could not understand; for if he who would comprehend Luther must be more than Luther, what must he be, who would comprehend God?

Look again, as a result of the disturbing force of genius, at the effects of great inventions—how unexpected, complex, subtle, all but miraculous—throwing out alike the path of human history, and the calculations of the student. If physical discoveries produced only physical or economic results—if the invention of printing had only produced more books, and more knowledge— if the invention of gunpowder had only caused more or less men to be killed—if the invention of the spinning-jenny had only produced more cotton-stuffs, more employment, and therefore more human beings,—then their effects would have been, however complex, more or less subjects of exact computation.

But so strangely interwoven is the physical and spiritual history of man, that material inventions produce continually the most unexpected spiritual results. Printing becomes a religious agent, causes not merely more books, but a Protestant Reformation; then again, through the Jesuit literature, helps to a Romanist count-

er-reformation; and by the clashing of the two, is one of
the great causes of the Thirty Years' War, one of the most
disastrous checks which European progress ever suffered. Gunpowder, again, not content with killing men,
becomes unexpectedly a political agent; 'the villanous
saltpetre,' as Ariosto and Shakespeare's fop complain,
'does to death many a goodly gentleman,' and enables
the masses to cope, for the first time, with knights in
armour; thus forming a most important agent in the rise
of the middle classes; while the spinning-jenny, not content with furnishing facts for the political economist,
and employment for millions, helps to extend slavery in
the United States, and gives rise to moral and political
questions, which may have, ere they be solved, the most
painful consequences to one of the greatest nations on
earth.

So far removed is the sequence of human history
from any thing which we can call irresistible or inevitable. Did one dare to deal in epithets, crooked, wayward,
mysterious, incalculable, would be those which would
rather suggest themselves to a man looking steadily not
at a few facts here and there, and not again at some hasty
bird's-eye sketch, which he chooses to call a whole, but
at the actual whole, fact by fact, step by step, and alas!
failure by failure, and crime by crime.

Understand me, I beg. I do not wish (Heaven forbid!) to discourage inductive thought; I do not wish
to undervalue exact science. I only ask that the moral
world, which is just as much the domain of inductive
science as the physical one, be not ignored; that the
tremendous difficulties of analyzing its phenomena

be fairly faced; and the hope given up, at least for the present, of forming any exact science of history; and I wish to warn you off from the too common mistake of trying to explain the mysteries of the spiritual world by a few roughly defined physical laws (for too much of our modern thought does little more than that); and of ignoring as old fashioned, or even superstitious, those great moral laws of history, which are sanctioned by the experience of ages.

Foremost among them stands a law which I must insist on, boldly and perpetually, if I wish (as I do wish) to follow in the footsteps of Sir James Stephen: a law which man has been trying in all ages, as now, to deny, or at least to ignore; though he might have seen it if he had willed, working steadily in all times and nations. And that is—that as the fruit of righteousness is wealth and peace, strength and honour; the fruit of unrighteousness is poverty and anarchy, weakness and shame. It is an ancient doctrine, and yet one ever young. The Hebrew prophets preached it long ago, in words which are fulfilling themselves around us every day, and which no new discoveries of science will abrogate, because they express the great root-law, which disobeyed, science itself cannot get a hearing.

For not upon mind, gentlemen, not upon mind, but upon morals, is human welfare founded. The true subjective history of man is the history not of his thought, but of his conscience; the true objective history of man is not that of his inventions, but of his vices and his virtues. So far from morals depending upon thought, thought, I believe, depends on morals. In proportion as a nation is righteous,—in proportion as common justice is done between man and man, will thought grow rapidly, securely, triumphantly; will its discoveries be cheerfully accepted, and faithfully obeyed, to the welfare of the whole commonweal. But where a nation is corrupt, that is, where the majority of individuals in it are bad, and justice is not done between man and man, there thought will wither, and science will be either crushed by frivolity and sensuality, or abused to the ends of tyranny, ambition, profligacy, till she herself perishes, amid the general ruin of all good things; as she had done in Greece, in Rome, in Spain, in China, and many other lands. Laws of economy, of polity, of health, of all which makes human life endurable, may be ignored and trampled under foot, and are too often, every day, for the sake of present greed, of present passion; self-interest may become, and will become, more and more blinded, just in proportion as it is not enlightened by virtue; till a nation may arrive, though, thank God, but seldom, at that state of frantic recklessness which Salvian describes among his Roman countrymen in Gaul, when, while the Franks were thundering at their gates, and starved and half-burnt corpses lay about the unguarded streets, the remnant, like that in doomed Jerusalem of old, were drinking, dicing, ravishing, robbing the orphan and the widow, swindling the poor man out of his plot of ground, and sending meanwhile to the tottering Cæsar at Rome, to ask, not for armies, but for Circensian games.

We cannot see how science could have bettered those poor Gauls. And we can conceive, surely, a nation falling into the same madness, and crying 'Let us eat and drink, for to-morrow we die,' in the midst of railroads, spinning-jennies, electric telegraphs, and crystal palaces, with infinite blue-books and scientific treatises ready to prove to them, what they knew perfectly well already, that they were making a very unprofitable investment, both of money and of time.

For science indeed is great: but she is not the greatest. She is an instrument, and not a power; beneficent or deadly, according as she is wielded by the hand of virtue or of vice. But her lawful mistress, the only one which can use her aright, the only one under whom she can truly grow, and prosper, and prove her divine descent, is Virtue, the likeness of Almighty God. This, indeed, the Hebrew Prophets, who knew no science in one sense of the word, do not expressly say: but it is a corollary from their doctrine, which we may discover for ourselves, if we will look at the nations round us now, if we will look at all the nations which have been. Even Voltaire himself acknowledged that; and when he pointed to the Chinese as the most prosperous nation upon earth, ascribed their prosperity uniformly to their virtue. We now know that he was wrong in fact: for we have discovered that Chinese civilization is one not of peace and plenty, but of anarchy and wretchedness. But that fact only goes to corroborate the belief, which (strange juxtaposition!) was common to Voltaire and the old Hebrew Prophets at whom he scoffed, name-ly, that virtue is wealth, and vice is ruin. For we have found that these Chinese, the ruling classes of them at least, are an especially unrighteous people; rotting upon the rotting remnants of the wisdom and virtue of their forefathers, which now live only on their lips in flowery maxims about justice and mercy and truth, as a cloak for practical hypocrisy and villany; and we have discovered also, as a patent fact, just what the Hebrew Prophets would have foretold us—that the miseries and horrors which are now destroying the Chinese Empire, are the direct and organic results of the moral profligacy of its inhabitants.

I know no modern nation, moreover, which illustrates so forcibly as China the great historic law which the Hebrew Prophets proclaim; and that is this:—That as the prosperity of a nation is the correlative of their morals, so are their morals the correlative of their theology. As a people behaves, so it thrives; as it believes, so it behaves. Such as his Gods are, such will the man be; down to that lowest point which too many of the Chinese seem to have reached, where, having no Gods, he himself becomes no man; but (as I hear you see him at the Australian diggings) abhorred for his foul crimes even by the scum of Europe.

I do not say that the theology always produces the morals, any more than that the morals always produce the theology. Each is, I think, alternately cause and effect. Men make the Gods in their own likeness; then they copy the likeness they have set up. But whichever be cause, and whichever effect, the law, I believe, stands true, that on the two together depends the physical welfare of a people. History gives us many examples, in which superstition, many again in which profligacy, have been the patent cause of a nation's deoradation. It does not, as far as I am aware, give us a single case of a nation's thriving and developing when deeply infected with either of those two vices.

These, the broad and simple laws of moral retribution, we may see in history; and (I hope) something more than them; something of a general method, something of an upward progress, though any thing but an irresistible or inevitable one. For I have not argued that there is no order, no progress—God forbid. Were there no order to be found, what could the student with a man's reason in him do, but in due time go mad?—Were there no progress, what could the student with a man's heart within him do, but in due time break his heart, over the sight of a chaos of folly and misery irredeemable?—I only argue that the order and the progress of human history cannot be similar to those which govern irrational beings, and cannot (without extreme danger) be described by metaphors (for they are nothing stronger) drawn from physical science. If there be an order, a progress, they must be moral; fit for the guidance of moral beings; limited by the obedience which those moral beings pay to what they know.

And such an order, such a progress as that, I have good hope that we shall find in history.

We shall find, as I believe, in all the ages, God educating man; protecting him till he can go alone, furnishing him with the primary necessaries, teaching him, guiding him, inspiring him, as we should do to our children; bearing with him, and forgiving him too, again and again, as we should do: but teaching him withal (as we shall do if we be wise) in great part by his own experience, making him test for himself, even by failure and pain, the truth of the laws which have been given him; discover for himself, as much as possible, fresh laws, or fresh applications of laws; and exercising his will and faculties, by trusting him to himself wherever he can be trusted without his final destruction. This is my conception of history, especially of Modern History—of history since the Revelation of our Lord Jesus Christ. I express myself feebly enough, I know. And even could I express what I mean perfectly, it would still be but a partial analogy, not to be pushed into details. As I said just now, were the true law of human progress revealed to us to-morrow, we could not understand it.

For suppose that the theory were true, which Dr. Temple of Rugby has lately put into such noble words: suppose that, as he says, 'The power whereby the present ever gathers into itself the results of the past, transforms the human race into a colossal man, whose life reaches from the creation to the day of judgment. The successive generations of men, are days in this man's life. The discoveries and inventions which characterize the different epochs of the world, are this man's works. The creeds and doctrines, the opinions and principles of the successive ages, are his thoughts. The state of society at different times, are his manners. He grows in knowledge, in self-control, in visible size, just as we do.' Suppose all this; and suppose too, that God is educating this his colossal child, as we educate our own children; it will hardly follow from thence that his education would be, as Dr. Temple says it is, precisely similar to ours.

Analogous it may be, but not precisely similar; and

for this reason: That the collective man, in the theory, must be infinitely more complex in his organization than the individuals of which he is composed. While between the educator of the one and of the other, there is simply the difference between a man and God. How much more complex then must his education be! how all-inscrutable to human minds much in it!—often as inscrutable as would our training of our children seem to the bird brooding over her young ones in the nest. The parental relations in all three cases may be—the Scriptures say that they are—expansions of the same great law; the key to all history may be contained in those great words—'How often would I have gathered thy children as a hen gathereth her chickens under her wings.' Yet even there the analogy stops short—'but thou wouldest not' expresses a new element, which has no place in the training of the nestling by the dam, though it has place in our training of our children; even that self-will, that power of disobedience, which is the dark side of man's prerogative as a rational and self-cultivating being. Here that analogy fails, as we should have expected it to do; and in a hundred other points it fails, or rather transcends so utterly its original type, that mankind seems, at moments, the mere puppet of those laws of natural selection, and competition of species, of which we have heard so much of late; and, to give a single instance, the seeming waste, of human thought, of human agony, of human power, seems but another instance of that inscrutable prodigality of nature, by which, of a thousand acorns dropping to the ground, but one shall become the thing it can become, and grow into a builder oak, the rest be craunched up by the nearest swine.

Yet these dark passages of human life may be only necessary elements of the complex education of our race; and as much mercy under a fearful shape, as ours when we put the child we love under the surgeon's knife. At least we may believe so; believe that they have a moral end, though that end be unseen by us; and without any rash or narrow prying into final causes (a trick as fatal to historic research as Bacon said it was to science), we may justify God by faith, where we cannot justify Him by experience.

Surely this will be the philosophic method. If we seem to ourselves to have discovered a law, we do not throw it away the moment we find phænomena which will not be explained by it. We use those phænomena to correct and to expand our law. And this belief that History is 'God educating man,' is no mere hypothesis; it results from the observation of thousands of minds, throughout thousands of years. It has long seemed—I trust it will seem still—the best explanation of the strange deeds of that strange being, man: and where we find in history facts which seem to contradict it, we shall not cast away rashly or angrily either it or them: but if we be Bacon's true disciples, we shall use them patiently and reverently to correct and expand our notions of the law itself, and rise thereby to more deep and just conceptions of education, of man, and—it may be—of God Himself.

In proportion as we look at history thus; searching for effective, rather than final causes, and content to see

God working everywhere, without impertinently demanding of Him a reason for His deeds, we shall study in a frame of mind equally removed from superstition on the one hand, and necessitarianism on the other. We shall not be afraid to confess natural agencies: but neither shall we be afraid to confess those supernatural causes which underlie all existence, save God's alone.

We shall talk of more than of an over-ruling Providence. That such exists, will seem to us a patent fact. But it will seem to us somewhat Manichæan to believe that the world is ill made, mankind a failure, and that all God has to do with them, is to set them right here and there, when they go intolerably wrong. We shall believe not merely in an over-ruling Providence, but (if I may dare to coin a word) in an under-ruling one, which has fixed for mankind eternal laws of life, health, growth, both physical and spiritual; in an around-ruling Providence, likewise, by which circumstances, that which stands around a man, are perpetually arranged, it may be, are fore-ordained, so that each law shall have at least an opportunity of taking effect on the right person, in the right time and place; and in an in-ruling Providence. too, from whose inspiration comes all true thought, all right feeling; from whom, we must believe, man alone of all living things known to us inherits that mysterious faculty of perceiving the law beneath the phænomena, by virtue of which he is a *man*.

But we can hold all this, surely, and equally hold all which natural science may teach us. Hold what natural science teaches? We shall not dare not to hold it. It will be sacred in our eyes. All light which science, political, economic, physiological, or other, can throw upon the past, will be welcomed by us, as coming from the Author of all light. To ignore it, even to receive it suspiciously and grudgingly, we shall feel to be a sin against Him. We shall dread no 'inroads of materialism;' because we shall be standing upon that spiritual ground which underlies—ay, causes—the material. All discoveries of science, whether political or economic, whether laws of health or laws of climate, will be accepted trustfully and cheerfully. And when we meet with such startling speculations as those on the influence of climate, soil, scenery on national character, which have lately excited so much controversy, we shall welcome them at first sight, just because they give us hope of order where we had seen only disorder, law where we fancied chance: we shall verify them patiently; correct them if they need correction; and if proven, believe that they have worked, and still work, ουκ ανευ Θεου, as factors in the great method of Him who has appointed to all nations their times, and the bounds of their habitation, if haply they might feel after Him, and find Him: though He be not far from any one of them; for in Him we live, and move, and have our being, and are the offspring of God Himself.

I thus end what it seemed to me proper to say in this, my Inaugural Lecture; thanking you much for the patience with which you have heard me: and if I have in it too often spoken of myself, and my own opinions, I can only answer that it is a fault which has been forced on me by my position, and which will not occur again. It seemed to me that some sort of statement of my belief was necessary, if only from respect to a University from which I have been long separated, and to return to which is to me a high honour and a deep pleasure; and I cannot but be aware (it is best to be honest) that there exists a prejudice against me in the minds of better men than I am, on account of certain early writings of mine. That prejudice, I trust, with God's help, I shall be able to dissipate.  At least whatever I shall fail in doing, this University will find that I shall do one thing; and that is, obey the Apostolic precept, 'Study to be quiet, and to do your own business.'

*Typeset in* ADOBE GARAMOND PREMIER
*a digital revival by Robert Slimbach*
*of the typefaces cut by Claude*
*Garamond in Paris in*
*the 16th century*